# THE COMPLETE GUIDE TO
# *Finishing* WALLS
# & CEILINGS

*Includes Plaster, Skim-coating, and Texture Ceiling Finishes*

**Creative Publishing international**

CHANHASSEN, MINNESOTA
www.creativepub.com

# Contents

**Creative Publishing international**

Copyright © 2007
Creative Publishing international, Inc.
18705 Lake Drive East
Chanhassen, Minnesota 55317
1-800-328-3895
www.creativepub.com

Printed in China

10 9 8 7 6 5 4 3 2

*President/CEO:* Ken Fund

*Publisher:* Bryan Trandem

*Senior Editor:* Mark Johanson
*Editor:* Tom Lemmer
*Assistant Managing Editor:* Tracy Stanley
*Creative Photography Director:* Tim Himsel
*Senior Art Director:* Dave Schelitzche
*Lead Photographer:* Steve Galvin
*Additional Photographers:* Andrea Rugg, Joel Schnell
*Scene Shop Carpenter:* Randy Austin
*Additional Shop Carpenter:* Glenn Austin
*Photo Editor:* Julie Caruso
*Technical Illustrator:* Earl Slack
*Production Manager:* Laura Hokkanen
*Proofreader:* Carolyn Henry-Johanson

THE COMPLETE GUIDE TO FINISHING WALLS & CEILINGS
*Created by:* The Editors of Creative Publishing international, Inc., in
cooperation with Black & Decker. Black & Decker® is a trademark of
The Black & Decker Corporation and is used under license.

Library of Congress
Cataloging-in-Publication Data
On file

Other titles from Creative Publishing international include:

*The Complete Guide to Home Wiring, The Complete Guide to Home Plumbing, The Complete Guide to Home Carpentry, The Complete Guide to Decks, The Complete Guide to Painting & Decorating, The Complete Guide To Bathrooms, The Complete Guide to Kitchens, The Complete Guide to Flooring, The Complete Guide to Roofing & Siding, The Complete Guide to Landscape Construction, The Complete Guide to Yard & Garden Features, The Complete Guide to Creative Landscapes, The Complete Guide to Windows & Doors, The Complete Guide to Wood Storage Projects, The Complete Guide to Easy Woodworking Projects, The Complete Guide to Trim & Finish Carpentry, The Complete Guide to Gazebos & Arbors, The Complete Guide to Ceramic & Stone Tile, The Complete Guide to Masonry & Stonework.*

**NOTICE TO READERS**

For safety, use caution, care, and good judgment when following the procedures described in this book. The publisher and Black & Decker cannot assume responsibility for any damage to property or injury to persons as a result of misuse of the information provided.

The techniques shown in this book are general techniques for various applications. In some instances, additional techniques not shown in this book may be required. Always follow manufacturers' safety warnings and instructions included with products. Deviation from the directions may create injury exposure and void warranties. The projects in this book vary widely as to skill levels required. Some may not be appropriate for all do-it-yourselfers, and some may require professional help. Consult your local building department for information on building permits, codes, and other laws as they apply to your project.

# Introduction

This book is a comprehensive guide to every aspect of building and finishing walls and ceilings, providing just about all the information most people are likely to need. It is an important reference for anyone who wants to understand the structural elements of home construction and surface finishes, but is first and foremost a how-to guide for homeowners who want to do this work themselves with a level of quality that rivals that achieved by professional frame-and-finish carpenters. Professionals may also find the book useful as a refresher, or as a helpful tool for explaining construction processes and finish options to their customers.

*The Complete Guide to Finishing Walls & Ceilings* is an indispensible guide to anyone interested in remodeling, especially those considering a major renovation or seeking to finish off unfinished space in their homes. It is organized to provide you with an encyclopedic understanding of this important element of the remodeling process.

Section One, *Building Basic Walls & Ceilings* gives the essential steps in planning, laying out, and framing walls and ceilings. You'll learn not only the basics of stud and joist construction, but how to frame with steel, how to attach walls to cement walls, and special techniques for soundproofing and for dealing with walls vulnerable to moisture.

Section Two, *Installing Wallboard*, leads you through the steps for covering framing with surface panels of wallboard or cementboard. It includes information on creating curves and architectural details.

Section Three, *Finishing Wallboard*, shows the classic techniques for taping, mudding and smoothing wallboard joints, but also gives important information on decorative skim coats and plaster veneers.

Section Four, *Installing Paneling & Ceiling Systems*, provides information on alternatives to wallboard: paneling, wainscotting, suspended ceilings, acoustical ceilings, and tin ceiling tiles.

Section Five, *Finishing Walls & Ceilings*, provides an overview of basic painting and wallpapering techniques, as well as the basics of wood trim installation.

Finally, Section Six, *Repairing Walls & Ceilings*, will show you how to keep wallboard, plaster, and tiled surfaces in good shape.

*The Complete Guide to Finishing Walls & Ceilings* is an essential reference for the homeowner who wants to understand wall and ceiling construction and finish processes. A helpful companion volume is *The Complete Guide to Trim & Finish Carpentry*, which offers additional information on creative trim carpentry and cabinet installation.

# Portfolio of Wall & Ceiling Ideas

Your walls and ceilings are much more than structural barriers dividing your house into separate areas. They are canvases awaiting an inspired treatment that can set mood, distinguish space, and reflect your personality within each individual room.

Through creative design and a thoughtful selection of colors, textures, and materials, nearly any wall and ceiling design you dream up can become a reality. From basic painted wallboard and traditional wood paneling to elegant glass block and distinct veneer plaster finishes, there is an ever-increasing variety of wall and ceiling finish materials available to you. Most home centers and lumberyards keep an impressive selection in stock and can easily accommodate special orders.

The photographs on the following pages show a few of the hundreds of ways you might use walls and ceilings as important design features in your home. As you gather ideas, keep in mind that good design doesn't have to be complicated or expensive—a little can go a long way. The key to creating truly attractive walls and ceilings is simple: if you like it, it's good design.

**Ordinary stock moldings** give plain walls a sense of depth and dimension when they are applied in a thoughtful manner, as with the faux wainscot panels seen here (right).

**Wall shape and the type of surface materials** used in the walls and ceilings contribute to excellent sound reproduction in this home theater.

(Top photo) **A raised panel ceiling** with fluting painted in complementary tones unifies this combined kitchen and social space.

**A striking lavender wainscot treatment** in this bathroom creates a cottage mood.

(Right) **Rounded walls** and a layered ceiling structure combine to form a truly unique entryway.

**Tongue-and-groove planks**, naturally finished, instill a warm, homey atmosphere in this attic, and provide contrast to the white-painted woodwork. Built-in shelves and bed make great use of limited space. A floral wallpaper used on the gable wall create a cottage mood.

**Archways are elegant.** From a modest curve at the top of a passage door to soaring masses of curvilinear wall supported by classic columns, an archway conveys timeless elegance in practically any setting. And with today's kits and preformed urethane millwork, you don't need to be Leonardo da Vinci to design and build an arch.

**An alcove** built into a wall can provide a spot to display artwork. In this example, a piece of Eastern religious art is framed by architectural columns for additional emphasis.

**Wood planks** aren't just for floors. Here, white planks contrast with darker ceiling beams to create drama in the kitchen.

**A simple raised-panel ceiling** can be created simply by arranging wood trim moldings in squares on a flat ceiling. The wall containing the fireplace is finished with paneled wood painted white for drama.

(Right) **Light-colored woods** used in ceiling beams, paneling, and edge trim contrast with white walls to create a modern-Scandinavian interior style.

(below) **Bare walls** can be beautiful. In this unusual treatment, walls stripped of wallpaper reveal an old plaster surface that is reminiscent of a castle or medieval monastery.

**Curved walls** can be used in all sorts of ways in today's remodeling. Here, a scalloped partition wall creates room boundaries while at the same time uniting adjoining spaces. A popular decor trend is to paint or finish walls with different colors or textures for contrast and drama.

**Wall texture** sets moods and establishes setting. The stucco-like texture of the wall covering seen here (left) creates an expansive transition between these rooms and puts forth an attitude of well-anchored security. And this finish can be accomplished on a wall with any internal structure, including a 2 × 4 stud wall covered in wallboard.

# Building Basic Walls & Ceilings

## A House with Platform Framing

- Shingles
- Roof sheathing
- Ridge board
- Skylight header
- Rafter
- Header
- Cripple stud
- Load-bearing wall
- Jack stud
- King stud
- Double top plate
- Header
- Sole plate
- Joist
- Cripple stud
- Rough sill
- Rim joist
- Subfloor
- Support beam
- Studs
- Joist
- Foundation
- Support posts

# Basic House Framing

Finishing walls and ceilings often requires fastening panel materials to your home's structural framing. A basic understanding of this framing will help you to properly plan and prepare for your wall and ceiling finishing projects.

The basic structure of a house is made up of four systems that work together to form a solid structure: the roof, the walls, the floors, and the foundation. Most houses are built using one of two framing styles—platform framing (left, below) or balloon framing (opposite page). Knowing your house's framing style makes it easier to locate framing members and anticipate blocking needs for panel materials. If changes to the structural framing are necessary, such as replacement of severely bowed or twisted studs, the framing style also determines what kind of temporary supports you will need to install and can affect the complexity of a project. If you have trouble determining what type of framing was used in your house, refer to the original blueprints, if you have them, or consult a building contractor or licensed home inspector.

## Platform Framing

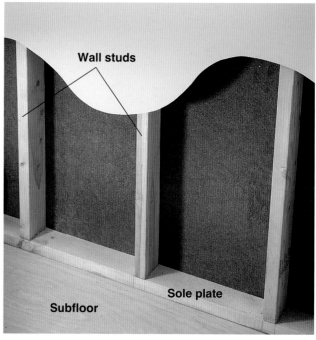

- Wall studs
- Sole plate
- Subfloor

**Platform framing** (left and above) is identified by the floor-level sole plates and ceiling-level top plates to which the wall studs are attached. Most houses built after 1930 use platform framing. If you do not have access to unfinished areas, you can remove the wall surface at the bottom of a wall to determine what kind of framing was used in your home.

There are two types of walls: load-bearing and partition (non-load-bearing). Load-bearing walls carry the weight of the house and require temporary support if alterations to the framing is required. Partition walls simply divide the space within the house to create rooms. They do not require temporary supports.

The on-center (O.C.) spacing of framing members determines the thickness of panel materials and size of fasteners you can use, as well as the fastening pattern. (Typically, the greater the O.C. spacing, the greater the panel thickness.) Modern building codes stipulate standard O.C. spacing for wall studs at 16-in. or 24-in., and for floor joists at 12-in., 16-in. or 24-in. When planning the layout of panel materials, make sure all joints between panels fall on the center of framing members. Install additional blocking where necessary to support panel ends.

Complete any changes or additions to your home's framing prior to covering the studs and joists.

## Balloon Framing

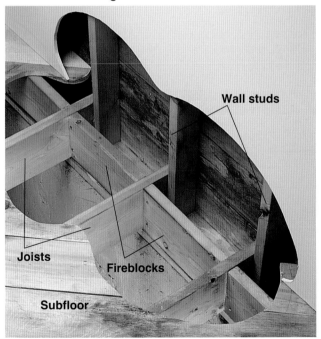

**Balloon framing** (right and above) is identified by wall studs that run uninterrupted from the roof to a sill plate on the foundation, without the sole plates and top plates found in platform-framed walls (page opposite). Balloon framing was used in houses built before 1930.

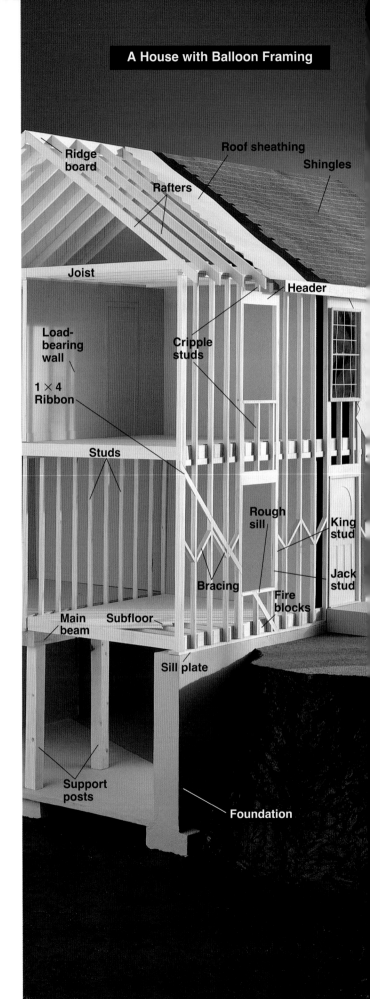

**A House with Balloon Framing**

## Flooring and Ceiling Framing

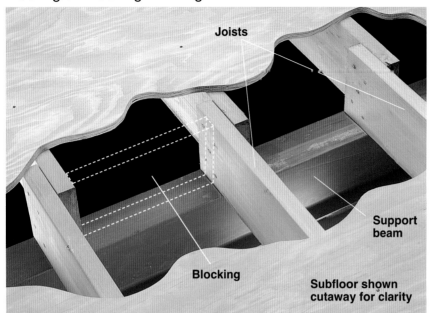

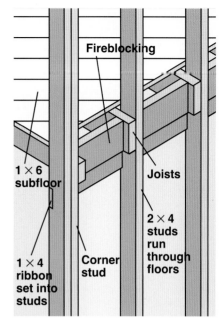

**Joists** carry the structural load of floors and ceilings. The ends of the joists rest on support beams, foundations, or load-bearing walls; joists always run perpendicular to their supports. Floor joists typically are 2 × 10 or larger lumber. Ceiling joists, which support only a ceiling finish and sometimes limited storage space, may be 2 × 4 or larger. Blocking or X-bridging is often installed between joists to provide additional support.

**Floor joists in balloon-frame houses** are nailed to the sides of continuous wall studs. Upper-story joists gain additional support from 1 × 4 ribbons notched into the studs. Solid blocking between the joists provides fire protection.

## Roof Framing

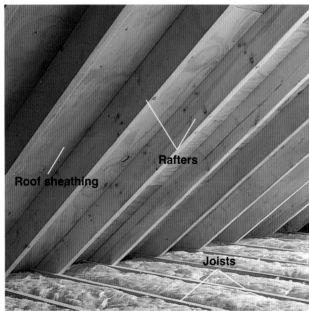

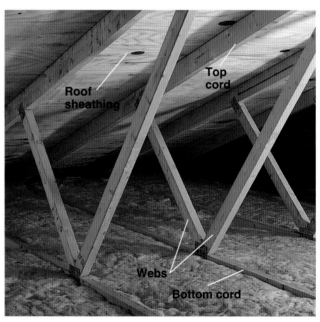

**Rafters**, typically made from 2 × 6 or larger lumber, span from the exterior walls to the ridge board (or beam) at the peak of the roof. In most rafter-frame roofs, the ceiling joists link the ends of opposing rafters to create a structural triangle; the frame may also have rafter ties or collar ties for additional support (see page 153). Rafters are usually spaced 16" or 24" apart.

**Trusses**, prefabricated frames made from 2 × lumber joined with metal plates or fasteners, are found in many houses built after 1950. Standard trusses contain bottom and top cords and interconnecting webs that provide rigidity. Trusses rely on the sum of their parts for support and cannot be cut or altered.

# Wall Framing

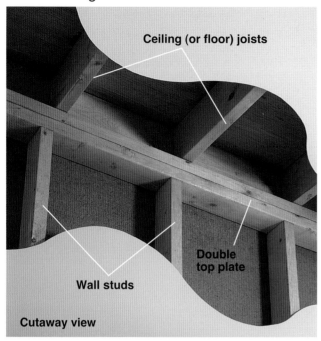

**Ceiling (or floor) joists**

**Double top plate**

**Wall studs**

Cutaway view

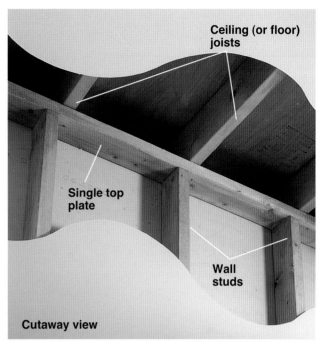

**Ceiling (or floor) joists**

**Single top plate**

**Wall studs**

Cutaway view

**Load-bearing walls** carry the structural weight of your home. In platform-frame houses, load-bearing walls can be identified by double top plates made from two layers of framing lumber. Load-bearing walls include all exterior walls and any interior walls that are aligned above support beams.

**Non-load-bearing, or partition, walls** are interior walls that do not carry the structural weight of the house. They have a single top plate and can be perpendicular to floor and ceiling joists but are not aligned above support beams. Any interior wall that is parallel to floor and ceiling joists is a partition wall.

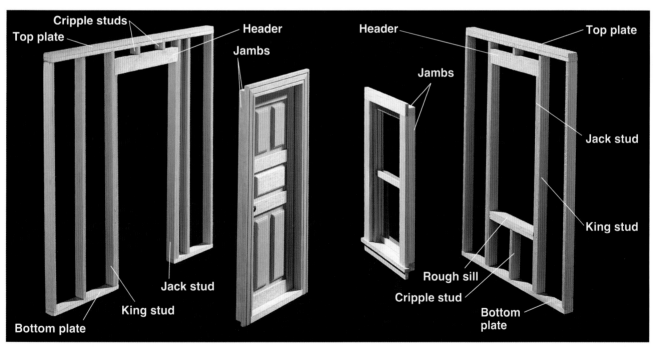

Cripple studs

Top plate

Header

Jambs

Jack stud

King stud

Bottom plate

Header

Top plate

Jambs

Jack stud

King stud

Rough sill

Cripple stud

Bottom plate

**Door and window frames**, called rough openings, are sized according to the dimensions of the door or window unit. In load-bearing walls, the weight from above the opening is borne by the cripple studs, which are supported by a header that spans the opening. A typical header is made with two pieces of 2 × lumber sandwiched around a layer of ½" plywood; some builders use oversized headers, which eliminate the need for cripples. Frames in non-load-bearing walls may have only a single 2 × 4 for a header. Each end of the header is supported by a jack stud that extends to the bottom plate and is nailed to a king stud for support. A window frame has a sill that defines the bottom of the opening.

A typical partition wall consists of top and bottom plates and 2 × 4 studs spaced 16" on- center. Use 2 × 6 lumber for walls that will hold large plumbing pipes (inset).

Labels on image: Wall studs, Top plate, Cripple stud, Header, King stud, Jack stud, Bottom plate

# Building Partition Walls

Partition walls are non-load-bearing walls typically built with 2 × 4 lumber, but they can also be built with 3⅝" steel studs (pages 28 to 31). Walls holding plumbing pipes can be framed with 2 × 6 lumber. On a concrete floor, use pressure-treated lumber for the bottom plates.

This project involves building a wall in place, rather than framing a complete wall on the floor and tilting it upright, as in new construction. The build-in-place method allows for variations in floor and ceiling levels and is generally much easier for remodeling projects.

If your wall will include a door or other opening, see pages 22 to 23. Check the local building codes for requirements about fireblocking in partition walls. And after your walls are framed and the mechanical rough-ins are completed, install metal protector plates where pipes and wires run through framing members.

## Everything You Need

Tools: Protective eyewear, chalk line, circular saw, framing square, plumb bob, powder-actuated nailer, T-bevel.

Materials: 2 × 4 lumber, blocking lumber, 16d and 8d common nails, concrete fasteners, wallboard screws.

## Variations for Fastening Top Plates to Joists

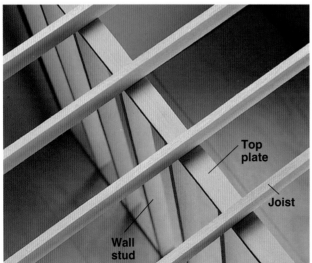

When a new wall is perpendicular to the ceiling or floor joists above, attach the top plate directly to the joists, using 16d nails.

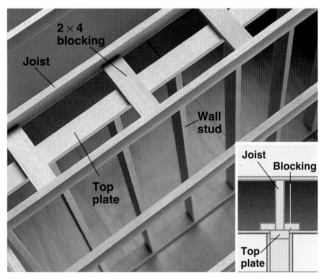

When a new wall falls between parallel joists, install 2 × 4 blocking between the joists every 24". If the new wall is aligned with a parallel joist, install blocks on both sides of the wall, and attach the top plate to the joist (inset).

## Variations for Fastening Bottom Plates to Joists

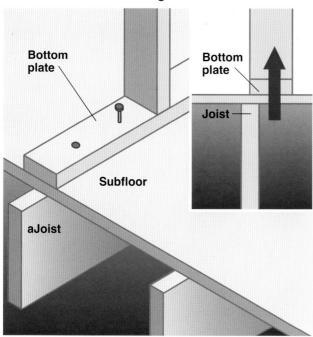

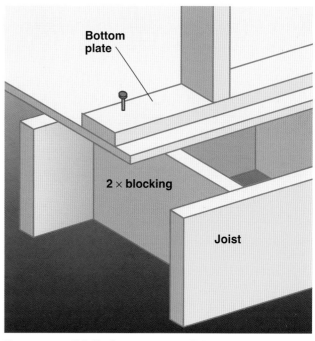

**If a new wall is aligned** with a joist below, install the bottom plate directly over the joist or off-center over the joist (inset). Off-center placement allows you to nail into the joist but provides room underneath the plate for pipes or wiring to go up into the wall.

**If a new wall falls between** parallel joists, install 2 × 6 or larger blocking between the two joists below, spaced 24" on center. Nail the bottom plate through the sub-floor and into the blocking.

## How to Build a Partition Wall

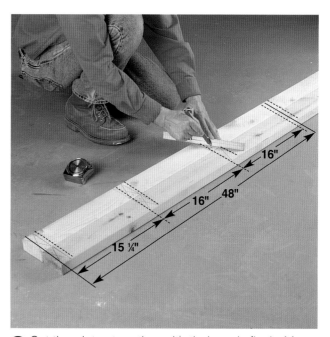

**1** Mark the location of the leading edge of the new wall's top plate, then snap a chalk line through the marks across the joists or blocks. Use a framing square, or take measurements, to make sure the line is perpendicular to any intersecting walls. Cut the top and bottom plates to length.

**2** Set the plates together with their ends flush. Measure from the end of one plate, and make marks for the location of each stud. The first stud should fall 15¼" from the end; every stud thereafter should fall 16" on center. Thus, the first 4 × 8-ft. wallboard panel will cover the first stud and "break" in the center of the fourth stud. Use a square to extend the marks across both plates. Draw an X at each stud location.

(continued next page)

**3** Position the top plate against the joists, aligning its leading edge with the chalk line. Attach the plate with two 16d nails driven into each joist. Start at one end, and adjust the plate as you go to keep the leading edge flush with the chalk line.

**4** To position the bottom plate, hang a plumb bob from the side edge of the top plate so the point nearly touches the floor. When it hangs motionless, mark the point's location on the floor. Make plumb markings at each end of the top plate, then snap a chalk line between the marks. Position the bottom plate along the chalk line, and use the plumb bob to align the stud markings between the two plates.

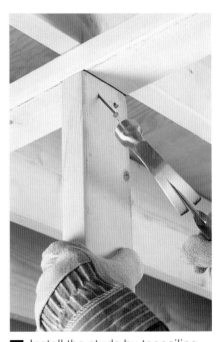

**5** Fasten the bottom plate to the floor. On concrete, use a powder-actuated nailer or masonry screws, driving a pin or screw every 16". On wood floors, use 16d nails driven into the joists below.

**6** Measure between the plates for the length of each stud. Cut each stud so it fits snugly in place but is not so tight that it bows the joists above. If you cut a stud too short, see if it will fit somewhere else down the wall.

**7** Install the studs by toenailing them at a 60° angle through the sides of the studs and into the plates. At each end, drive two 8d nails through one side of the stud and one more through the center on the other side.

## How to Frame Corners (shown in cutaways)

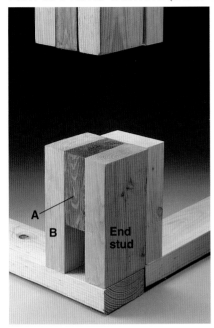

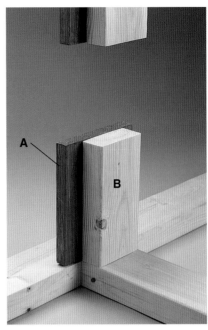

**L-corners:** Nail 2 × 4 spacers (A) to the inside of the end stud. Nail an extra stud (B) to the spacers. The extra stud provides a surface to attach wallboard at the inside corner.

**T-corner meets stud:** Fasten 2 × 2 backers (A) to each side of the side-wall stud (B). The backers provide a nailing surface for wallboard.

**T-corner between studs:** Fasten a 1 × 6 backer (A) to the end stud (B) with wallboard screws. The backer provides a nailing surface for wallboard.

## How to Frame an Angled Partition Wall in an Attic

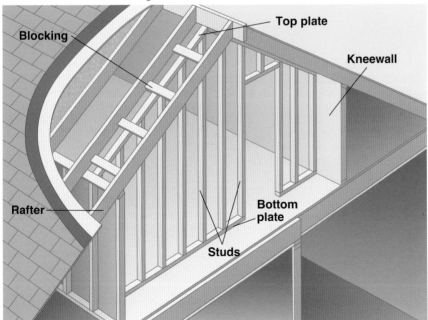

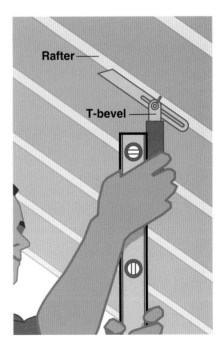

**Full-size attic partition walls** typically run parallel to the rafters and have sloping top plates that extend down to knee walls on either side. To build one, cut the top and bottom plates, and mark the stud locations on the bottom plate only. Nail the top plates in place, and use a plumb bob to position the bottom plate, as with a standard wall. Use the plumb bob again to transfer the stud layout marks from the bottom to the top plate. To find the proper angle for cutting the top ends of the studs, set a level against the top plate (or rafter) and hold it plumb. Then, rest the handle of a T-bevel against the level, and adjust the T-bevel blade to follow the plate. Transfer the angle to the stud ends, and cut them to length.

21

# How to Frame a Rough Opening for an Interior Prehung Door

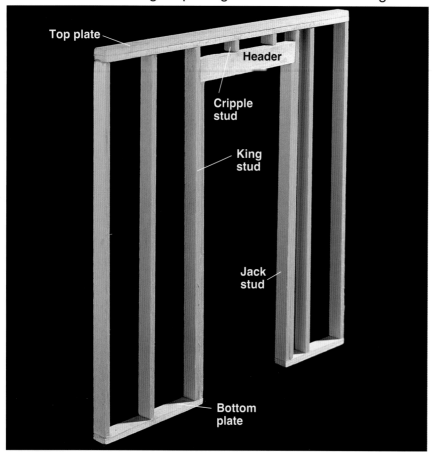

**Door frames** for prehung doors (left) start with *king* studs that attach to the top and bottom plates. Inside the king studs, *jack* studs support the *header* at the top of the opening. *Cripple* studs continue the wall-stud layout above the opening. In non-load-bearing walls, the header may be a 2 × 4 laid flat or a built-up header (below). The dimensions of the framed opening are referred to as the *rough opening*.

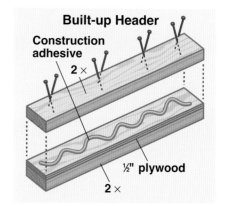

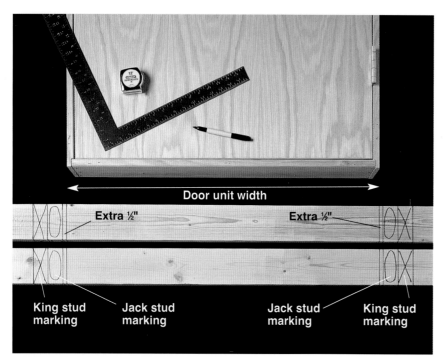

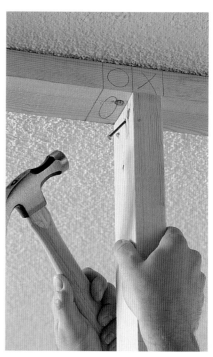

**1** To mark the layout for the door frame, measure the width of the door unit along the bottom. Add 1" to this dimension to determine the width of the rough opening (the distance between the jack studs). This gives you a ½" gap on each side for adjusting the door frame during installation. Mark the top and bottom plates for the jack and king studs.

**2** After you've installed the wall plates (see page 20), cut the king studs and toenail them in place at the appropriate markings.

**3** Measure the full length of the door unit, then add ½" to determine the height of the rough opening. Using that dimension, measure up from the floor and mark the king studs. Cut a 2 × 4 header to fit between the king studs. Position the header flat, with its bottom face at the marks, and secure it to the king studs with 16d nails.

**4** Cut and install a cripple stud above the header, centered between the king studs. Install any additional cripples required to maintain the 16" on-center layout of the standard studs in the rest of the wall.

**5** Cut the jack studs to fit snugly under the header. Fasten them in place by nailing down through the header, then drive 10d nails through the faces of the jack studs and into the king studs, spaced 16" apart.

**6** Saw through the bottom plate so it's flush with the inside faces of the jack studs. Remove the cut-out portion of the plate. NOTE: If you're finishing the wall with drywall, hang the door after the drywall is installed.

## How to Install Archways in Wall Openings

Arches add a touch of elegance to doorways, windows, and other wall openings. A number of preformed arches are currently available on the market, turning a once specialized and labor-intensive building technique into an easy, do-it-yourself project.

Preformed arches are fabricated from various materials, in a variety of styles, for a number of applications. Steel track arches are ideal for new framing, while wallboard forms are great for creating archways in remodels. Forms are also available for applications involving plaster. You can find forms to accommodate just about any arch radius, from a perfect half-circle at a doorway to a subtle elliptical arc for a kitchen pass-through. You can even use a series of preformed arches to create a barrel-arch ceiling in a hallway or entryway.

Whether made from metal track or wallboard, the installation of most preformed arches is the same: Frame the opening as you normally would, then center the form in the opening and fasten it to the framing with wallboard screws. Some products require additional blocking and others are installed after the wallboard is hung. Once installed, preformed arches are finished using traditional wallboard techniques.

Although installing a preformed arch is simple, always follow the manufacturer's instructions for the product you choose.

**Preformed wallboard arches** are typically installed after wallboard is in place. One-piece forms create an unbroken arch, while two-piece forms can be used to round-off corners. Joints are finished with wallboard tape and joint compound (see pages 106 to 115).

## Products for Making Archways

**Steel track arches** are installed during wall construction to create a variety of archways and barrel-arched ceilings. To finish steel track arches with wallboard, follow the curved walls techniques on page 88.

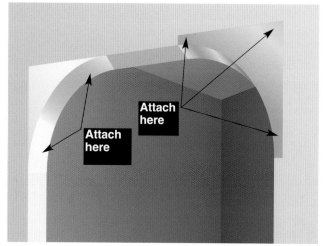

Attach here

Attach here

**Corner forms** are installed in the top corners of a wall opening to create an arch. Some (left) are affixed into the corner and fit flush with the walls; others (right) snap over the walls and are screwed to the door jambs. Cover with joint compound and paint.

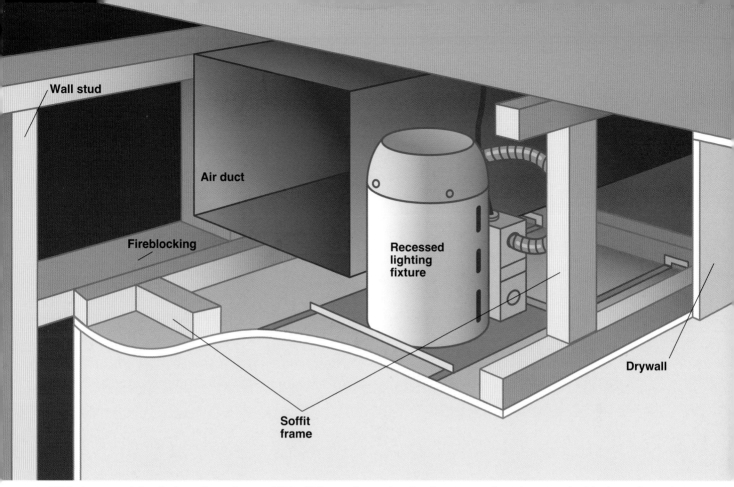

**Wall stud**

**Air duct**

**Fireblocking**

**Recessed lighting fixture**

**Drywall**

**Soffit frame**

**Hide immovable obstructions** in a soffit built from dimension lumber or steel and covered with drywall or other finish material. An extra-wide soffit is also a great place to install recessed lighting fixtures.

# Framing Soffits & Chases

Unfinished basements and other areas often contain elements like beams, pipes, and ductwork, that may be vital to your house but become big obstacles to finishing the space. When you can't conceal the obstructions within walls, and you've determined it's too costly to move them, hide them inside a framed soffit or chase. This can also provide a place to run smaller mechanicals, like wiring and water supply lines.

You can frame a soffit with a variety of materials. 2 × 2 lumber and 1⅝" steel studs both work well, because they're small and lightweight (though steel is usually easier to work with because it's always straight). For large soffits that will house lighting fixtures or other elements, you might want the strength of 2 × 4s or 3⅝" steel studs. Chases should be framed with 2 × 4s or 3⅝" steel studs, so they're as rigid as walls.

The following pages show you some basic techniques for building soffits and chases, but the design of your framing is up to you. For example, you may want to shape your soffits for a decorative effect or build an oversized chase that holds bookshelves. Just make sure the framing conforms to local building codes.

There may be code restrictions about the types of mechanicals that can be grouped together, as well as minimum clearances between the framing and what it encloses. Most codes also specify that soffits, chases, and other framed structures have fireblocking every 10 ft. and at the intersections between soffits and neighboring walls. Remember, too, that drain cleanouts and shutoff valves must be accessible, so you'll need to install access panels at these locations.

# Variations for Building Soffits

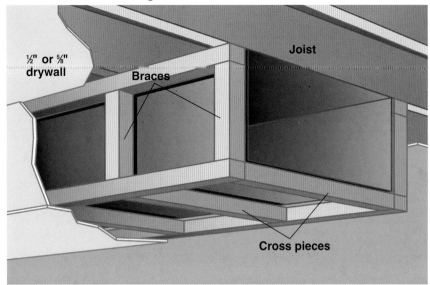

**2 × 2 soffit:** Build two ladder-like frames for the soffit sides, using standard 2 × 2s. Install braces every 16" or 24" to provide nailing support for the edges of the dry-wall. Attach the side frames to the joists on either side of the obstruction, using nails or screws. Then, install cross pieces beneath the obstacle, tying the two sides together.

Labels in image: ½" or ⅝" drywall · Braces · Joist · Cross pieces

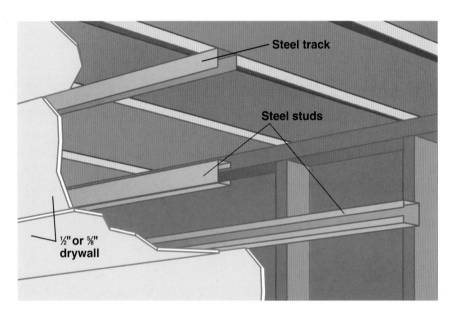

**Simple steel-frame soffit:** With ½" drywall, this construction works for soffits up to 16" wide; with ⅝" drywall, up to 24" wide. Use 1⅝", 2½", or 3⅝" steel studs and tracks (see pages 28 to 31). Fasten a track to the ceiling and a stud to the adjoining wall, using drywall screws. Cut a strip of dry-wall to form the side of the soffit, and attach a steel stud flush with the bottom edge of the strip, using type S screws. Attach the assembly to the ceiling track, then cut and install drywall panels to form the soffit bottom.

Labels in image: Steel track · Steel studs · ½" or ⅝" drywall

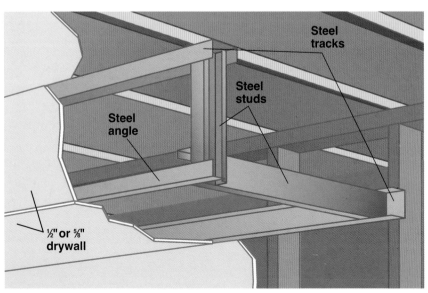

**Steel-frame soffit with braces:** Use 1⅝", 2½", or 3⅝" steel studs and tracks. Fasten a track to the ceiling and wall with drywall screws. Cut studs to form the side and bottom of the soffit, fasten them to the tracks every 16" or 24" on-center, using type S pan-head screws, then join the pieces with metal angle (you can use a steel track cut in half lengthwise). Use a string line and locking clamps to help keep the frame straight and square during construction.

Labels in image: Steel tracks · Steel studs · Steel angle · ½" or ⅝" drywall

## How to Frame a Chase

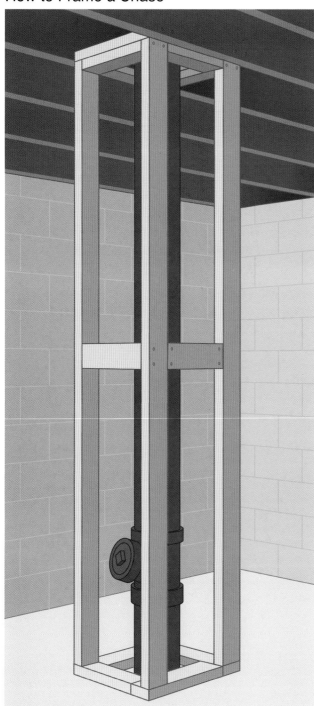

**Build chases** with 2 × 4s or 3⅝" steel framing. Use steel or pressure-treated lumber for bottom plates on concrete floors, attaching them with construction adhesive and powder-actuated nailer fasteners (see page 20). Add top plates, then install studs to form the corners of the chase. If desired, block in between the studs for stability. To make the chase smaller, notch the top and bottom plates around the obstruction, and install the studs flat. If you're framing around a vertical drain pipe (especially the main DWV stack), leave room around the pipe for soundproofing insulation; plastic pipes can be especially noisy.

## Making Access Panels

**Make access panels** after installing drywall. *In a horizontal surface*, cut out a square piece of drywall at the access location, and set it inside the soffit. Glue mitered trim around the opening so it overhangs the edges by ½". Rest the cutout on the trim overhang to cover the opening. *In a vertical surface*, glue the trim to the cutout to create the panel. Install plywood strips to the back of the drywall at two sides of the opening. Secure the panel to the strips with screws.

## Attaching Framing to Steel Members

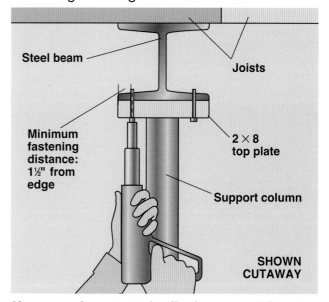

Steel beam

Joists

Minimum
fastening
distance:
1½" from
edge

2 × 8
top plate

Support column

**SHOWN
CUTAWAY**

**Use a powder-actuated nailer** (see page 20) to attach wood and steel framing to steel I-beams and columns. Hold the nailer at a right angle to the surface and drive the fastener at least 1½" from the edge of the steel. Use a fastener and power load appropriate to the tool and each application. The tool manufacturer should supply a manual, fastener charts, and load charts with the tool. Always wear eye and ear protection when working with these tools.

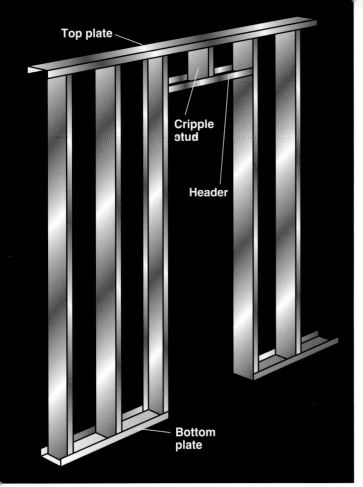

Steel framing, when coupled with wallboard, creates a rigid wall system as solid and strong as wood-framed walls. Steel track is used to create plates, headers and sills. Steel studs are installed so the open side faces in the same direction, except at door, window or other openings. The knockouts in studs are for running utility lines through the framing.

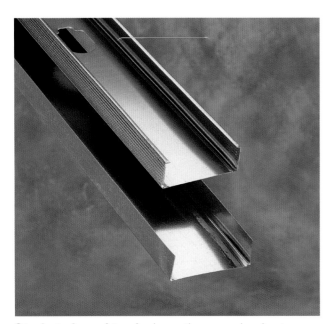

Steel studs and tracks have the same basic structure—a web that spans two flanges sides—however, studs also contain a ¼" lip to improve their rigidity.

# Framing with Steel

Steel framing is quickly becoming a popular alternative to wood in residential construction due to the rising cost of wood and the advantages that steel offers. Steel framing is fireproof, insect proof, highly rot-resistant, and lightweight. But the most significant advantage is that steel, unlike lumber, is always perfectly uniform and straight.

Steel studs and tracks (or plates) are commonly available at home centers and lumberyards in nominal widths comparable to their wooden counterparts: 1⅝" (2 × 2), 2½" (2 × 3), 3⅝" (2 × 4), and 5½" (2 × 6). 25-gauge (or 18-mil) and 20-gauge (or 33-mil) steel framing is suitable for most non-load-bearing partition walls and soffits that will be covered with wallboard, but 20-gauge results in a somewhat sturdier wall. Use 20-gauge studs for walls that will receive cementboard.

With a few exceptions, the layout and framing methods used for a steel-frame partition wall are the same as those used for a wood-frame wall. For more information on framing partition walls, see pages 18 to 21; for help with framing soffits, see pages 25 to 26.

Here are a few tips for working with steel:

• Steel framing is fastened together with screws, not nails. Attach steel tracks to existing wood framing using long drywall screws.

• Even pressure and slow drill speed make it easy to start screws. Drive the screws down tight, but be careful not to strip the steel. Don't use drill-point screws with 25-gauge steel, which can strip easily.

• Most steel studs have punch-outs for running plumbing and electrical lines through the framing. Cut the studs to length from the same end, to keep the punch-outs lined up.

• The hand-cut edges of steel framing are very sharp; wear heavy gloves when handling them.

• To provide support for electrical receptacle boxes, use boxes with special bracing for steel studs, or fasten boxes to wood framing installed between the studs.

• Use 16"-wide batts for insulating between steel studs. The added width allows for a friction fit, whereas standard batts would slide down.

## Tools & Materials for Framing with Steel

**Steel framing requires** a few specialty tools and materials. Aviation snips (A) are needed to cut tracks and studs, though a miter saw outfitted with a steel-cutting abrasive blade (B) can speed up the process. A drill or screwgun (C) is required for fastening framing. Handy for large projects, a stud crimper (D) creates mechanical joints between tracks and studs. Plastic grommets (E) are placed in knockouts to help protect utility lines.

Protective eyewear and heavy work gloves (F, G) are necessities when working with the sharp edges of hand-cut steel framing. Use self-tapping screws (inset) to fasten steel components. To install wood trim, use type S trim-head screws (H); to fasten wallboard, type S wallboard screws (I); and to fasten studs and tracks together, $^7/_{16}$" type S pan-head screws (J).

## Tips for Framing with Steel

**When running metal** plumbing pipe and electrical cable through steel studs, use plastic grommets at knockouts to prevent galvanic action and electrification of the wall. Install wood blocking between studs for hanging decorative accessories or wainscoting.

**Frame door openings** 3" wider and 1½" taller than normal, then wrap the insides with 2 × 4s to provide a nailing surface for hanging the door and installing the casing.

# How to Frame a Steel Partition Wall

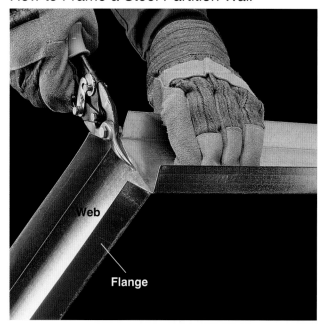

Web

Flange

**1** Mark the wall location on the floor or ceiling, following the same procedure used for a wood-frame wall. Cut the top and bottom tracks to length with aviation snips. Cut through the side flanges first, then bend the waste piece back and cut across the web. Use a marker to lay out the tracks with 16" on-center spacing (see page 19).

**2** Fasten the bottom track to the floor. For wood floors, use 2" coarse-thread drywall screws. For concrete floors, pin the track down with a powder-actuated nailer (see page 20), or use 1¼" masonry screw. Drill pilot holes for screws using a masonry bit. Drive a fastener at each end of the track, then every 24" in between.

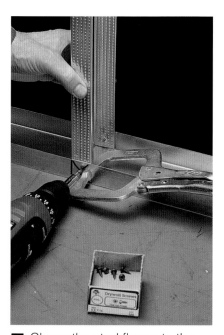

**3** Plumb up from the bottom track with a plumb bob to position the top track. Fasten the top track to the ceiling joists with 1⅝" drywall screws. Drive two screws at each joist location.

**4** At the first stud location, measure between the tracks and cut a stud to length. Insert the stud into the tracks at a slight angle and twist into place. NOTE: Cut all subsequent studs from the same end so the knockouts align.

**5** Clamp the stud flange to the track with C-clamp pliers and drive a ⁷⁄₁₆" type S pan-head screw through the tracks into the stud. Drive one screw on each side, at both ends of the stud. Install remaining studs so the open sides face the same direction (except at door-frame studs).

**6** To install a door header, cut track 8" longer than the opening. Measure in 4" at each end, cut the flanges at an angle toward the mark, then bend down the ends at 90°. Fasten the header in place with three screws at each stud—two through the fastening tab and one through the overlapping flange.

**7** To provide running blocking for cabinets, wainscoting, or other fixtures, snap a chalkline across the face of the studs at the desired height, hold a track level at the line, then notch the flanges of the track to bypass the studs. Fasten the track in place with two screws at each stud location.

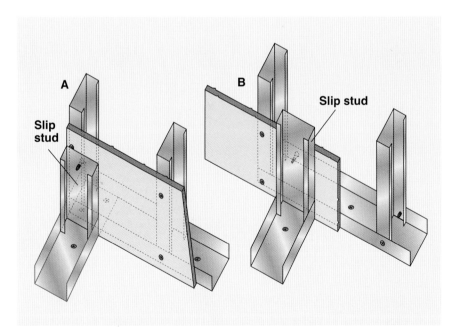

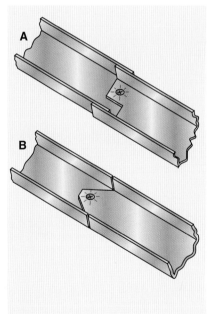

**Build corners using a slip stud:** A slip stud is not fastened until the adjacent drywall is in place. Form L-shaped corners (A) by overlapping the tracks. Cut off the flange on one side of one track, removing enough to allow room for the overlapping track and drywall. Form a T-shaped corner (B) by leaving a gap between the tracks for the drywall. Secure each slip stud by screwing through the stud into the tracks of the adjacent wall. Also screw through the back side of the drywall into the slip stud, if possible. Where there's no backing behind the slip stud, drive screws at a 45° angle through the back corners of the slip stud and into the drywall.

**Join sections** with a spliced joint (A) or notched joint (B). Make a spliced joint by cutting a 2" slit in the web of one track. Slip the other track into the slit and secure with a screw. For a notched joint cut back the flanges of one track and taper the web so it fits into the other track; secure with a screw.

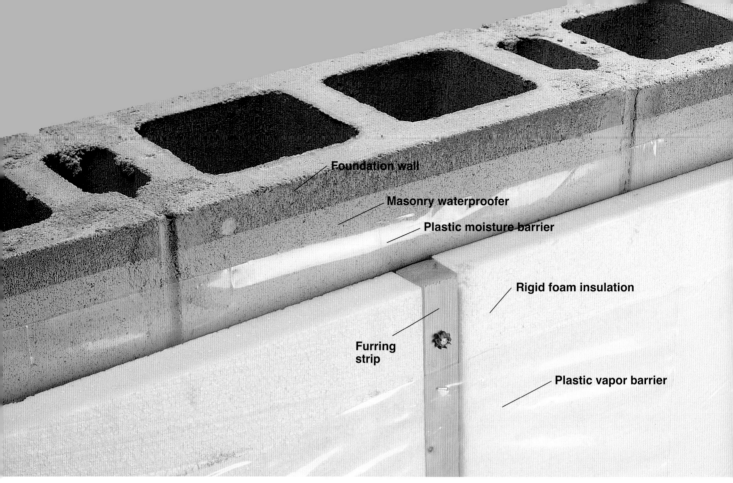

Labels on image:
- Foundation wall
- Masonry waterproofer
- Plastic moisture barrier
- Rigid foam insulation
- Furring strip
- Plastic vapor barrier

**Local building codes** may require a barrier to prevent moisture from damaging wood and insulation covering foundation walls. This may be masonry waterproofer, or plastic sheeting placed behind or in front of the framing.

# Covering Foundation Walls

There are two common methods for covering foundation walls. Because it saves space, the more popular method is to attach 2 × 2 furring strips directly to the masonry wall. These strips provide a 1½"-deep cavity between strips for insulation and service lines, as well as a framework for attaching drywall. The other method is to build a complete 2 × 4 stud wall or steel-frame wall just in front of the foundation wall. This method offers a full 3½" for insulation and lines, and it provides a flat, plumb wall surface, regardless of the foundation wall's condition.

To determine the best method for your project, examine the foundation walls. If they're fairly plumb and flat, you can consider furring them. If the walls are wavy or out of plumb, however, it may be easier to build stud walls. Also check with the local building department before you decide on a framing method. There may be codes regarding insulation minimums and methods of running service lines along foundation walls.

A local building official can also tell you what's recommended, or required, in your area for seal-ing foundation walls against moisture. Common types of moisture barriers include masonry waterproofers that are applied like paint, and plastic sheeting installed between masonry walls and wood framing. The local building code will also specify whether you need a vapor barrier between the framing and the drywall.

Before you shop for materials, decide how you'll fasten the framing to your foundation walls and floor. If you're covering a large wall area, it will be worth it to buy or rent a powder-actuated nailer for the job.

## Everything You Need

Tools: Circular saw, drill, powder-actuated nailer, plumb bob.

Materials: 2 × 2 and 2 × 4 lumber, 2½" drywall screws, construction adhesive, concrete fasteners, insulation.

## Options for Attaching Wood to Masonry

**Webs**

**Powder-actuated nailers** fasten framing to block, poured concrete, and steel. They use gunpowder caps (*loads*) to drive hardened-steel nails (*pins*). Trigger types (shown) and hammer types are available for sale or rental. NOTE: With block, drive pins into the solid webs, not into the voids.

**Masonry nails** are the cheapest way to attach wood to concrete block walls. Drive the nails into the mortar joints for maximum holding power and to avoid cracking the blocks. Drill pilot holes through the strips if the nails cause splitting. Masonry nails are difficult to drive into poured concrete.

**Self-tapping masonry screws** hold well in block or poured concrete, but they must be driven into predrilled holes. Use a hammer drill to drill holes of the same size in both the wood and the concrete, after the wood is positioned. Drive the screws into the block webs, not into the voids.

## How to Install Furring Strips on Masonry Walls

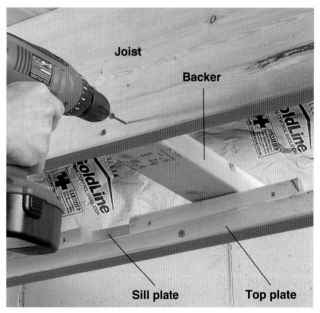

**Joist**

**Backer**

**Sill plate**　　**Top plate**

**1** Cut a 2 × 2 top plate to span the length of the wall. Mark the furring strip layout onto the bottom edge of the plate, using 16"-on-center spacing. Attach the plate to the bottom of the joists with 2½" drywall screws. The back edge of the plate should line up with the front of the blocks.

**Variation:** If the joists run parallel to the wall, install backers between the outer joist and the sill plate to provide support for ceiling drywall. Make T-shaped backers from short 2 × 4s and 2 × 2s. Install each so the bottom face of the 2 × 4 is flush with the bottoms of the joists. Attach the top plate to the foundation wall with its top edge flush with the tops of the blocks.

(continued next page)

**2** Install the bottom plate cut from pressure-treated 2 × 2 lumber. Apply construction adhesive to the back and bottom of the plate, then attach it to the floor with a nailer or masonry screws. Use a plumb bob to transfer the furring-strip layout marks from the top plate to the bottom plate.

**3** Cut 2 × 2 furring strips to fit between the top and bottom plates. Apply construction adhesive to the back of each strip, and position it on the layout marks on the plates. Fasten along the length of each strip every 16".

**Variation:** Install shorter strips to leave a 2"-wide channel for adding wires or supply pipes. NOTE: Consult local codes to ensure proper installation of electrical or plumbing materials.

**4** Fill the cavities between furring strips with rigid insulation board. Cut the pieces so they fit snugly within the framing. If necessary, make cutouts in the insulation to fit around service lines, and cover any channels with metal protector plates before closing up the wall.

# Tips for Covering Foundation Walls with Stud Walls

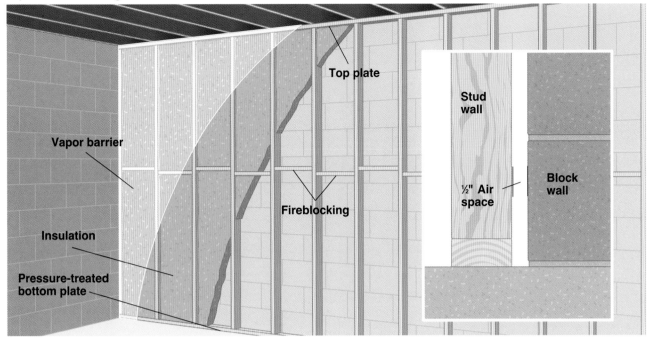

**Vapor barrier**

**Top plate**

**Stud wall**

**½" Air space**

**Block wall**

**Fireblocking**

**Insulation**

**Pressure-treated bottom plate**

**Build a standard partition wall** with 2 × 4s or 3⅝" steel framing, following the basic steps on pages 18 to 21 (see pages 28 to 31 for help with steel framing). Use pressure-treated lumber for wood bottom plates that rest on concrete. To minimize moisture problems and avoid unevenness in foundation walls, leave a ½" air space between the stud wall and masonry wall (inset). Insulate the stud wall with fiberglass blankets, and install a vapor barrier and fireblocking if required by local code.

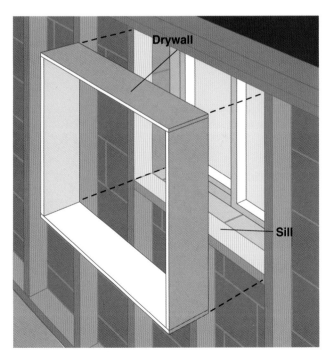

**Drywall**

**Sill**

**Frame around a basement window** so the framing is flush with the edges of the masonry on all sides. Install a sill at the base of the window opening, and add a header, if necessary. Fill the space between the framing members and the masonry with fiberglass insulation or non-expanding foam insulation. Install drywall so it butts against the window frame.

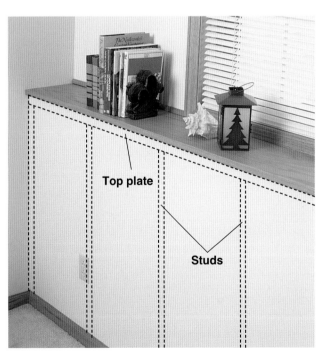

**Top plate**

**Studs**

**Build a short stud wall** to cover a low foundation wall in a walkout or "daylight" basement. Install the top plate flush with the top of the foundation wall. Cover the wall with drywall or other finish, then cap it with finish-grade lumber or plywood to create a decorative shelf.

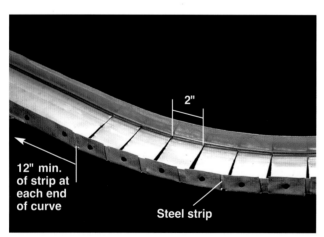

**Flexible steel track** makes it easy to build walls of almost any shape. Tracks come in 10-ft. lengths and fit with 2 × 4s or 3⅝" steel studs.

# Framing Curved Walls

Curved walls have obvious appeal and are surprisingly easy to build. Structurally, a curved wall is very similar to a standard non-load-bearing partition wall, with two key differences: the stud spacing, and the materials used for the top and bottom wall plates.

Traditionally, plates for curved walls were cut from ¾" plywood—a somewhat time-consuming and wasteful process—but now a flexible track product, made of light-gauge steel, has made the construction much easier (see page 234 for supplier information). Using the steel track, frame the wall based on a layout drawn onto the floor. Shape the track to follow the layout, screw together the track pieces to lock-in the shape, then add the studs.

The best stud spacing for your project depends upon the type of finish material you plan to use. If it's wallboard, ¼" flexible panels require studs spaced a maximum of 9-in. O.C. for curves with a minimum radius of 32-in. For radii less than 32-in., you may have to wet the panels; contact the wallboard manufacturer to learn the bending properties of their product. (See pages 88 to 89.) If you will be covering the wall with plywood, space the studs at 2-in. per foot of outer radius. For example, a wall with a 36" outer radius should have studs spaced 6" O.C.

By virtue of their shape, curved walls provide some of their own stability, so that half-walls with pronounced curves may not need additional support if they're secured at one end. If your wall needs additional support, look for ways to tie it into the existing framing, or install cabinets or other permanent fixtures for stability.

If you are planning a curved wall of full height, use a plumb bob to transfer the layout of the bottom track to ceiling for the layout of the top track. Check the alignment of using a few studs at the ends and middle, then fasten the top track to the ceiling joists with wallboard screws.

**12" min. of strip at each end of curve**

**2"**

**Steel strip**

**As a substitute for flexible track,** use standard 20- or 25-gauge steel track. Along the curved portion of the wall, cut the web and flange along the outside of the curve at 2" intervals. From the web of a scrap piece, cut a 1"-wide strip that runs the length of the curve, plus 8". Bend the track to follow the curve, then screw the strip to the inside of the outer flange, using ⁷⁄₁₆" type S screws. This construction requires 12" of straight (uncut) track at both ends of the curve.

### Everything You Need

Tools: Framing square, chalk line, marker, aviation snips, drill, 2-ft. level.

Materials: Flexible metal track, masking tape, ⁷⁄₁₆" Type S pan-head screws, 2 × 4 lumber, 1¼" coarse-thread drywall screws.

## How to Frame a Curved Half-wall

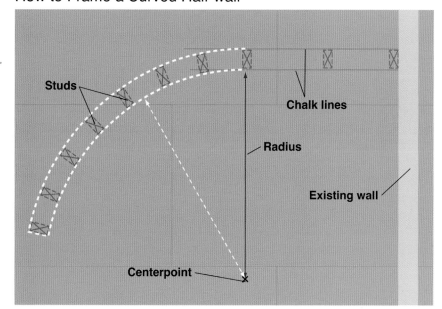

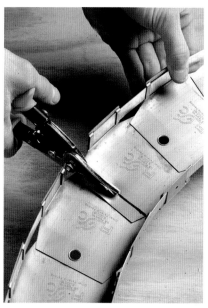

**1** Draw the wall layout. Mark straight portions with parallel chalk lines representing the outside edges of the wall track. Use a framing square to make sure the lines are perpendicular to the adjoining wall. At the start of the curve, square off from the chalk line and measure out the distance of the radius to mark the curve's centerpoint. For small curves (4 ft., or so), drive a nail at the centerpoint, hook the end of a tape measure on the nail, and draw the curve using the tape and a pencil as a compass; for larger curves, use a straight board nailed at the centerpoint.

**2** Position the track along the layout lines, following the curve exactly. Mark the end of the wall onto the track, using a marker, then cut the track to length with aviation snips. Cut the top track to the same length.

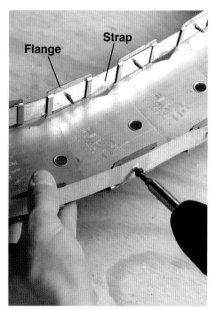

**3** Reposition the bottom track on the layout, then apply masking tape along the outside flanges. Secure the track by driving a type S screw through each flange and into the strap. Screw both sides of the track. Turn over the bottom track, then set the top track on top and match its shape. Tape and screw the top track.

**4** Fasten the bottom track to the floor, using 1¼" drywall screws. Mark the stud layout onto both tracks. Cut the studs to length. Install the studs one at a time, using a level to plumb each along its narrow edge, then driving a 1¼" screw through the flange or strap and into the stud on both sides.

**5** Fit the top track over the studs and align them with the layout marks. Fasten the studs to the top track with one screw on each side, checking the wall for level and height as you work. Set the level on top of the track, both parallel and perpendicular to the track, before fastening each stud.

# Building Glass Block Walls

With its ability to transmit light, a glass block partition wall defines separate living areas while maintaining a sense of openness. You can find glass block at specialty distributors and home centers in a variety of patterns, shapes, and sizes, along with all the products needed for the installation.

You can build your wall to any height. Top a low wall with a course of bullnose blocks to give it a finished rounded edge, or with flat block to create a shelf. To build a full-height wall, calculate the number of courses of block you'll have, then frame-in a header to fill the remaining space between the finished block and the ceiling.

Follow these tips for a successful installation: When laying out your wall, keep in mind that glass block cannot be cut, so measure carefully. Lay-up the wall using plastic spacers set between the blocks. These ensure consistent mortar joints, and they support the weight of the block to prevent the mortar from squeezing out before it sets. Use premixed glass block mortar, available in dry-mix bags, in white and mortar-gray. When mixing the mortar, follow the manufacturer's directions carefully to achieve the ideal working consistency.

Because of its weight, a glass block wall requires a sturdy foundation. A 4"-thick concrete basement floor should be strong enough, but a wood floor may need to be reinforced. Contact the local building department for requirements in your area. Also bear in mind that glass block products and installation techniques vary by manufacturer—ask a glass block retailer or manufacturer for advice about the best products and methods for your project.

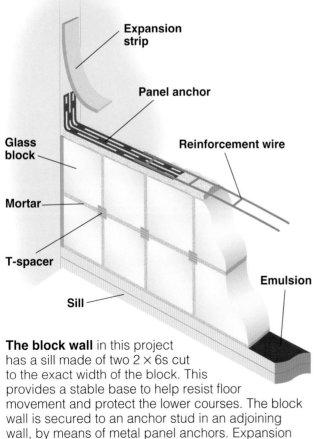

Expansion strip

Panel anchor

Glass block

Reinforcement wire

Mortar

T-spacer

Emulsion

Sill

**The block wall** in this project has a sill made of two 2 × 6s cut to the exact width of the block. This provides a stable base to help resist floor movement and protect the lower courses. The block wall is secured to an anchor stud in an adjoining wall, by means of metal panel anchors. Expansion strips between the two walls allow for movement.

## Everything You Need

Tools: Chalk line, circular saw, jig saw, paintbrush, drill, mixing box, trowel, level, pliers, jointing tool, nylon- or natural-bristle brush, sponge.

Materials: 2 × 6 lumber, 16d common nails, water-based asphalt emulsion, panel anchors, 2½" drywall screws, foam expansion strips, glass block mortar, 8" glass blocks, ¼" T-spacers, board, reinforcement wire, 16-gauge wire, caulk or wall trim, baseboard.

# How to Build a Glass Block Wall

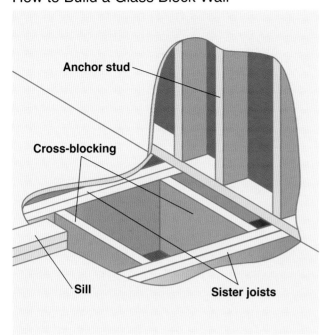

**Tip:** If necessary, reinforce the floor joists nearest the new wall by installing sister joists and blocking that are the same size as the existing joists. If the new wall is not aligned with an existing wall stud, add an anchor stud centered at the new wall location. You can install the sill directly over the subfloor or over a suitable floorcovering.

**1** Dry-lay the first course of glass block, using a $\frac{3}{8}$" wood spacer between the wall and the first block, and $\frac{1}{4}$" spacers between the remaining blocks, to set the gaps for the mortar joints. Mark the wall position onto the floor, then remove the blocks. Snap chalk lines along the marks to create the sill outline.

**2** Determine the sill thickness based on the size of your baseboard and thickness of the floorcovering. Rip 2 × 6 lumber to the width of the block. If the end blocks are shaped, trim the sill pieces to match, using a jig saw. Fasten the sill to the subfloor and framing below with 16d common nails. Apply asphalt emulsion to the sill, using a paintbrush.

**3** Mark plumb lines on the adjoining wall, straight up from sides of the sill. Mark the finished height of each course along the lines. Fasten a panel anchor to the anchor stud at the top of every second course, using 2$\frac{1}{2}$" drywall screws. Cut expansion strips to size and adhere them to the wall between the anchors.

(continued next page)

**4** Mix only as much mortar as you can apply in about 30 minutes. Lay a ⅜"-thick mortar bed on the sill, enough for three or four blocks. Set the first block, using ¼" T-spacers at the mortar joint locations (follow the manufacturer's directions for modifying T-spacers at the bottom and sides of the wall). Do not place mortar between blocks and expansion strips. Butter the trailing edge of each subsequent block with enough mortar to fill the sides of both blocks.

**5** Lay the remainder of the course. If the wall has a corner, work from both ends toward the center, and install the corner piece last. Use ¼" T-spacers between blocks to maintain proper spacing. Plumb and level each block as you work, then check the entire course, using a flat board and a level. Tap blocks into place using a rubber mallet—do not strike them with a metal tool.

**6** At the top of the course, fill the joints with mortar, and then lay a ¼" bed of mortar for the second course. Lay the block for the second course, checking each block for level and plumb as you work.

**7** Apply a ⅛" bed of mortar over the second course, then press the panel anchor into the mortar. Repeat this process at each anchor location.

**8** Add reinforcement wire in the same joints as the panel anchors, overlapping the anchors by 6". Also overlap the wire by 6" where multiple pieces are needed. At corners, cut the inner rail of the wire, bend the outer rail to follow the corner, then tie the inner rail ends together with 16-gauge wire. Add another ⅛" mortar bed, then lay the next course of block.

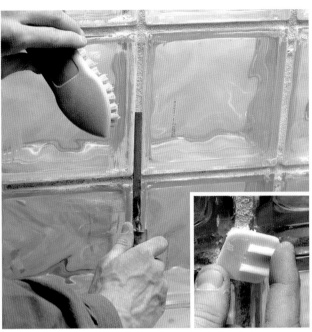

**9** Build the wall in complete courses, checking the mortar after each course. When it is hard enough to resist light finger pressure (usually within 30 minutes), twist off the T-spacer tabs (inset) and pack mortar in the voids. Then, tool all of the joints with a jointing tool. Remove excess mortar from the glass, using a brush or damp sponge.

**10** Clean the glass block thoroughly, using a wet sponge and rinsing it often. Allow the surface to dry, then remove cloudy residue with a clean, dry cloth. After the mortar has cured for two weeks, apply a sealant. Caulk the seam between the glass block and the adjoining wall, or cover the gap with trim.

**11** Reinstall the flooring, if necessary, then cut baseboard to fit around the sill (see pages 200 to 205). If the end of your wall has curved (bullnose) block, wrap the end with three pieces of trim.

# Installing Fiberglass Insulation

Before you insulate your walls, ceilings, or floors (or even buy insulation), ask the local building department about two things: R-value and vapor barriers. All insulation has an R-value clearly printed on its packaging. This is the measure of how well the insulation keeps in the heat and keeps out the cold, and vice versa. The higher the R-value, the better the insulation works—and the thicker it is. The building department will tell you what R-values you need for your walls, ceilings, and floors, and whether the insulation job must be inspected before you cover it.

Vapor barriers come in a few different forms, but all have a common purpose. They prevent the water vapor present in warm indoor air from passing beyond wall or ceiling surfaces and through the framing, where it would contact cold exterior surfaces and condense. This condensation promotes mildew growth that can rot the framing and insulation. Vapor barriers are required in most climates and are typically installed on the "warm-in-winter" side of exterior walls and ceilings, between the insulation and the interior finish material.

Paper-faced, foil-faced, and encapsulated insulation have their own vapor barriers, but a layer of 6-mil polyethylene sheeting stapled to framing members over unfaced insulation provides a more effective, continuous barrier. If you decide to use faced insulation be aware that it comes with a few drawbacks: the paper tears easily, and facings make it difficult to cut around obstacles. Also, if you trim a batt to fit into a narrow bay, you lose the facing flange—and thus the vapor seal—on one side. Most facings are flammable and must be covered with wallboard or another approved finish, even in unfinished areas, such as storage rooms. One alternative is to use insulation with an approved flame-resistant foil facing.

When installing insulation, make sure there are no gaps between the insulation and framing, around obstructions, or between pieces of insulation. The idea is to create a continuous "thermal envelope" that keeps interior air from coming into contact with outdoor temperatures.

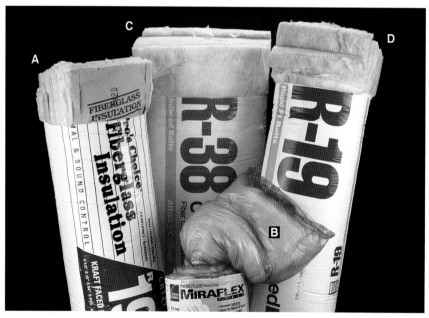

**Fiberglass insulation** comes in batts cut to length for standard stud-wall bays, as well as long rolls. Various options include: kraft-paper and foil facings (A), which serve as vapor barriers (some foils are flame-resistant); plastic-encapsulated blankets (B); high density blankets (for rafters) (C); and standard, unfaced rolls and batts (D). Standard widths fit between 16"- or 24"-on-center framing.

**Handling fiberglass** is a lot less uncomfortable when you're dressed for it. Wear long pants, a long-sleeve shirt, gloves, goggles, and a good-quality dust mask or respirator. Shower as soon as you finish working.

## Tips for Installing Fiberglass Insulation

**Never compress insulation** to fit into a narrow space. Instead, use a sharp utility knife to trim the blanket about ¼" wider and longer than the space. To trim, hold the blanket in place and use a wall stud as a straightedge and cutting surface.

**Insulate around pipes**, wires, and electrical boxes by peeling the blanket in half and sliding the back half behind the obstruction. Then, lay the front half in front of the obstruction. Trim the front half to fit snugly around boxes.

**Use scraps** of insulation to fill gaps around window and door jambs. Fill the cavities loosely to avoid compressing the insulation. Fill narrow gaps with expanding spray-foam insulation, following manufacturer's instructions.

## Tips for Adding Vapor Barriers

**Provide a vapor barrier** using faced insulation by tucking in the edges of the insulation until the facing flanges are flush with the edges of the framing. Make sure the flanges lie flat, with no wrinkles or gaps, and staple them to the faces of the framing members about every 8". Patch any gaps or facing tears with packing tape or a construction tape supplied by the manufacturer.

**Install a polyethylene vapor barrier** by draping the sheeting over the entire wall or ceiling, extending it a few inches beyond the perimeter and overlapping the sheets at least 12". Staple the sheeting to the framing, then carefully cut around obstructions. Seal around electrical boxes and other penetrations with packing tape. Trim excess sheeting along the ceiling and floor after you install the surface material.

# Soundproofing Walls & Ceilings

In making homes quieter, building professionals add soundproofing elements to combat everything from the hum of appliances to the roar of airliners. Many of the techniques they use are simple improvements involving common products and materials. What will work best in your home depends upon a few factors, including the types of noises involved, your home's construction, and how much remodeling you have planned. For starters, it helps to know a little of the science behind sound control.

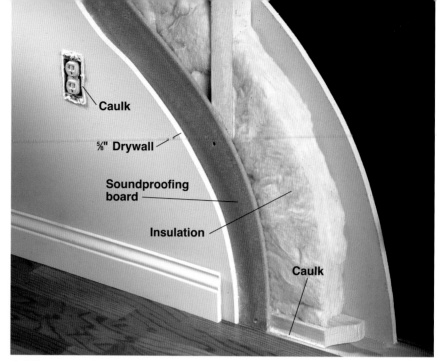

**Caulk**

**⅝" Drywall**

**Soundproofing board**

**Insulation**

**Caulk**

**Adding soundproofing board** and insulation are among the many simple ways you can reduce noise in your home.

Sound is created by vibrations traveling through air. Consequently, the best ways to reduce sound transmission are by limiting airflow and blocking or absorbing vibrations. Effective soundproofing typically involves a combination of methods.

Stopping airflow—through walls, ceilings, floors, windows, and doors—is essential to any soundproofing effort. (Even a 2-ft.-thick brick wall would not be very soundproof if it had cracks in the mortar.) It's also the simplest way to make minor improvements. Because you're dealing with air, this kind of soundproofing is a lot like weatherizing your home: add weatherstripping and door sweeps, seal air leaks with caulk, install storm doors and windows, etc. The same techniques that keep out the cold also block exterior noise and prevent sound from traveling between rooms.

After reducing airflow, the next level of soundproofing is to improve the sound-blocking qualities of your walls and ceilings. Engineers rate soundproofing performance of wall and ceiling assemblies using a system called Sound Transmission Class, or STC. The higher the STC rating, the more sound is blocked by the assembly. For example, if a wall is rated at 30 to 35 STC, loud speech can be understood through the wall. At 42 STC, loud speech is reduced to a murmur. At 50 STC, loud speech cannot be heard through the wall.

Standard construction methods typically result in a 28 to 32 STC rating, while soundproofed walls and ceilings can carry ratings near 50. To give you an idea of how much soundproofing you need, a sleeping room at 40 to 50 STC is quiet enough for most people; a reading room is comfortable at 35 to 40 STC. For another gauge, consider the fact that increasing the STC rating of an assembly by 10 reduces the perceived sound levels by 50%. The chart on page 45 lists the STC ratings of several wall and ceiling assemblies.

Improvements to walls and ceilings usually involve increasing the mass, absorbancy, or resiliency of the assembly; often, a combination is best. Adding layers of drywall increases mass, helping a wall resist the vibrational force of sound (⅝" fire-resistant drywall works best because of its greater weight and density). Insulation and soundproofing board absorb sound. Soundproofing board is available through drywall suppliers and manufacturers (see page 234). Some board products are gypsum-based; others are lightweight fiberboard. Installing resilient steel channels over the framing or old surface and adding a new layer of drywall increases mass, while the channels allow the surface to move slightly and absorb vibrations. New walls built with staggered studs and insulation are highly effective at reducing vibration.

In addition to these permanent improvements, you can reduce noise by decorating with soft materials that absorb sound. Rugs and carpet, drapery, fabric wall hangings, and soft furniture help reduce atmospheric noise within a room. Acoustical ceiling tiles effectively absorb and help contain sound within a room but do little to prevent sound from entering the room.

## STC Ratings for Various Wall & Ceiling Constructions*

| Assembly | STC Rating | Assembly | STC Rating |
|---|---|---|---|
| *Wood-frame Walls* | | *Steel-frame Walls* | |
| • 2 × 4 wall; ½" drywall on both sides; no caulk | 30 | • 3⅝" metal studs, spaced 24" on-center; ⅝" fire-resistant drywall on both sides | 40 |
| • 2 × 4 wall; ½" drywall on both sides; caulked | 35 | • 3⅝" metal studs, spaced 24" on-center, ½" fire-resistant drywall single layer on one side, doubled on other side; insulated | 48 |
| • 2 × 4 wall; ½" drywall on both sides; additional layer of ⅝" fire-resistant drywall on one side | 38 | • 2½" metal studs, spaced 24" on-center; soundproofing board (base layer) and ½" fire-resistant drywall on both sides; insulated | 50 |
| • 2 × 4 wall; ½" drywall on both sides; additional layer of ⅝" fire-resistant drywall on both sides | 40 | *Wood-frame Floor/Ceiling* | |
| • 2 × 4 wall; ½" drywall on both sides; insulated | 39 | • Drywall below; subfloor and resilient (vinyl) flooring above | 32 |
| • Staggered-stud 2 × 4 wall; ⅝" fire-resistant drywall on each side; insulated | 50 | • ⅝" fire-resistant drywall attached to resilient steel channels below; subfloor, pad, and carpet above | 48 |
| • 2 × 4 wall, soundproofing board (base layer) and ⅝" fire-resistant drywall on each side; insulated | 50 | • Double layer ⅝" fire-resistant drywall attached to resilient steel channels below; subfloor, pad, and carpet above | Up to 60 |
| • 2 × 4 wall with resilient steel channels on one side; ⅝" fire-resistant drywall on both sides; insulated | 52 | | |

*All assemblies are sealed with caulk, except where noted. Ratings are approximate.

## Tips for Reducing Exterior Noise

**Install weatherstripping** on doors and windows to seal off any air leaks. If the wall framing around the door or window is exposed, make sure all cavities are filled with loosely packed insulation.

**Add storm doors and windows** to minimize air leaks and create an additional sound barrier. Use high-performance (air-tight) storm units and maintain a 2" air gap between the storm and the primary unit.

**Seal around pipes,** A/C service lines, vents, and other penetrations in exterior walls, using expanding foam or caulk. Make sure through-wall A/C units are well-sealed along their perimeters.

45

# Tips for Reducing Interior Noise

**Stop airflow** between rooms by sealing the joints where walls meet floors. With finished walls, remove the shoe molding and spray insulating foam, acoustic sealant, or non-hardening caulk under the baseboards. Also seal around door casings. With new walls, seal along the top and bottom plates.

**Cover switch and receptacle boxes** with foam gaskets to prevent air leaks. Otherwise, seal around the box perimeter with acoustic sealant or caulk and seal around the knockout where the cables enter the box.

**Soundproof doors between rooms** by adding a sweep at the bottom and weatherstripping along the stops. If doors are hollow-core, replacing them with solid-core units will increase soundproofing performance. Soundproof workshop and utility room doors with a layer of acoustical tiles.

**Reduce sound transmission through ductwork** by lining ducts with special insulation (see page 234). If a duct supplying a quiet room has a takeoff point close to that of a noisy room, move one or both ducts so their takeoff points are as distant from each other as possible.

## How to Install Resilient Steel Channels

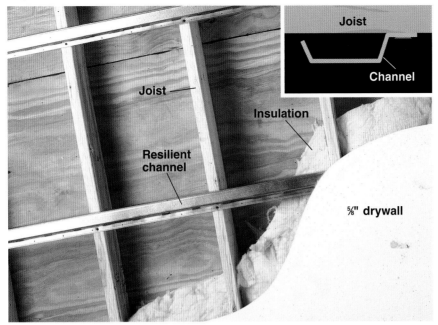

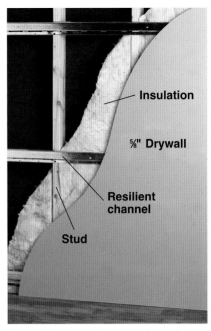

**On ceilings,** install channels perpendicular to the joists, spaced 24" on-center. Fasten at each joist with 1¼" type W drywall screws, driven through the channel flange. Stop the channels 1" short of all walls. Join pieces on long runs by overlapping the ends and fastening through both pieces. Insulate the joist bays with R-11 unfaced fiberglass or other insulation and install ⅝" fire-resistant drywall, run perpendicular to the channels. For double-layer application, install the second layer of drywall perpendicular to the first.

**On walls,** use the same installation techniques as with the ceiling application, installing the channels horizontally. Position the bottom channel 2" from the floor and the top channel within 6" of the ceiling. Insulate the stud cavities and install the drywall vertically.

## How to Build Staggered-stud Partition Walls

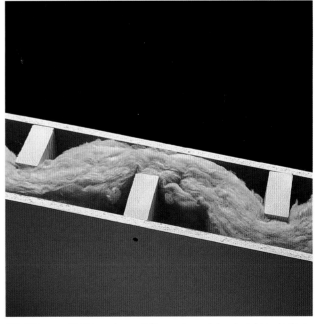

**1** Frame new partition walls using 2 × 6 plates. Space the studs 12" apart, staggering them so alternate studs are aligned with opposite sides of the plates. Seal under and above the plates with acoustic sealant.

**2** Weave R-11 unfaced fiberglass blanket insulation horizontally between the studs. Cover each side with one or more layers of ⅝" fire-resistant drywall.

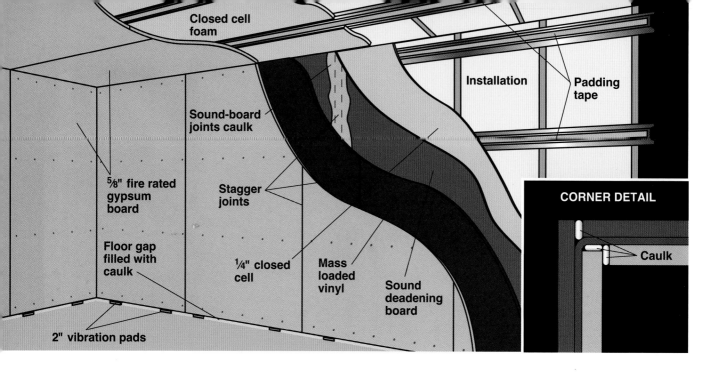

**Closed cell foam**

**Installation**

**Padding tape**

**Sound-board joints caulk**

**CORNER DETAIL**

**⅝" fire rated gypsum board**

**Stagger joints**

**Caulk**

**Floor gap filled with caulk**

**¼" closed cell**

**Mass loaded vinyl**

**Sound deadening board**

**2" vibration pads**

# Soundproofing Home Theaters

Home theaters are quickly becoming a common feature in many homes. And while finding an affordable yet impressive multimedia system is no longer a problem, finding a space within your home to enjoy it may not be so easy. The walls of the average house are not designed to contain extreme sound levels. To combat this issue, there are numerous soundproofing products and materials available to help keep those on both sides of a home theater wall happy.

As discussed on page 44, engineers rate the soundproofing performance of wall and ceiling assemblies using a system called Sound Transmission Class (STC). Standard partition walls carry STC ratings of 28 to 32. Determining an appropriate STC rating for your home theater is dependent on a number of factors, such as the power of your multimedia system and the type of room opposite the wall, but a minimum of 60 STC is adequate for most. Remember: The higher the STC rating, the more sound is blocked.

But blocking sound is not the only consideration. The low frequencies generated by subwoofers cause vibrations, which in turn create unwanted noise within the room. The most effective approach for soundproofing a home theater is to install both sound barriers to minimize sound escaping and sound absorbers to reduce noise within the room.

Adding mass to walls and ceilings is an effective way to block sound. In new construction, staggered-stud partitions (page 47) or double stud partitions (two adjacent rows of studs) are

possibilities. Hanging soundproofing board, sound-rated wallboard, or multiple layers of wallboard can increase STC ratings significantly. Two of the most effective systems are resilient channels (page 47) and mass loaded vinyl (MLV) underlayment, a heavy vinyl sheeting which many manufacturers claim can more than double a wall's STC rating.

For sound absorption, closed-cell acoustical foam matting can be used to insulate between wallboard panels and framing. Similarly, padded tape minimizes transmission of sound vibration between wall panels and framing, and can be used to line resilient channels for added insulation. Sound isolation mounting clips contain molded neoprene to provide added insulation between resilient channels and framing. Vibration pads made of cork and closed-cell acoustical foam or neoprene isolates sound vibration to reduce transmission between objects.

When fastening soundproofing and wallboard panels to resilient channels, leave a ¼-in. between all panels at corners, and fill the gaps with acoustical caulk. All gaps, seams, and cracks should be filled with acoustical caulk. The more airtight a home theater, the more soundproof it is.

Whichever soundproofing products or materials you choose, make sure to follow the manufacturer's installation instruction to achieve the optimal performance. For more information regarding soundproofing board and sound-rated wallboard, see pages 55 and 84 to 85.

## Tips for Soundproofing a Home Theater

**Use contact cement** to glue ¼" closed-cell acoustical matting directly to existing wall and ceiling surfaces or to the backside of wallboard panels in new construction.

**Apply self-adhesive** padded tape to resilient channels or directly to the edges of framing members.

**Staple MLV** (mass loaded vinyl) underlayment directly to framing members, between layers of wallboard and soundproofing board, or directly to existing wall and ceiling surfaces. Overlap seams by at least 6".

**Install 2" vibration pads** every 2 feet between flooring and installed wallboard panels. Fasten baseboard into framing only, not into vibration pads.

**Seal all gaps** between panels and at wall and ceiling joints with acoustical caulk.

**Plastic sheeting, sheet membrane, building paper, and trowel-applied membrane** are all options for adding waterproofing to walls. Isolation membranes in strips or sheets also protect tile surfaces from cracking due to small movements in the underlayment.

# Installing Wall Membranes

Wall membranes may provide waterproofing or isolation from small underlayment movement, or both. Because water does not sit on wall surfaces as it does on floors, waterproofing of walls is not as critical. In most cases, plastic sheeting or building paper behind cement backer board is sufficient. Saunas and steam rooms may need additional waterproofing.

Isolation membrane comes in roll- or trowel-on forms as well as in sheet form. It can be applied to existing cracks or potential areas of movement. Check the product directions for the maximum width crack or expansion joint that can be spanned and the type of substrate on which it can be used.

It is important to apply isolation membrane to concrete walls to prevent hairline cracks from being transferred outward to the tile or grout surface. Some products combine waterproofing and isolation properties. The tile adhesive is applied directly to the isolation membrane after it has cured.

Be sure to check for compatibility between the roll- or trowel-on membranes and your particular application needs. Fountains and pools have specific waterproofing needs—check with your tile dealer if you plan on using wall tile for a pool wall.

**A water barrier of 4-mil plastic sheeting** can be stapled to studs before installing cementboard or fiber-cement board.

**Building paper (15#)** can also be used as a water barrier behind cementboard and fiber-cement board. Start from the bottom and install horizontally so each layer overlaps the previous one by two inches.

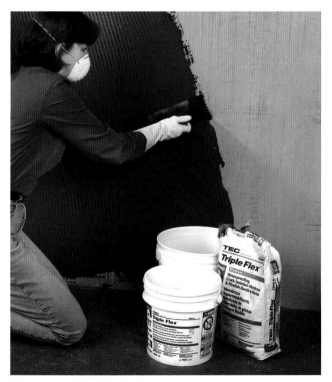

**Waterproofing/isolation membranes** are an easy way to add waterproofing and crack protection to existing walls. This application is especially suited to smooth, solid concrete surfaces. The tile adhesive is applied directly to the membrane after it dries.

**Isolation membrane** may be used on wall and ceiling surfaces in areas such as steam rooms and saunas that have extreme temperature fluctuation and high humidity. The membrane is typically installed with mortar, but some membranes must be used with a specific bonding agent.

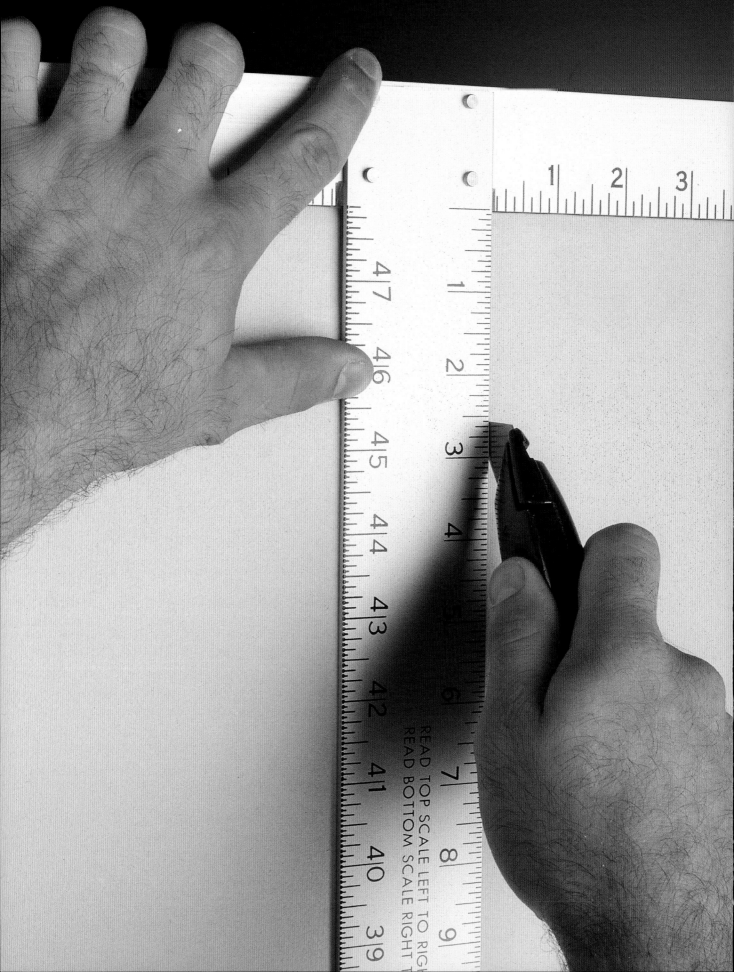

# Installing Wallboard

**Most home centers and lumberyards** have ample supplies of common wallboard products and materials in stock. If you can't find what you need, call a wallboard supplier, usually listed in the phone book under "Building Materials," "Wallboard," or "Drywall."

# Wallboard & Wallboard Installation Materials

Drywall in its present form was developed in 1917 as an economical substitute for plaster. It became popular during the 1940s and today has all but replaced plaster in new construction. Because drywall is inexpensive, perfectly uniform, and easy to install, it's also the best choice for do-it-yourselfers working on remodeling projects.

Drywall panels consist of a core of solid gypsum (a natural mineral product) wrapped in paper. The paper, which is thick, smooth, and white on the panel face and rougher and gray on the back, provides most of the panel's strength, so it's important that the paper remains intact.

The long edges of drywall panels are tapered about $2\frac{1}{2}$" from the edge. When two panels are butted together, the tapered edges create a recess for the joint tape and drywall compound that cover the seam and make the panels appear continuous. The ends of the panels, which are not tapered, are more difficult to finish when butted together.

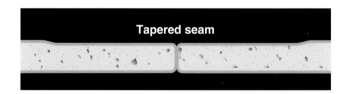

**Tapered seam**

## Wallboard Panels

Know by several common names, such as gypsum board, plasterboard, drywall, and Sheetrock, wallboard comes in a variety of types and sizes, each designed to perform best under specific conditions.

*Standard drywall* is used for most walls and ceilings in dry, interior areas. It comes in 4-ft.-wide panels in lengths ranging from 8 ft. to 16 ft. and in thicknesses of $\frac{1}{4}$", $\frac{3}{8}$", $\frac{1}{2}$", and $\frac{5}{8}$". There are also 54"-wide panels for horizontal installations on walls with 9-ft. ceilings.

Standard $\frac{1}{2}$" panels are appropriate for walls and for ceilings with standard 16" on-center framing. Where ceiling framing is 24" on-center, $\frac{5}{8}$" standard panels or $\frac{1}{2}$" *ceiling panels* are recommended to prevent sagging (ceiling panels are specifically designed for this application, and for when heavy, water-based textures will be applied). The ¼" and ⅜" panels are useful for adding a smooth veneer over old, rough surfaces and for curved walls.

*Flexible drywall,* specially made for curved walls, is a more flexible version of standard ¼"-thick drywall. It can be installed dry or dampened with water to increase its flexibility.

*Fire-resistant drywall* has a dense, fiber-reinforced core that helps contain fire. Thicknesses are ½", ⅝", and ¾". Your local building department may require fire-resistant panels in garages, on walls adjacent to garages, and in furnace and utility rooms.

*Moisture-resistant drywall,* commonly called greenboard or blueboard, for the color of its face paper, is made to hold up in areas of high-humidity and against occasional contact with moisture. It is used most often in bathrooms, behind kitchen sinks, and in laundry rooms. For 16" on-center framing, ½"-thick panels are appropriate for walls, and ⅝" panels for ceilings. For wet areas that will receive tile, it's better to use a tile backer (see page 56) rather than greenboard.

*Abuse-resistant drywall* withstands surface impacts and resists penetrations better than standard drywall. It's available in ½" regular and ⅝" fire-resistant types.

*Foil-backed drywall* has a foil layer in its back side that serves as a vapor barrier to prevent interior water vapor from migrating outward into the wall cavity. These panels are not recommended for tile applications or for use in hot, humid climates.

*Decorative drywall* products are available from various major and specialty manufacturers. Popular options include prefinished vinyl-coated panel systems, decorative corner treatments, prefabricated arches, and drywall panels that look like traditional paneling.

Blueboard is the common name of the wallboard panels used with veneer plaster systems. Panels are actually wrapped in two layers of paper. The blue-colored face paper is highly absorptive while the second layer is moisture-resistant to protect the gypsum core. The wet-mix plaster soaks into the face layer, but stops at the base layer, thereby bonding with the former to create a solid, monolithic surface that is stronger and more consistent than wallboard.

High-density gypsum and cellulose fiber sound-proofing board provide excellent noise attenuation for home theaters, media rooms, and other

**¼" flexible drywall**

**⅝" fire-resistant drywall**

**Moisture-resistant drywall**

**½" standard drywall**

quiet spaces. Both types are available in common thicknesses up to ⅝-in.; when used in multi-layer installations, their sound-deadening capabilities increase.

Mold-resistant wallboard is a specialty board designed for areas that are regularly damp, have high humidity or that are otherwise susceptible to mold and mildew growth. There are two main types available: paperless and "purpleboard." Paperless wallboard is a gypsum panel faced with glass matting that replaces the paper mold feeds on. "Purpleboard" is a paper-faced panel treated with a number of moisture-, mold-, and mildew-resistant chemicals, and can be used as a tile backer.

## TILE BACKER

If you're planning to tile new walls in wet areas, such as tub and shower enclosures, use tile backer board as a substrate rather than drywall. Unlike drywall, tile backer won't break down—and ruin the tile job—if water gets behind the tile. There are three basic types of tile backer (see page 234 for supplier information):

*Cementboard* is made from portland cement and sand reinforced by a continuous outer layer of fiberglass mesh. It's available in ½" and ⅝" thicknesses. See page 92 to 93 for installation instructions.

*Fiber-cement board* is similar to cementboard but is somewhat lighter, with fiber reinforcement integrated throughout the panel material. It comes in ¼" and ½" thicknesses. Cementboard and fiber-cement board cannot be damaged by water, but water can pass through them. To prevent damage to the framing, install a water barrier of 4-mil plastic or 15# building paper behind the backer.

*Dens-Shield®*, commonly called glass mat, is a water-resistant gypsum board with a waterproof fiberglass facing. Dens-Shield cuts and installs much like standard drywall but requires galvanized screws to prevent corrosion. Because the front surface provides the water barrier, all untaped joints and penetrations must be sealed with caulk before the tile is installed. Do not use a water barrier behind Dens-Shield.

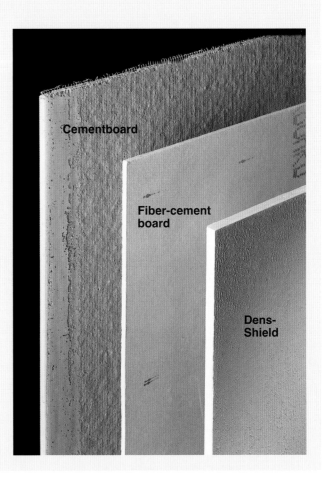

Cementboard

Fiber-cement board

Dens-Shield

**TIP: Pre-bowing panels** helps ensure a tight seal with the framing when using adhesives. The day before installation, stack panels face up, supporting each end with a pair of 2 × 4s. This helps create pressure between the panel and the studs as the memory of the panel tries to revert to the bowed shape.

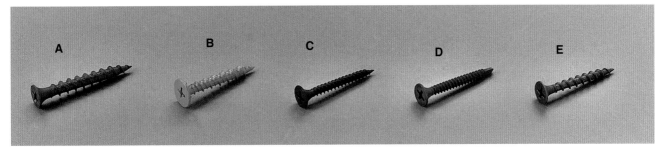

**Screws for attaching wallboard** include (from left): type-G for multi-layer installations (A), cementboard screws (B), type-S standard and self-tapping for attaching panels to steel framing (C, D), and type-W screws for screwing panels to wood framing (E).

## Fasteners

**Wallboard screws** have replaced nails as the fastener-of-choice for most professionals, and for good reason. Screws hold better than nails and are less likely to "pop," they install faster, and they're easier to drive without damaging the wallboard. Wallboard screws have bugle-shaped heads that help them countersink into the panel surface without breaking the face paper. There are four types of screws common to wallboard installation:

**Type-W screws** have coarse threads for securing panels to wood framing. They offer tremendous holding power when properly installed. Type-W screws must be long enough to penetrate wood framing by a minimum of $\frac{5}{8}$"

**Type-G screws** have a thicker shank and a coarse thread pattern for holding together panels in multi-layer installations that do not require fastening to framing. To use type-G screws, the base layer must be a minimum of $\frac{1}{2}$" thick.

**Type-S screws** are fine-threaded fasteners for securing wallboard to steel framing resilient channels. Make sure type-S screws penetrate steel framing by at least $\frac{3}{8}$"

**Cementboard screws** are made from stainless steel with ridges beneath the head that cut into the backer board to countersink the screw head.

**Wallboard screws** are sold by the pound at home centers and lumberyards. Typically, you'll use a Phillips drive to install screws, though the square drive (or "Robertson) is finding popularity. Outfit your screwgun or drill with the proper bit and change it out for a new one at the first sign of wear.

## Adhesives

Adhesives can be used in wallboard installation, and offer a number of benefits: they create a much stronger bond between framing and panels,

they reduce the number of fasteners needed by up to 75%, and they can bridge minor irregularities in framing members. Adhesives are available in tubes and applied in $\frac{3}{8}$" using a caulk gun.

There are three types of adhesives used for installing wallboard. Construction adhesive is used with screws for gluing panels directly to framing or a solid base, such as concrete basement walls. Panel or laminating adhesive is used for gluing wallboard panels to other panels in multi-layer installations, or to bond wallboard with concrete walls or rigid foam insulation. A few type-G wallboard screws may be needed to support panels while the adhesive sets up. Contact cement is used for attaching other coverings to wallboard panels, such as mass loaded vinyl sheeting for soundproofing (see pages 48 to 49).

While not an adhesive, acoustical caulk is used during multiple layer installations to seal all gaps around the perimeter of installed panels, along corners, ceilings, and floors. Acoustical caulk also comes in tubes and is applied with a caulk gun.

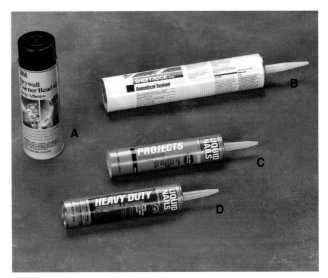

**Adhesives used for wallboard** include: contact cement A), acoustical caulk (B) and panel adhesive (C) and construction adhesive (D).

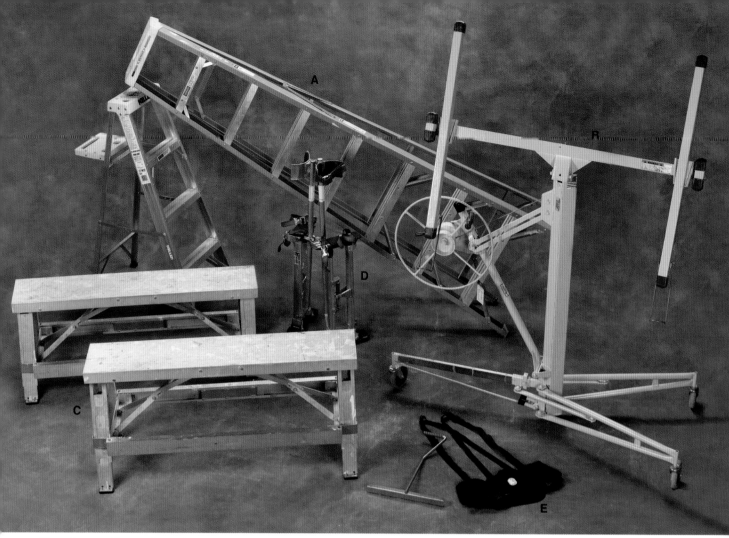

**Hanging wallboard** requires a number of support and safety tools and equipment. While stepladders (A) are the most readily available for accessing ceilings and upper walls, a wallboard lift (B) can hoist a panel tight against the framing. The lift's frame can also be tilted to accommodate the pitch of attic and cathedral ceilings. Wallboard benches (C) and wallboard stilts (D) are other options, bringing you within reach of ceilings for easy panel installation. To avoid injury to your back, use a panel carrier and lower-back support (E) when moving or lifting panels.

# Tools for Installing Wallboard

To hang wallboard you'll need a variety of tools to measure, mark, and cut panels to size, as well as fasten them to the framing. A tape measure is a necessity for measuring and marking wallboard. A T-square saves time by helping you make straight, square cuts across the entire width of a panel, while a chalk line creates layout and cutting lines across greater spans. To check the framing for plumb and square, a framing square and 4-ft. level are handy.

The main tool for cutting wallboard is a utility knife. Make sure you have plenty of extra sharp blades on hand, swapping out the dull ones often. Use a wallboard rasp to smooth cut panel edges. A standard compass is necessary for scribing adjacent surfaces onto a panel and creating small circles for cutouts. For larger circles,

use a wallboard compass to score the panel. A drill can also be outfitted with a hole saw for pipes and other small round cutouts. A keyhole saw makes quick work of small holes, such as those for electrical boxes. A wallboard saw cuts notches for doors, windows, and other openings quickly. But for genuine speed in making cutouts, use a wallboard router to cut through panels after they have been installed.

The best tool for hanging wallboard is a screwgun. Similar to a drill, a screw gun has an adjustable clutch that stops driving the screw at a preset depth. For large jobs, it's practical to rent a screwgun; otherwise, use a variable speed 3/8" drill and drive the screws carefully. A wallboard lifter helps you prop up panels while fastening them, but a flat bar can perform the same func-

**Tools for installing wallboard include:** plumb bob (A), drywall rasp (B), compass (C), wallboard compass (D), protective masks (E), drill with hole saw (F), drywall router (G), drywall gun (H), utility knife (I), eye protection (J), tape measure (K), wallboard lifter (L), caulk gun (M), pry bar (N), wallboard saw (O), keyhole saw (P), framing square (Q), level (R), wallboard T-square (S).

tion. Apply adhesives and caulking using a caulk gun.

Wallboard hand tools can be purchased at home centers at reasonable prices. If you don't wish to buy power tools, most of them can be can be found at rental centers, along with a variety of the specialty tools. During every phase of a wallboard project, make sure to protect yourself from the dust and debris generated—always wear protective eyewear, with a dust mask or respirator when cutting wallboard.

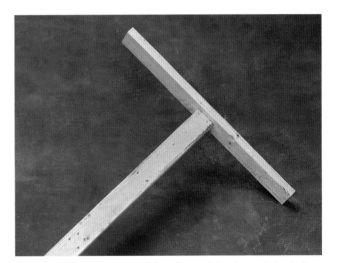

**A pair of T-braces or "deadmen"** that are 1-in. taller than the ceiling height can help hold wallboard against the framing during ceiling installations. Cut a straight 2 × 4 so it's a ½" shorter than the ceiling height, then fasten a 36-in.-long 2 × 4 to the end for the bracing arm.

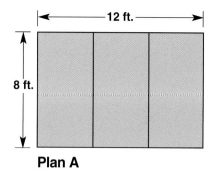

**Plan A**

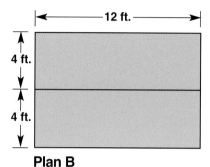

**Plan B**

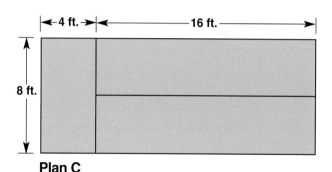

**Plan C**

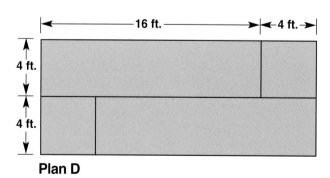

**Plan D**

## Wallboard Grain

Gypsum wallboard actually has a grain that runs parallel to its long tapered sides, giving panels more strength along their length then across their width. Installing panels perpendicular to the framing provides stronger, more rigid wall and ceiling surfaces.

# Devising a Layout Plan

Planning the layout of wallboard panels prior to installation makes it a lot easier to create a materials list, minimize seams and solve problems before they crop up. Take careful measurements and make a sketch of each wall and ceiling to be covered. Note the O.C. spacing of the framing, which can affect the thickness of wallboard you can install as well as how you install it (either parallel or perpendicular to the framing). See the chart on the opposite page for maximum framing spacing allowances.

Standard wallboard is commonly available in widths of 4-ft. and 54-in. (4-ft. 6-in.), and lengths of 8-ft., 10-ft., 12-ft., 14-ft., and 16-ft. It's in your best interest to use the longest wallboard panels you can: it'll save you a lot of work during the finishing phase. While home centers and lumberyard always have 4-ft. × 8-ft. in stock, they often carry smaller quantities of the other sizes or can special order them.

The trick to planning the optimal wallboard layout is to minimize seams. Seams require joint tape, compound, and sanding, which means the less of them there are, the less work you have ahead of you. For wall or ceiling surfaces 48-in. wide or less, cover the entire area using a single wallboard panel. With no seams to tape, you'll only have to cover the screw heads with a few thin coats of compound.

Walls that are wider than 48-in. will require at least two panels. While there are a number of ways you could hang them, some possibilities yield better results than others. For example, take a wall that is 8-ft. high and 12-ft. long, as shown in first two plans at the top left. Three panels could be installed vertically (Plan A), resulting in only tapered seams and no butt joints. However, this plan requires 16 linear ft. of vertical taping, working from floor to ceiling, which is more difficult than taping a horizontal seam. Using two 4-ft. × 12-ft. panels (Plan B) reduces the amount of taping by 25% and places the seam about waist high, easing the finishing process. While a reduction of 25% of the finish work may not mean much on a small project, on a large remodel or new construction it can save you a lot of time and money.

Avoid butt joints where possible, but if they are necessary, locate them as far from the center of the wall as possible to help mask the seam. While it is best to use full panels, do not butt a tapered edge to panel ends (Plan C). This configuration produces an 8-ft. long butt seam that

## How to Devise a Drywall Layout

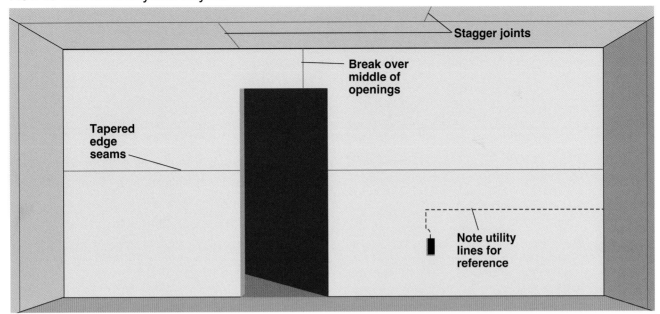

**Wallboard seams** must fall on the centers of framing members, so measure the framing when planning your layout. Use long sheets to span an entire wall, or hang sheets vertically. Avoid butted end joints whenever possible; where they do occur, stagger them between rows so they don't fall on the same framing member.

Don't place seams over the corners of doors, windows, and other openings: joints here often crack or cause bulges that interfere with trim. Where framing contains utility lines, draw a map for future reference, noting locations of wiring, pipes and shutoff valves.

## Maximum Framing Spacing

| Panel Thickness | Installation | Maximum Framing Spacing |
|---|---|---|
| 3⁄8" | Ceilings, perpendicular to Framing<br>Walls | 16-in. O.C.<br>16-in. O.C. |
| 1⁄2" | Ceilings, parallel to Framing<br>Ceilings, perpendicular to Framing<br>Walls | 16-in. O.C.<br>24-in. O.C.<br>24-in. O.C. |
| 5⁄8" | Ceilings, parallel to Framing<br>Ceilings, perpendicular to Framing<br>Walls | 16-in. O.C.<br>24-in. O.C.<br>24-in. O.C. |

will be difficult to finish. The best solution is to stagger the long panels and fill in with pieces cut from another (Plan D). For all butt joints, panel ends must break on a framing member unless you plan to use back blocking to recess the seam (see page 83).

In rooms with ceilings over 8-ft in height, use 54-in. wide panels. If ceilings are 9-ft. or more, consider using longer panels installed vertically.

## Estimating Materials

To estimate the number of wallboard panels you'll need, you can simply count the number used in your layout sketch. For larger projects, you can do a quick estimation for using 4-ft. × 8-ft. panels by measuring the length of the walls and divide the total by 4. For each window, subtract 1⁄4 panel; for doors, a 1⁄2 panel. Keep in mind that panels are sold in pairs, so round odd numbered totals up to an even amount.

The amount of screws you'll need depends on the O.C. spacing of your framing and the fastener spacing schedule required (see page 73). For a rough estimate, calculate the square footage of the wall and ceiling surfaces and multiply by 1 fastener per every 1 sq. ft. Wallboard screws are sold in pounds—one pound of screws equals roughly 320 screws. Construction adhesive is available is tubes. Check the manufacturer's specifications on the tube for coverage.

# Preparing for Wallboard Installation

Begin your installation project by checking the framing—and adding blocking, if necessary—and planning the layout of the panels. Minor flaws in the framing can be hidden by the wallboard and joint compound, but a severely bowed or twisted stud or crowned or sagging joists will result in an uneven wallboard surface.

Check the straightness and alignment of the framing using your eye, a level, a straight board, or a string. Bad studs can be corrected or replaced, but for serious joist problems it's usually easiest to add a grid of furring strips or install a steel channel ceiling system (see page 65).

> ### Everything You Need
>
> Tools: Hammer, tape measure, 4-ft. level, framing square, handsaw, plane, screwgun or drill, chalkline.
>
> Materials: 2× framing lumber, 10d framing nails, wood shims, wallboard screws, suspended ceiling system.

**Following your layout plan**, measure and mark the location of wallboard seams to ensure there is adequate backing for panels. Install 2× blocking where needed to provide additional fastening support.

## Tips for Drywall Preparation

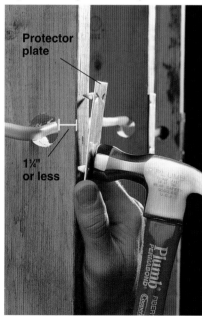

**Install protector plates** where wires or pipes pass through framing members and are less than 1¼" from the front edge. The plates keep drywall screws from puncturing wires or pipes.

Protector plate

1¼" or less

**Wrap cold-water pipes** along the ceiling with foam insulation before covering them with drywall. This prevents condensation on the pipes that can drip onto the drywall and cause staining.

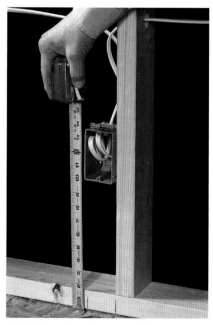

**Mark the location** and dimensions of electrical boxes on the floor. This makes it easier to locate them during wallboard installation.

## Tips for Installing Blocking

**Add backing** to support panel edges that won't fall over framing. When installing new panels next to an existing wall surface, or where the framing layout doesn't coincide with the drywall edges, it's often easiest to add an extra stud for backing. See page 33 for adding backing above foundation walls.

**Add crossblocking** between framing members with 24-in. O.C. spacing where needed, to help support edges of wallboard panels ⅜-in.-thick or less.

**Fasten 2 × 4 nailers** to the top plate of walls that run parallel to joints. This provides a fastening surface for ceiling panels. The nailer should overhang the plate by half its width.

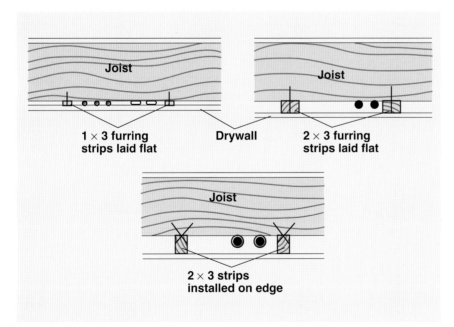

Joist

1 × 3 furring strips laid flat

Drywall

Joist

2 × 3 furring strips laid flat

Joist

2 × 3 strips installed on edge

**Attach furring strips** where service lines and other obstacles project beyond the framing. The strips create a flat surface for attaching drywall and can also be used to compensate for uneven joists. Use 1 × 3 or 2 × 3 furring strips and attach them perpendicularly to the framing with drywall screws. Space the strips 16" on-center and use wood shims secured behind the strips to adjust for unevenness.

**Use plywood strips** to join panel edges in problem areas between framing, creating a floating seam. This method does not provide a substitute for structural backing; the panels still must be supported by framing or blocking.

## How to Straighten Bowed Studs

**Use a long, straight 2 × 4** as a guide to check the alignment of studs. Hold the 2 × 4 against the studs both horizontally and diagonally, looking for gaps. To check a corner for square, use a 24-in. framing square.

**For studs that bow slightly**, use a plane or chisel to trim the facing edge just enough so it is flush with the surrounding framing.

## How to Straighten Bowed Studs

**Studs in non-load-bearing** walls bowed inward more than ¼" can be straightened. Using a handsaw, make a 2" cut into the stud at the midpoint of the bow. Pull the stud outward, and glue a tapered wood shim into the saw cut to hold the stud straight. Attach a 2-ft.-long 2 × 4 brace to one side of the stud to strengthen it, then trim off the shim. For studs that bow outward, plane down the stud surface with a portable power plane or hand plane. Replace any studs that are severely twisted.

**Variation:** Staple cardboard strips to stud faces. Use solid strips (not corrugated), which are available from drywall suppliers, or mat board from an art supply store. For extreme bows, start with a 12" to 24" strip and add layers of successively longer strips.

# Installing a Suspended Ceiling System for Wallboard

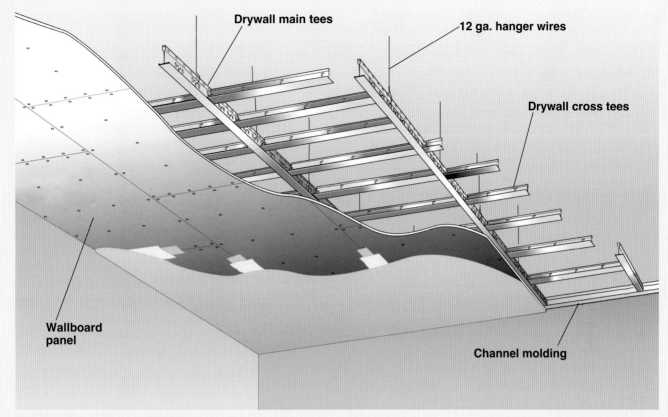

**Drywall main tees**

**12 ga. hanger wires**

**Drywall cross tees**

**Wallboard panel**

**Channel molding**

**Suspended ceiling systems** for wallboard are installed similarly to suspended acoustical ceilings (see pages 154 to 157). The resilient steel tees, channels, and heavy-gauge wire work together to create a base grid strong enough to support up to two layers of ⅝" fire-rated wallboard. Like steel framing, steel channels and tees can be cut to length using aviation snips or a saw outfitted with a metal cutting blade. Once the ceiling system is in place, wallboard panels are installed as in a conventional installation. For ½" and ⅝" panels, use 1" type-S (fine thread) wallboard screws.

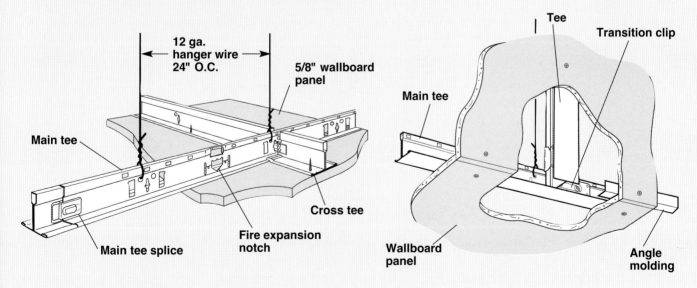

**12 ga. hanger wire 24" O.C.**

**5/8" wallboard panel**

**Main tee**

**Cross tee**

**Main tee splice**

**Fire expansion notch**

**Tee**

**Transition clip**

**Main tee**

**Wallboard panel**

**Angle molding**

**Main tees** should be supported every 24-in. O.C. for ½-in. and ⅝-in. ceiling panels, and a maximum of 16-in. O.C. for thicker panels. Use 12-gauge hanger wires fastened to the ceiling joists. Fasten the molding to framing members with 1¼" wallboard screws.

**Form vertical surfaces** for ceiling soffits or ductwork raceways by screwing wallboard panels to tees that are attached to the main tees with transition clips.

# Measuring & Cutting Wallboard

Wallboard is one of the easiest building materials to install, partly because it allows so much margin for error. Most professionals measure and cut to the nearest 1/8-in., and it's perfectly acceptable to trim off a little extra from a panel to make it easier to get into a tight space. The exceptions to this are cutouts for electrical boxes and recessed light fixtures, which must be accurate, because the coverplates usually hide less then you think they will.

Make sure your utility knife is sharp. A sharp blade ensures clean, accurate cuts that slice through the face paper and score the gypsum core in one pass. A dull blade can slip from the cutting line to snag and rip the face paper, and is more likely to cause injury.

With a sharp utility knife, you can make cuts from either side of panels. But when using wallboard and keyhole saws, make all cuts from the front side to prevent tearing the face paper. For projects that require a number of cutouts, use a wallboard router. They make short work of large openings and electrical boxes, though they generate a lot of dust, so make sure to wear a dust mask. Wallboard routers are available at rental centers, or you can use a standard router outfitted with a piloted wallboard bit.

## Everything You Need

Tools: Tape measure, T-square, pencil, chalkline, utility knife, wallboard rasp, wallboard saw, keyhole saw, compass, wallboard router.

Materials: Wallboard panels.

## How to Make Straight Cuts

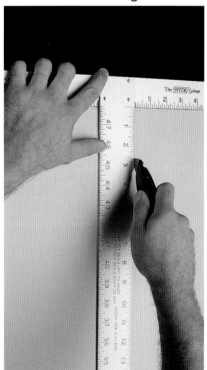

**1** Mark the length on the face of the panel, then set a T-square at the mark. Hold the square in place with your hand and foot, and cut through the face paper, using a utility knife with sharp blade.

**2** Bend the scored section backward with both hands to snap the gypsum core.

**3** Fold back the waste piece and cut through the back paper with the utility knife.

## How to Make Angled Cuts

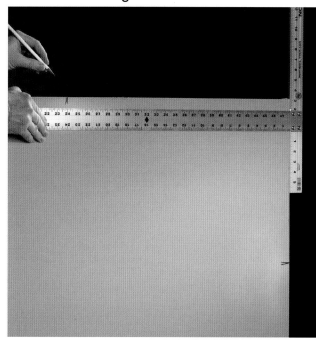

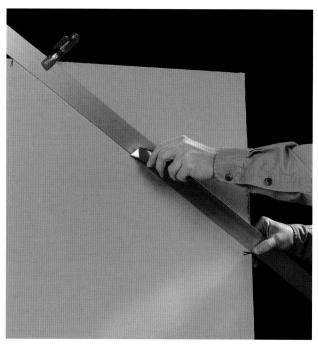

**1** Measure both the vertical "rise" and horizontal "run" of the area and mark the dimensions along the corresponding edges of the wallboard.

**2** Connect the marks with a T-square, hold down firmly, and score the wallboard from point to point. Finish the cut using the "snap cut" method on page 66; be careful not to damage the pointed ends.

## Tips for Making Straight Cuts

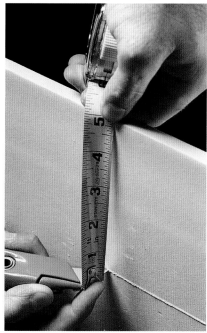

**Variation:** Make horizontal cuts using a tape measure and utility knife. With one hand, hold the knife blade at the end of the tape. With the other hand, grip the tape at the desired measurement—slide this hand along the panel edge as you make the cut.

**3** Smooth rough edges with a drywall rasp. One or two passes with the rasp should be sufficient. To help fit a piece into a tight space, bevel the edge slightly toward the back of the panel.

**Tip:** Where untapered panel ends will be butted together, bevel-cut the outside edges of each panel at 45°, removing about 1/8" of material. This helps prevent the paper from creating a ridge along the seam. Peel off any loose paper from the edge.

## How to Cut Notches

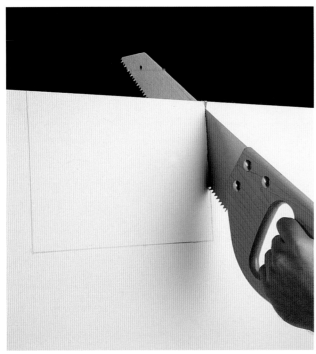

**1** Using a large drywall saw, cut the vertical sides of the notch. (These saws are also handy for cutting out door and window openings after the drywall is installed.)

**2** Cut the face paper along the bottom of the notch, using a utility knife. Snap the waste piece backward to break the core, then cut through the back paper.

## How to Cut Large Openings

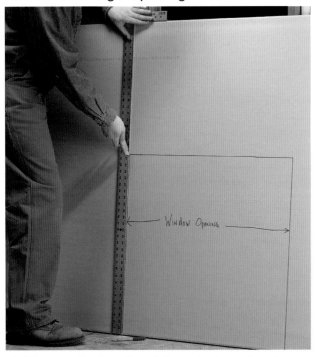

**1** Measure the location of the cutout and transfer the dimensions to the backside of the panel. Score along the line that represents the header of the opening, using a straightedge and utility knife.

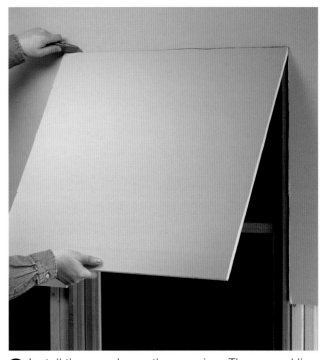

**2** Install the panel over the opening. The scored line should fall at the header. Cut the wallboard along the jambs and up to the header, using a wallboard saw. Snap forward the waste piece to break the core, then cut through the face paper and remove.

## How to Cut an Electrical Box Opening: Coordinate Method

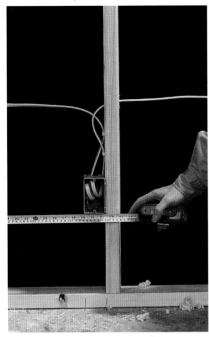 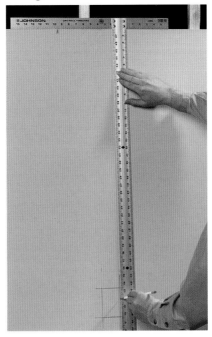 

**1** Locate the four corners of the box by measuring from the nearest fixed edge—a corner, the ceiling, or the edge of an installed panel—to the outside edges of the box.

**2** Transfer the coordinates to the panel and connect the points, using a T-square. Measure from the panel edge that will abut the fixed edge you measured from. If the panel has been cut short for a better fit, make sure to account for this in your measurements.

**3** Drill a pilot hole in one corner of the outline, then make the cutout with a keyhole saw.

## How to Cut an Electrical Box Opening: Chalk Method

**1** Rub the face of the electrical box with chalk, then position the panel where it will be installed, and press it into the box.

**2** Pull the panel back from the wall; a chalk outline of the box is on the back of the panel. Drill a pilot hole in one corner of the outline, then make the cut with a keyhole saw.

## How to Cut Holes in Drywall

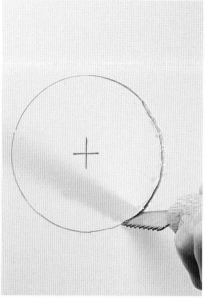

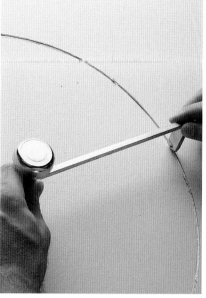

**1** To make round cutouts, measure to the center of the object, then transfer the centerpoint to the drywall panel. Use a compass set to ½ the diameter of the cutout to mark the circle on the panel face.

**2** Force the pointed end of a drywall saw through the panel from the face side, then saw along the marked line. (These saws work well for all internal cuts.)

**Variation:** Drive the point of a drywall compass into the center marking, then rotate the compass wheel to cut the face paper. Tap a nail through the centerpoint, score the back paper, then knock out the hole through the face.

## How to Make a Cutout for a Round Fixture Box

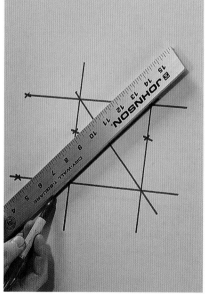

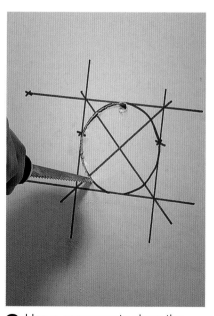

**1** Locate the four outmost edges of the round box by measuring from the nearest fixed edge—a corner, the ceiling, or the edge of an installed panel—to the outermost edges of the box.

**2** Transfer the coordinates to the panel, measuring from the panel edge that will abut the fixed edge you measured from, then connect the points using a T-square. The point where the lines intersect is the centerpoint of the circle. Note: If the panel has been cut short for a better fit, make sure to account for this in your measurements.

**3** Use a compass to draw the outline of the round box on the panel (see above). Drill a pilot hole at one point of the outline, then make the cutout with a keyhole saw.

## How to Make Cuts with a Compass

**For out-of-square corners**, cut the panel 1" longer than necessary, then hold it in position so it is plumb. Set a compass at 1¼", then run it along the wall to scribe the corner onto the face of the panel. Snap cut along the line, using a utility knife (see page 66).

**Irregular surfaces** can be scribed onto panels using the same method. Cut along the scribe line with a keyhole saw, then test fit the piece and make adjustments as necessary.

## How to Cut Drywall with a Router

**Standard or drywall routers** are handy for cutting holes for electrical boxes and openings. You can use a router made for the purpose or outfit a standard router by removing the router base and installing a piloted drywall bit (typically a ¼" shank).

**For electrical boxes**, mark the floor at the locations of the box centers. Hang the drywall, fastening only at the top edge. Plunge the router bit into the box center, move the bit sideways to the edge, then carefully work the bit to the outside. Follow the outside of the box, cutting counterclockwise.

**For doorways** and other openings, install the drywall over the opening. Moving clockwise, let the router bit follow the inside of the frame to make the cutout. Always work clockwise when cutting along the inside of a frame; counterclockwise when following the outside of an object, like an electrical box.

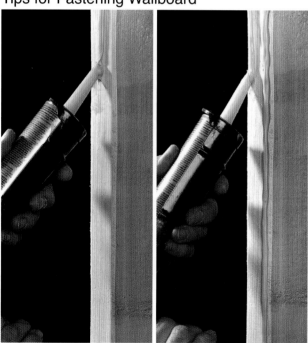

**Pre-drive fasteners** along the top edge of panels, at the location of each framing member, to help facilitate installation. Drive fasteners deep enough to hold their place but not enough to penetrate the backside of the panel.

## Tips for Fastening Wallboard

**Adhesives create** stronger bonds than fasteners, and reduce the number of screws need for panel installation. Apply a ⅜" bead along framing members, stopping 6-in. from panel edges (left). At butt joints, apply beads to both sides of the joint (right). Panels are then fastened along the perimeter.

# Fastening Wallboard

The key to fastening wallboard is to countersink screwheads to create a slight recess, or "dimple," without breaking the face paper. The best tool for the job is a screwgun, which has an adjustable clutch that can be set to stop screws at a preset depth. A variable speed drill/driver and a light touch will also get the job done.

When driving screws, hold the screwgun or drill at a right angle to the framing, placing the fastener ⅜" from the panel edge. Space screws evenly along the perimeter and across the field of the panel, following the chart on the opposite page. Do not fasten the entire perimeter and then fasten the field; work along the length or width of the panel, moving across to the sides as you push the push the wallboard tight against the framing. In addition to screws, construction adhesive can be used to create a stronger bond between wallboard and framing.

**Everything You Need**

Tools: Screwgun or ⅜-in. drill, caulk gun.

Materials: Wallboard, wallboard nails, wallboard screws, construction adhesive.

**At panel edges,** drive fasteners ⅜-in. from the edges, making sure to hit the framing squarely. If the fastener tears the paper or crumbles the edge, drive another about 2-in. away from the first.

**Recess all screws** to provide a space, called a "dimple," for the joint compound. However, driving a screw too far and breaking the paper renders it useless. If this happens, drive another screw about 2" away.

## Size of Fasteners

| Fastener type | Wallboard thickness | Minimum fastener length |
|---|---|---|
| **Wood screws** (Type W; coarse thread) | $3/8$" | 1" |
| | $1/2$" | $1 1/8$" |
| | $5/8$" | $1 1/4$" |

| Fastener type | Wallboard thickness | Minimum fastener length |
|---|---|---|
| **Steel screws** (Type S; fine thread, self-tapping) | $3/8$" | $3/4$" |
| | $1/2$" | $7/8$" |
| | $5/8$" | 1" |

*For multiple layers of wallboard, fasteners must penetrate the framing by $7/8$-in. Add the thickness of the two layers plus $7/8$-in. to determine the minimum fastener length.

## Fastening Schedules

| Framing | O. C. spacing | Installation style | Maximum screw spacing |
|---|---|---|---|
| Wood joists | 16" O.C. | Single panel w/screws | 12" O.C. |
| | | Single panel w/adhesive & screws | 16" O.C. |
| | | Multiple layers w/screws  Base layer:  Face layer: | 24" O.C.  12" O.C. |
| | | Multiple layers w/adhesive & screws:  Base layer:  Face layer: | 12" O.C.  12" O.C. (perimeter)  16" O.C. (field) |
| | 24" O.C. | Single panel w/screws | 12" O.C. |
| | | Single panel w/adhesive & screws | 16" O.C. |
| | | Multiple layers w/screws | 12" O.C. |
| | | Multiple layers w/adhesive & screws:  Base layer:  Face layer: | 12" O.C.  12" O.C. (perimeter)  16" O.C. (field) |
| Wood studs | 16" O.C. | Single panel w/screws | 16" O.C. |
| | | Single panel w/adhesive & screws:  Load-bearing partitions  Non-load-bearing partitions |  24" O.C.  24" O.C. |
| | | Multiple layers w/screws  Base layer:  Face layer: | 24" O.C.  16" O.C. |
| | | Multiple layers w/adhesive & screws:  Base layer:  Face layer: | 16" O.C.  16" O.C. (at top & bottom only) |
| | 24" O.C. | Single panel w/screws | 12" O.C. |
| | | Single panel w/adhesive & screws:  Load-bearing partitions  Non-load-bearing partitions |  16" O.C.  24" O.C. |

| Framing | O. C. spacing | Installation style | Maximum screw spacing |
|---|---|---|---|
| | | Multiple layers w/screws  Base layer:  Face layer: | 24" O.C.  12" O.C. |
| | | Multiple layers w/adhesive & Screws:  Base layer:  Face layer: | 12" O.C.  16" O.C. (at top & bottom only) |
| Steel studs | 16" O.C. | Single panel w/screws | 16" O.C. |
| | | Multiple layers w/screws:  Base layer:  Parallel panels  Perpendicular  Face layer: | 24" O.C.  *(See below)  16" O.C. |
| | | Multiple layers w/adhesive & screws:  Base layer:  Face layer: | 24" O.C.  12" O.C. (perimeter)  16" O.C. (field) |
| Steel studs & resilient channel: walls | 24" O.C. | Single panel w/screws  Multiple layers w/screws:  Base layer:  Parallel panels  Perpendicular  Face layer: | 12" O.C.   24" O.C.  *(See below)  12" O.C. |
| | | Multiple layers w/adhesive & screws:  Base layer:  Face layer: | 24" O.C.  12" O.C. (perimeter)  16" O.C. (field) |
| Resilient channel: ceilings | 24" O.C. | Single panel w/screws  Multiple layers w/screws:  Base layer:  Parallel panels  Perpendicular  Face layer: | 12" O.C.    24" O.C.  *(See below)  12" O.C. |
| | | Multiple layers w/adhesive & screws:  Base layer:  Face layer: | 24" O.C.  12" O.C. (perimeter)  16" O.C. (field) |

*1 screw at each end and 1 screw centered in the field, at each fastener location.

Note: The above information is subject to manufacturer installation specifications.

# Hanging Standard Wallboard

Hanging wallboard is a project that can be completed quickly and easily with a little preplanning and a helping hand.

Planning the layout of panels will help you reduce waste and deal with problem areas. Where possible, install full panels perpendicular to the framing to add strength and rigidity to walls and ceilings. To save yourself time and trouble during the finishing process, avoid joints where two untapered panel ends are butted together. These are difficult to finish because there's no recess for the compound and tape. In small areas, you can avoid butt joints by installing long sheets horizontally that run the full length of the walls. Or you can hang the panels vertically, which produces more seams that need taping but eliminates butted end joints. If butted joints are unavoidable, as they often are, stagger the seams and locate them away from the center of the wall, or install back blocking to help mask their unflattering effects (see page 83).

If you're installing wallboard on both the ceilings and the walls, do the ceilings first, so the wall panels add extra support for the ceiling panels. When it comes time to install the walls, hang all full panels first, then measure and cut the remaining pieces about ⅛" too small, to allow for easy fit.

In nearly every installation, you'll deal with corners. For standard 90° corners, panels most often can butt against one another. But other corners, such as those lacking adequate nailing surfaces or that are prone to cracking, may require the use of wallboard clips or specialty beads.

Wallboard is heavy. While it's possible to hang wallboard by yourself, work with a helper whenever possible. A wallboard lifter is also a time saver, simplifying installation to ceilings and the upper portion of walls. If you don't want to rent a wallboard lift, you can make a pair of T-braces, called "Deadmen" (see page 59) to hold ceiling panels tight against framing for fastening.

**Use a panel lifter** to position wallboard for fastening. Slide the front end of the lifter beneath the panel edge, then rock backward with your foot to raise the panel into place.

**Where untapered panel ends** will be butted together, bevel-cut the outside edges of each panel at 45°, removing about ⅛-in. of material. This helps prevent the paper from creating a ridge along the seam. Peel off any loose paper from the edge.

**Everything You Need**

Tools: T-square, utility knife, wallboard saw, keyhole say, wallboard rasp, compass, screwgun or drill, wallboard lifter, rented wallboard lift (for ceilings), chalk line.

Materials: Wallboard panels, wallboard screws.

## How to Install Wallboard on Flat Ceilings

**1** Snap a chalk line perpendicular to the joists, 48⅛" from the starting wall.

**2** Measure to make sure the first panel will break on the center of a joist. If necessary, cut the panel on the end that abuts the side wall so the panel breaks on the next farthest joist. Load the panel onto a rented drywall lift, or use a helper, and lift the panel flat against the joists.

**3** Position the panel with the leading edge on the chalk line and the end centered on a joist. Fasten the panel with appropriately sized screws and following the fastener spacing shown on page 73.

**4** After the first row of panels is installed, begin the next row with a half-panel. This ensures that the butted end joints will be staggered between rows.

**Tip:** Drywall stilts bring you within reach of ceilings, so you can fasten and finish the drywall without a ladder. Stilts are commonly available at rental centers and are surprisingly easy to use.

## How to Install Ceiling Panels Using a Deadman

**1** Construct two 2 × 4 deadmen (see page 59). Lean one against the wall where the panel will be installed, with the top arm a couple inches below the joists. Have a helper assist in lifting the panel and placing the lead edge on the arm. Angle the deadman to pin the panel flush against the joists, but don't use so much pressure you risk damage to the panel.

**2** As the helper supports the panel, use the other deadman to hoist the panel against the joists 24-in. from the back end. Place ladders at each deadman location and adjust the panel's position by loosening the braces with one hand and moving the panel with the other. Replace the braces and fasten the panel to the framing, following the fastener spacing shown on page 73.

## How to Install Wallboard on Ceilings Using a Wallboard Lift

**1** Cut the first wallboard panel to size, if necessary, then rest the panel in the lift and pivot it into a horizontal position. Hoist the panel upward by rotating the wheel. Use adhesive to eliminate sagging panels and a wallboard lift to ease installation.

**2** When the panel is within a few inches of the ceiling, roll the lifter into position so the edges of the panel run along the center of a joist, then hoist the panel tight against the ceiling and secure it with wallboard screws. with wallboard screws. On subsequent panels, stagger panels so joints are offset.

## Tips for Installing Floating Ceiling Joints

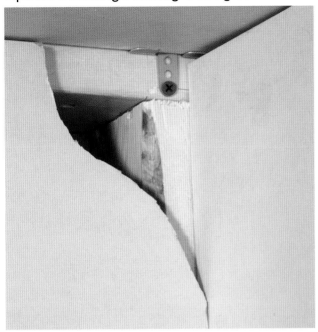

**Use a "floating corner"** to reduce the chances of popped fasteners and cracks. Install the ceiling panel, locating the first row of screws 7-in. from the wall. Push the top edge of the wall panel against the ceiling to support the unfastened edge. Fasten the wall, locating the first row of screws 8-in. from the ceiling.

**For a ceiling with trusses,** use wallboard clips to eliminate cracks caused by "truss uplift," the seasonal shifting caused by weather changes. Slip clips on the edge of the panel prior to installation, then fasten the clips to the top plate. Fasten the panel to the trusses not less than 18-in. from the edge of the panel.

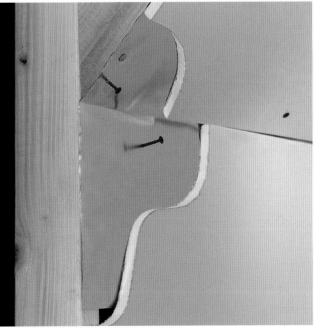

**Use metal flashing** to prevent cracks along the peak of pitched and cathedral ceilings (left) and the angle between pitched ceilings and sidewalls (right). For both applications, cut metal flashing 16-in.-wide and to the length of the joint, then bend it lengthwise to match the angle of the peak or corner. Fasten flashing to the framing on one side only, then fasten the panels on that side to the framing. However, fasten the panels at the unfastened side to the flashing only, using self-taping steel screws. Drive the first row of screws into the framing not less than 12-in. from the "floating" edge of the panels. NOTE: Flexible vinyl bead can also be used for corners prone to cracking.

# How to Install Wallboard on Wood-framed Walls

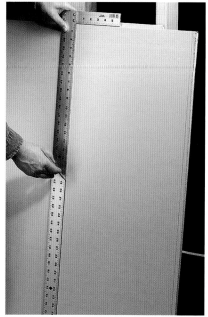

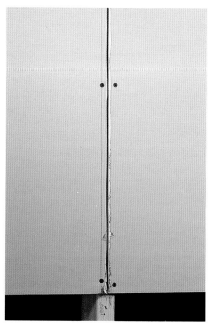

**1** Measure from the wall end or corner to make sure the first panel will break on the center of the stud. If necessary, trim the sheet on the side or end that will be placed in the corner. Mark the stud centers on the panel face and pre-drive screws at each location along the top edge to facilitate fastening. Apply adhesive to the studs, if necessary (see page 73).

**2** With a helper or a wallboard lift, hoist the first panel tight against the ceiling, making sure the side edge is centered on a stud. Push the panel flat against the framing and drive the starter screws to secure the panel. Make any cutouts, then fasten the field of the panel, following the screw spacing on page 73.

**3** Measure, cut and install the remaining panels along the upper wall. Bevel panel ends slightly, leaving a ⅛" gap between them at the joint. Butt joints can also be installed using back blocking to create a recess (see page 83).

**4** Measure, cut and install the bottom row, butting the panels tight to the upper row and leaving a ½" gap at the floor. Secure to the framing along the top edge using the starter screws, then make all cutouts before fastening the rest of the panel.

**Variation:** When installing wallboard vertically, cut each panel so it's ½" shorter than the ceiling height to allow for expansion. (The gap will be covered by base molding.) Avoid placing tapered edges at outside corners, which makes then difficult to finish.

# How to Install Wallboard at Inside Corners

**Standard 90° inside corners** are installed with the first panel butted against the framing and the adjacent panel butted against the first. The screw spacing remains the same as on a flat wall (see page 73). If the corner is out of plumb or the adjacent wall has an irregular surface, see page 71 for cutting instructions.

**Use a "floating corner"** to reduce the chances of popped fasteners and cracks. Install the first panel, fastening only to within one stud bay of the corner. Push the leading edge of the adjacent panel against the first to support the unfastened edge. Fasten the second panel normally, including the corner.

**Wallboard clips** can be used at corners that lack an adequate nailing surface, allowing two panels to be secured to the same stud. Slide clips onto the leading edge of the first panel, with the metal nailing flange outward. Install the panel, fastening the flange to the stud on the adjacent wall with ¾" steel screws. Install the adjacent panel normally.

**For off-angle corners,** do not overlap panel ends. Install so the panel ends meet at the corner with a ⅛" gap between them.

## How to Install Wallboard at Outside Corners

**At outside corners,** run panels long so they extend past the corner framing. Fasten the panel in place, then score the backside and snap cut to remove the waste piece.

**For standard 90° outside corners,** install the first panel so the outside edge is flush with the framing, then install the adjacent panel so it overlaps the end of the first panel.

**For off-angle corners** or corners where bullnose bead will be installed, no not overlap panel ends. Install each panel so it's leading edge breaks 1⁄8" from the outside edge of the framing. NOTE: Bullnose beads with a slight radius may require a larger reveal.

**For wallboard that abuts a finished edge,** such as paneling or wood trim, install panels 1⁄8" from the finished surface, then install a an L-bead to cover the exposed edge (see page 103).

## How to Install Wallboard Abutting a Finished Surface

**1** Cut the J-bead (see page 96) to size, then position it flush against the finished surface. Fasten it to the adjacent framing with ¾-in. steel screws. Note: Make sure to install J-bead that matches the thickness of your wallboard.

**2** Cut a piece of wallboard to size, but let the end run long for final trimming. Slide the end of the wallboard into the J-bead (see page 96) until it fits snugly, then fasten the panel to the framing. Score the backside flush with the face of the wall, then snap cut to remove the waste (opposite page).

## Installing Wallboard On Gable Walls

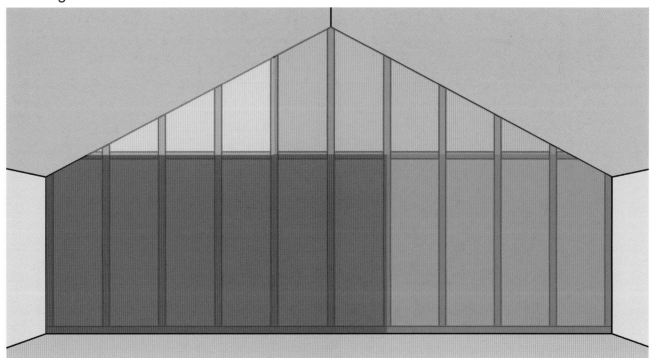

**Gables and cathedral ceilings** present unique challenges when installing wallboard. A few pointers that will help you be successful include: use as many of the panel's factory edges as possible; test-fit each piece directly on the wall; do not force pieces into place, but trim edges as needed instead; install pieces horizontally, with 2 × 4 blocking between the framing member; align horizontal seams, but not vertical seams—stagger these to minimize any twisting in the framing members.

## How to Install Wallboard on Steel Framed Walls

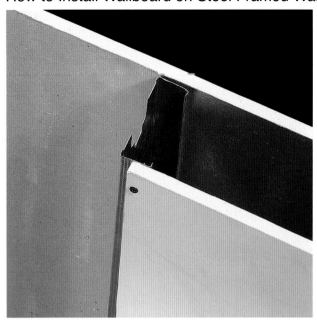

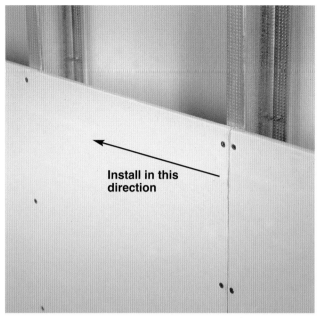

**1** Position the first panel so you'll attach it along the open half of the stud rather than on the webbed side. This will make the stud more rigid and make it easier to attach the adjoining panel. Fasten in the field and along the edges completely before installing the adjacent panel. For screw size and spacing, see page 73.

**2** Butt the next panel against the first, fastening the panel end at the joint to the webbed side of the stud. Secure the top edge of the panel to the framing, then make cutouts as needed (see pages 66 to 71) before fastening the rest of the panel Continue installing panels, making sure that seams are offset as you move up the wall.

## Tips for Hanging Specialty Wallboard

**Moisture-resistant wallboard** is installed like standard wallboard, but with a few requirements: framing must be 16-in. O.C. for walls and 12-in. O.C. for ceilings. Space screws 12-in. O.C., or 8-in. O.C. if you're installing tile. Do not install over a vapor barrier if you're using MR board as a tile backer. Treat all cut edges with a water-resistant tile adhesive or waterproof caulk before finishing with joint compound.

**Gypsum base**, also called blueboard, is a gypsum-core wallboard used as a base for veneer plaster (see pages 128 to 133). Install as you would standard wallboard, with the following exceptions: allow 1/8" clearance on all sides of cutouts, and space screws 12" O.C. on both walls and ceiling.

## Installing Back Blockers

No matter how good a job you do installing and finishing a butt joint, there's always a chance it'll be visible, even after a coat of paint or layer of wallcovering. Wallboard panels can expand and contract as the temperature and humidity in your home changes, causing butted panel ends to push outward and create ridges. While ridging eventually stops (up to a year after installation), you can install back blocking to help prevent the problem before it even starts.

Back blocking creates a recessed butt joint by slightly bending panel ends into the bay between framing members, where they are secured to a floating blocking device with wallboard screws. The result is a recessed joint that approximates a tapered joint and can be finished just as easily using standard techniques. And because the joint floats between framing members, it's unlike to crack or ridge. Back blocking can be used for both walls and ceilings.

Although commercial back blockers are available, you can easily make your own back blocker by attaching narrow strips of hardboard to the edges of a 6-in. to 10-in. wide strip of 3/4" plywood. When placed behind a wallboard butt joint, the backer board will create a thin space, into which the edges of the wallboard will be deflected when it's screwed to the back blocker. The instructions below show a home-made back blocker in use.

### Everything You Need

Tools: Screwgun or ⅜-in. drill; to build your own: tape measure, circular saw, hammer.

Materials: Wallboard panels, back blocker, wallboard screws; to build your own: 10" × 48" plywood, ¼-in. × ¾" × 48".

### How to Install a Back Blocker

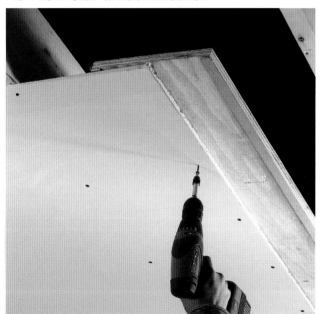

**1** Hang the first wallboard panel so the end breaks midway between the framing members. Position the back blocker behind the panel so the end covers half of the wood center strip, then fasten every 6-in. along the end.

**2** Install the second panel so it butts against the first panel. Fasten the end of the second panel to the back blocker with wallboard screws every 6-in.; the screws will pull the end of the panel into the blocker, creating the recessed joint.

# Hanging Wallboard in Multiple Layers

Installing wallboard in multiple layers is an effective means of soundproofing and also increases the fire-rating of walls and ceilings. Wallboard can be heavy, especially when installed in layers, so it's important to install panels correctly to prevent sagging, cracks, and popped fasteners. Always fasten both the base layer (which can be standard wallboard or a soundproofing board) and the face layer with the correct number of screws (see page 73). Panels can be secured with fasteners alone, though many manufacturers recommend the use of panel adhesive. It's best to install the base layer vertically and the face layer horizontally, staggering the joints. If panels must be hung in the same direction, stagger parallel seams between layers by at least 10"

See pages 44 to 49 for more on soundproofing walls and ceilings.

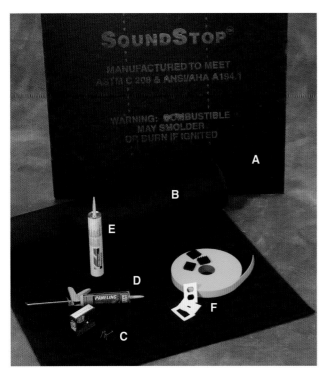

**Specialty materials** can help eliminate sound transmission better than wallboard alone. High-density gypsum and cellulose fiber soundproofing board (A) provides excellent noise attenuation. MLV (mass-loaded vinyl) sheeting (B) can double a wall's soundproofing value. Type-G wallboard screws (C) have coarse threads to hold wallboard panels together as the panel adhesive (D) sets to create a strong bond. Acoustical caulk (E) seals gaps to absorb noise vibrations. And for added protection, install closed cell foam gaskets (F) behind electrical coverplates.

## Everything You Need

Tools: Tape measure, T-square, utility knife, drywall saws, screwgun or 3/8-in. drill, wallboard lifter, caulk gun.

Materials: Wallboard panels, wallboard screws, acoustical caulk.

**Building Code** requires that the front face of electrical boxes be flush with the finished wall surface. In new construction, attach boxes so they extend past the framing the combined thickness of the wallboard layers. If you're covering an old surface, use extension rings to bring existing boxes flush.

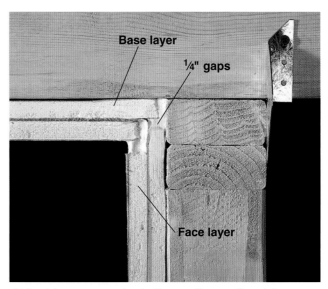

**At inside corners,** including wall-to-ceiling joints, stagger the joints between the layers, leaving a 1/4" gap between panels. Seal all gaps with acoustical caulk to help absorb sound vibration. See pages 44 to 49 for more information.

# How to Hang Multiple Layers of Wallboard for Soundproofing

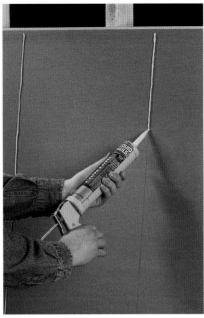

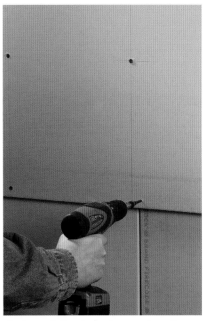

**1** Install the base layer of wallboard or soundproofing board parallel to the framing, using the screws and spacing found on page 73. Leave a ¼" gap around the perimeter of each surface (at corners, ceilings, and along floors). After panels are installed, seal the perimeter gaps with acoustical caulk.

**2** To install the face layer, use adhesive to ensure a strong bond to the base. Apply ⅜" beads of adhesive every 16" across the backside of the panels.

**3** Install the face layer of wallboard perpendicular to the framing and joints of the base layer, spacing screws as recommended on page 73. Make sure to stagger the seams between layers. Use Type-G screws to temporarily hold panels together as the adhesive sets up.

**4** Seal the perimeter gaps at corners, ceiling and along floors with acoustical caulk. Also seal around electrical boxes and HVAC ducts.

**Variation:** If you're installing wallboard to resilient steel channels (see page 47), install the base layer panels perpendicular to the channels, and the face layer perpendicular to the base layer. For both layers, use type-S screws driven into the channels only, not into the framing.

# Hanging Decorative Wallboard Panels

Another option for adding decorative detail to walls and ceilings is to use designer wallboard. When installed, these panels replicate the look of raised panel walls and ceilings. Designer wallboard can be used to add a wainscot, bring interest to upper walls, or create a coffered ceiling.

Designer wallboard is installed like standard wallboard, though the layout must be carefully planned. The raised panels need to be in alignment across the entire surface to look right. Standard wallboard is used to fill strips between or around panels, and all seams are finished using standard techniques. Do not get compound in the raised-panel area of wallboard. If you do, carefully clean it out immediately with a clean wallboard knife and a damp towel.

### Everything You Need

Tools: Tape measure, chalk line, T-square, utility knife, wallboard saws, caulk gun, screwgun or ⅜" drill, wallboard lifter.

Materials: Designer wallboard panels, construction adhesive, wallboard screws.

## How to Install Decorative Wallboard Panels

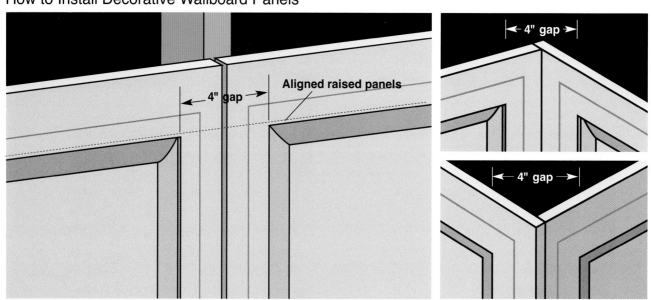

**When planning your designer wallboard installation,** the key to a good layout is symmetry. Panels should be installed so the raised areas break at equal distances from the corners. Standard wallboard can be used to fill in between panels to create a workable layout. Treat both inside and outside corners similarly, so that the raised areas fall the same distance from the corner on each side of the wall. Panels also can be installed to "wrap" inside corners if necessary (opposite page). Take careful measurements of your walls and ceilings and make accurate sketches to guide your project.

## How to Install Decorative Wallboard Panels

**1** Measure and mark the location of the first panel on the framing. At one end of the wall, measure and mark the top edge of the panel's raised area. Drive a nail and run a level mason's line across the wall at 1-in. from the framing. Install the first panel with wallboard screws, so the top edge of the raised area is level with the mason's line.

**2** Install subsequent panels not only so the raised top edge is level with the mason's line, but also with an equal distance between the sides of the raised areas of each panel. At corners, make sure to account for panel overlap when making cuts.

**Variation:** To wrap an inside corner, score the back of a panel using a T-square and sharp utility knife, being careful not to pierce the front face of the panel. Gently snap back the panel, leaving the face paper intact. Fill the void with a bead of adhesive to reinforce the panel, then install it immediately.

**3** After all designer panels are installed, finish the rest of the wall and fill gaps with standard wallboard of the same thickness. The designer panels can be taped and finished in the same manner as standard wallboard. At outside corners, install metal corner bead.

# Hanging Wallboard on Curves

Curves and arches add an elegant touch to a room, and they are easier than ever to create. Two layers of ¼-in. flexible wallboard are installed over the framing (see pages 36 to 37) to form curved walls and archways. If the radius of the curve is less than 32-in., dampen the panels before installing them (see below). The minimum radius for inside (concave) curves is 20-in.; the minimum for outside (convex) curves is 15-in. NOTE: Bending limitations may vary by manufacturer.

When hanging wallboard on curved walls, it's best to install the panels perpendicular to the framing. Try to avoid joints. Though if it's unavoidable, vertical seams are much easier to hide in the curve than horizontal seams. If panels have been wetted for the installation, allow them to dry thoroughly before taping seams.

### Everything You Need

Tools: Tape measure, T-square, utility knife, screwgun, paint roller and tray or spray bottle.

Materials: ¼" flexible wallboard panels, 1¼" wallboard screws.

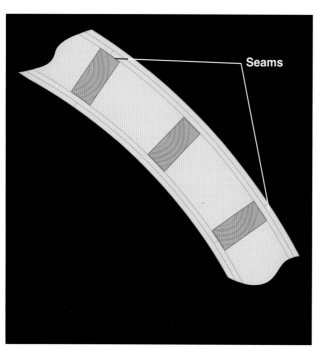

**Use two layers** of ¼" flexible wallboard for curved walls and arches. If there are butted seams, stagger the seams between layers.

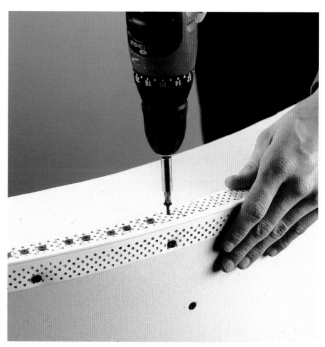

**Finish curved edges** with flexible vinyl corner bead, which has one segmented flange that allows it to bend. Install the bead as you would standard corner bead, but drive a screw every 2". To substitute for flexible bead, snip one flange of standard bead at 1" intervals.

## How to Hang Flexible Wallboard

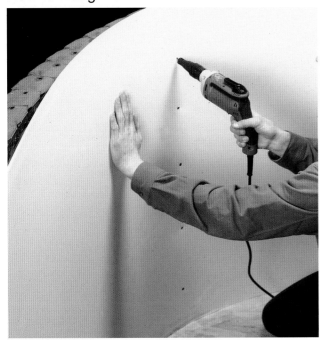

**Start at the center for concave curves.** Cut the first panel a little long and position it lengthwise along the wall. Carefully bend the panel toward the midpoint of the curve and fasten it to the center stud. Work toward the ends to fasten the rest of the panel. Install the second panel over the first, then trim along the top of the wall with a drywall saw.

**Start at one end for convex curves.** Cut the panel long and fasten it lengthwise along the wall, bending the panel as you work. Add the second layer, then trim both to the framing. To cover the top of a curved wall, set a ½" panel on the wall and scribe it from below.

## How to Hang Wallboard on Archways

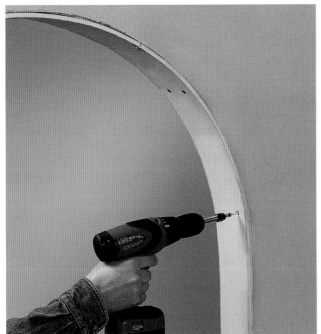

**Cut ¼" flexible wallboard** to width and a couple inches longer then needed. Fasten to the arch with 1¼" wallboard screws, working from the center out to the ends. Trim the ends of the piece and install a second to match the thickness of the surrounding wallboard.

**Variation:** Score the backside of ½" wallboard every inch (or more for tighter curves) along the length of the piece. Starting at one end, fasten the piece along the arch; the scored wallboard will conform to the arch.

# Adding Architectural Detail with Wallboard

Wallboard can be installed in layers or in conjunction with a 2× framework to bring a wide variety of architectural detail to a room. From a simple series of tiers wrapping the perimeter of a room (shown here) to curved soffits or raised panels on walls, you can replicate designs you've seen in high-end homes or bring your own creation to life.

The same basic technique used to hang wallboard in multiple layers applies to adding built-up wallboard detail. Use a sharp utility knife and a rasp for cutting as panel edges must be clean for finishing. The use of adhesive is highly recommended to create strong bonds between layers so the pieces hold together tightly. Use

type-G screws to hold panels together while the adhesive sets up. Use L-bead to create sharp, clean panel ends. Finish all seams and beads with joint tape and at least three coats of compound, following standard finishing techniques.

See pages 84 to 85 for more information on installing wallboard in multiple layers.

### Everything You Need

Tools: Tape measure, T-square, utility knife, wallboard rasp, chalk line, screwgun or ⅜" drill.

Materials: Wallboard, wallboard screws, L-bead.

## Tips for Creating Built-up Wallboard Details

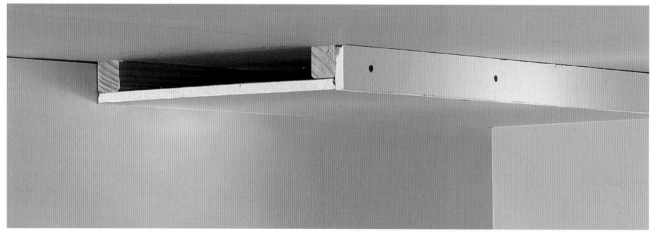

**For a more substantial step soffit,** build a 2× framework as a base for the wallboard. As you lay out the placement of the new framing, make sure to account for the thickness of the wallboard in all final dimensions.

## How to Add Decorative Tiers to a Ceiling

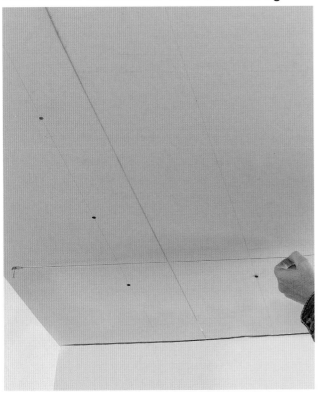

**1** Measure and mark the width of the first tier on the ceiling along each wall, then snap chalk lines to mark the perimeter.

**2** Cut pieces of wallboard to size, apply ⅜" beads of adhesive to the backside, and install with wallboard screws, following the spacing chart on page 73.

**3** Snap chalk lines for the second tier perimeter, then cut and install the wallboard as described in step 2. Stagger all seams at corners and along tier runs.

**4** Install L-bead on all exposed edges of each tier, then finish with three coats of joint compound. Edges can also be finished with flexible corner tape.

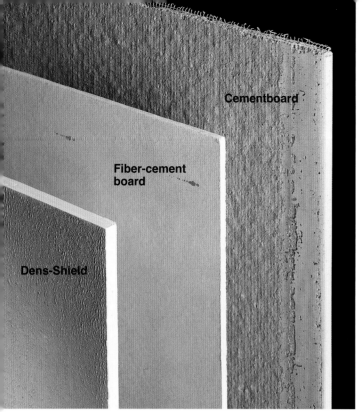
Cementboard

Fiber-cement board

Dens-Shield

**Common tile backers** are cementboard, fiber-cement board, and Dens-Shield. Cementboard is made from portland cement and sand reinforced by an outer layer of fiberglass mesh. Fiber-cement board is made similarly, but with a fiber reinforcement integrated throughout the panel. Dens-Shield is a water-resistant gypsum board with a waterproof acrylic facing.

# Hanging Cementboard

Use tile backer board as the substrate for tile walls in wet areas. Unlike wallboard, tile backer won't break down and cause damage if water gets behind the tile. The three basic types of tile backer are cementboard, fiber-cement board, and Dens-Shield.

Though water cannot damage either cementboard or fiber-cement board, it can pass through them. To protect the framing members, install a water barrier of 4-mil plastic or 15# building paper behind the backer.

Dens-Shield has a waterproof acrylic facing that provides the water barrier. It cuts and installs much like wallboard, but it requires galvanized screws to prevent corrosion and must be sealed with caulk at all untaped joints and penetrations.

## Everything You Need

Tools: Utility knife, T-square, drill with a small masonry bit, hammer, jig saw with a bimetal blade, wallboard knife, stapler, drill.

Materials: 4-mil plastic sheeting, cementboard, 1¼" cementboard screws, cementboard joint tape, latex-portland cement mortar.

**1** Staple a water barrier of 4-mil plastic sheeting or 15# building paper over the framing. Overlap seams by several inches, and leave the sheets long at the perimeter. NOTE: Framing for cementboard must be 16" on-center; steel studs must be 20-gauge.

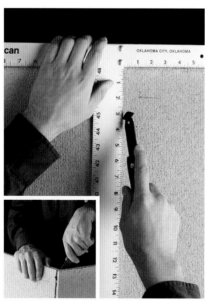

**2** Cut cementboard by scoring through the mesh just below the surface, using a utility knife or carbide-tipped cutter. Snap the panel back, then cut through the back-side mesh (inset). NOTE: For tile applications, the rough face of the board is the front.

**3** Make cutouts for pipes and other penetrations by drilling a series of holes through the board, using a small masonry bit. Tap the hole out with a hammer or a scrap of pipe. Cut holes along edges with a jig saw and bimetal blade.

**4** Install the sheets horizontally. Where possible, use full pieces to avoid cut-and-butted seams, which are difficult to fasten. If there are vertical seams, stagger them between rows. Leave a ⅛" gap between sheets at vertical seams and corners. Use spacers to set the bottom row of panels ¼" above the tub or shower base. Fasten the sheets with 1¼" cementboard screws, driven every 8" for walls and every 6" for ceilings. Drive the screws ½" from the edges to prevent crumbling. If the studs are steel, don't fasten within 1" of the top track.

**5** Cover the joints and corners with cementboard joint tape (alkali-resistant fiberglass mesh) and latex-portland cement mortar (thin-set). Apply a layer of mortar with a wallboard knife, embed the tape into the mortar, then smooth and level the mortar.

## Variation: Finishing Cementboard

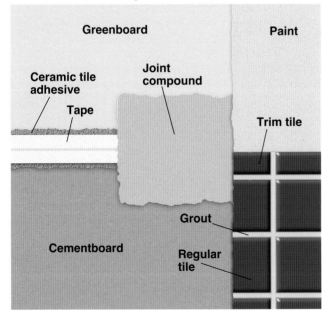

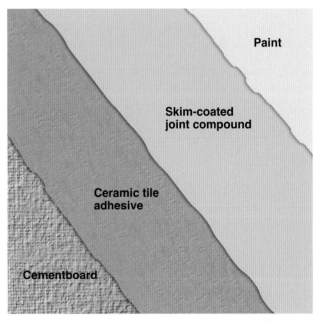

**To finish a joint** between cementboard and greenboard, seal the joint and exposed cementboard with ceramic tile adhesive, a mixture of four parts adhesive to one part water. Embed paper joint tape into the adhesive, smoothing the tape with a tape knife. Allow the adhesive to dry, then finish the joint with at least two coats of all-purpose wallboard joint compound.

**To finish small areas** of cementboard that will not be tiled, seal the cementboard with ceramic tile adhesive, a mixture of four parts adhesive to one part water, then apply a skim-coat of all-purpose wallboard joint compound, using a 12" wallboard knife. Then paint the wall.

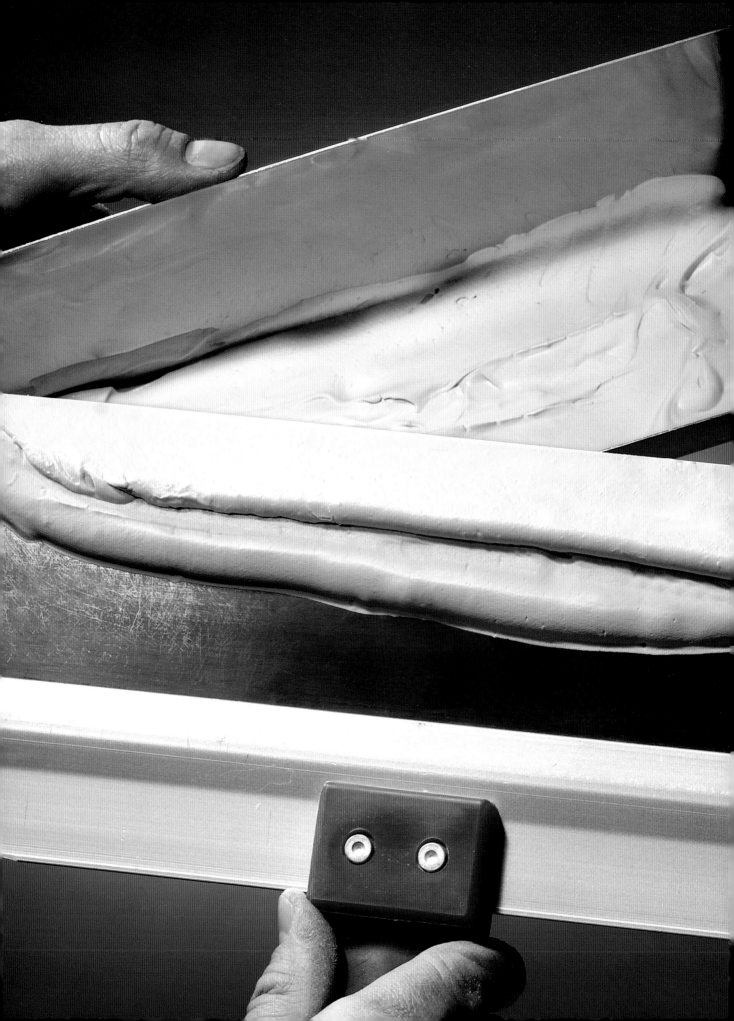

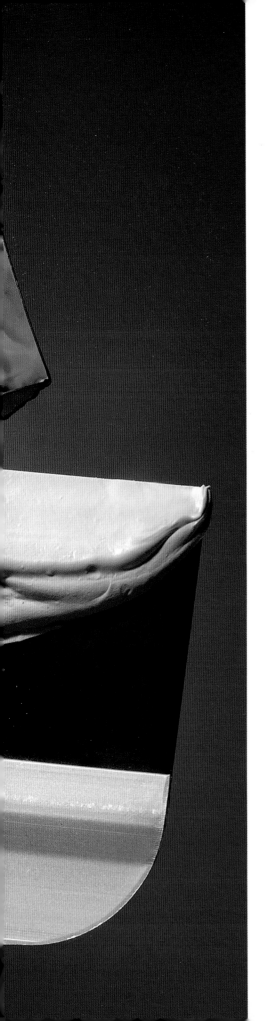

# Finishing Wallboard

# Wallboard Finish Materials

Finishing wallboard is easily the more difficult phase of surfacing walls and ceilings, but it's a project well within the ability of any homeowner. Armed with a basic understanding of the variety of finish materials available, you'll be able to walk out of your local home center or wallboard supplier with the exact supplies you need to cover all joints, corners and fasteners for a successful wallboard finish project.

**Corner bead** is the angle strip, usually made of metal or vinyl, that covers a wallboard corner, creating a straight, durable edge where walls intersect. Most corner beads are installed over the wallboard and are finished with compound. In addition to standard 90° outside-corner bead, there's an ever-growing variety of bead types designed for specific situations and easy application. There are beads for inside corners, flexible beads for off-angles and curves, J-bead and L-beads for flat panel edges, and bullnose beads for creating rounded inside and outside corners. While metal beads are installed with fasteners, vinyl beads can be installed with vinyl adhesive and staples, or be embedded in joint compound, using the same techniques for installing paper-faced beads.

**Joint tape** is combined with joint compound to create a permanent layer that covers the wall-

board seams, as well as small holes and gaps. Without tape, thick applications of compound are highly prone to cracking. There are two types of joint tape—paper and self-adhesive fiberglass mesh.

Paper tape comes in 2-in.-wide rolls. It has a crease down its center, making it easy to fold in half lengthwise for taping inside corners. Paper tape can be used for all taping situations, but because it must be adhered to the wall with compound and is somewhat more difficult to use, many wallboard installers use mesh tape on all tapered seams. Paper tape is stronger than mesh and is the better choice for taping butted seams and inside corners. Also available is paper tape reinforced with a metal center strip for finishing off-angle corners.

Fiberglass mesh tape comes in 2" and 2½"-wide rolls and has an adhesive backing that sticks to bare wallboard. This simplifies the taping coat because you can apply the tape before applying any compound. Store unused mesh tape in a plastic bag to prevent the adhesive from drying out.

Fire-rated tape is another convenient self-adhesive tape, used for surfaces that are finished just enough to meet fire codes. It doesn't need a coat of compound to achieve its fire rating.

**Wallboard finishing products** include metal, paper and vinyl outside corner beads (A), flexible corner bead for arches (B), L- and J-beads (C), vinyl bullnose bead (D), fiber joint tape (E), paper joint tape (F) ½" staples (G), vinyl adhesive spray (H), paper-faced inside corner bead (I), fire-rated joint tape (J).

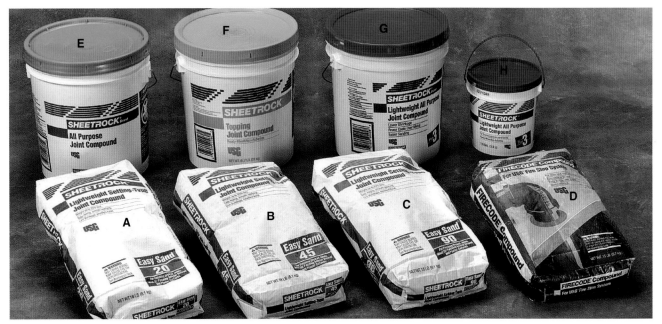

**Wallboard joint compounds** include: setting-type joint compounds in 20-minute, 45-minute and 90-minute grades (A, B, C); fireproof taping compound (D); premixed all-purpose joint compound (E); premixed topping compound (F); premixed lightweight taping compound (G); premixed lightweight all-purpose joint compound (H).

**Joint compound**, commonly called *mud*, seals and levels all seams, corners, and depressions in a wallboard installation. It's also used for skim coating and some texturing treatments. There are several types of compounds, with important differences among them, but the two main forms are setting-type and drying-type.

Setting-type compound is sold in dry powder form that is mixed with water before application. Because it dries through chemical reaction, setting compound dries quickly (from twenty minutes to six hours, depending on the product) and is virtually unaffected by humidity and temperature. Setting compounds generally shrink less, bond better, and become harder than drying types, but they're more difficult to sand, a characteristic that makes them a better choice for the taping coat than for the filler and final coats. Manufacturers now also offer lighter weight setting compounds formulated to be easier to sand.

Drying-type compounds dry through evaporation and usually take about 24 hours to dry completely. Available in dry powder and convenient premixed forms in re-sealable one- and five-gallon buckets, drying compounds are highly workable and consistent. There are three formulas of drying compound: "taping" is a hard-drying formula made for the taping coat; "topping" is somewhat softer and is best for the filler and final coats; and "all-purpose" is a compromise between the other two and is suitable for all coats.

Ideally, you'll use a setting-type compound for the tape coat, then a topping or all-purpose compound for both the filler and final coats. But for small jobs and repairs it's more convenient to use all-purpose compound for all three layers—using one material versus three is less expensive and less wasteful.

## Estimating Materials

The following tips will help you determine how much of each material you need for your project. Add ten to fifteen percent to your estimate to cover error and omissions.

**Corner Beads:** Count the number of corners and the lengths of each, and purchase enough bead to cover each in one piece. Beads are available in standard lengths of 6-ft.-10-in. to 10 ft.

**Joint Tape:** Approx. 375 ft. of tape will finish 1000 sq. ft. of wallboard.

**Compound:** The following are estimates. Check with the manufacturer for actual coverage information. For every 100 sq. ft. of wallboard, you'll need approx.:

- 1 gallon of pre-mixed drying-type compounds (taping, topping, and all-purpose).
- 8 lbs. of powder drying-type compounds
- 7.5 lbs. of standard powder setting-type compounds
- 5.5 lbs. of lightweight powder setting-type compounds

# Tools for Finishing Wallboard

A successful wallboard finish job is one that isn't seen once the paint or wallcovering is applied. Achieving a flawless finish is a lot easier when you use the proper tools for the job. Joint compound can be mixed with a ½-in. heavy-duty drill and a mixing paddle, or by hand, using a hand masher. A mud pan holds the compound while you work. It fits nicely into your hand and has sharp edges for scraping excess mud from taping knives.

As for knives, the minimum you'll need are a 6-in. knife for taping and a 12-in. knife for the filler and final coats—though a 4-in. taping knife is handy for tight spots, and some prefer a 10-in. knife for the filler coat. There are a number of specialty knives available that can help make taping easier, such as a double-bladed knife for inside corners and angled knives for tight spots. Many wallboard installers also find a 12-in. finishing trowel handy for feathering the final coat.

Don't buy bottom-line or plastic knives, even for a small job, because the money saved won't justify the frustration.

Sanding completes the job. Professionals use a pole sander with replaceable fiberglass sanding screens—a versatile and effective tool, and quite handy for ceilings. For hand sanding, sanding blocks and dry sanding sponges will take care of the finish work, and a bright work light can help draw attention to overlooked areas in need of sanding.

If you will be skim-coating surfaces, you'll also need a 5-gallon bucket for thinning down compound and a paint roller with a tight-nap roller cover for application. Finally, keep a few general tools on hand for making adjustments as you work, such as a utility knife for trimming tape or panels at butt joints, and a screwdriver to drive protruding heads.

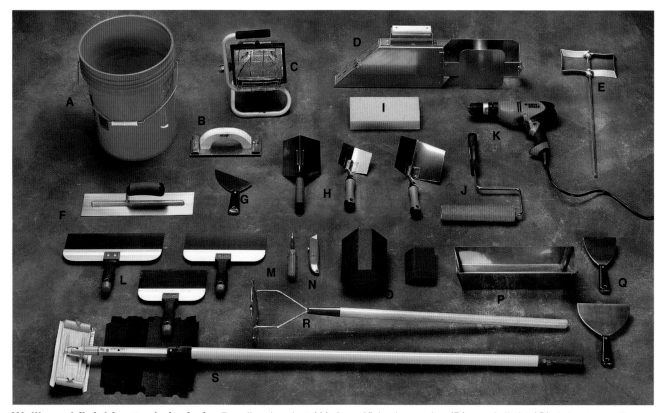

**Wallboard finishing tools include:** 5-gallon bucket (A); hand/block sander (B); work light (C); joint tape dispenser (D); mixing paddle (E); 12-in. finishing trowel (F); 6-in. angled taping knife (G); insider corner taping knifes (H); wet sanding sponge (I); paint roller with tight-nap roller cover (J); ½" drill (K); joint taping knives (4-in., 6-in., 12-in.) (L); screwdriver (M); utility knife (N); dry sanding sponges (O); mud pan (P); taping knives (Q); hand masher (R); 120-, 150-, 220-grit sanding screens and sandpaper; pole sander (S).

## Specialty Equipment for Finishing Wallboard

**Sanding systems** can reduce airborne dust by up to 95%. Most systems are available with both pole and hand sanding attachments that connect to a wet/dry vacuum. Water filters are also available for catching dust before it reaches the vacuum.

**Air compressors and sprayguns** with handheld hoppers are used to apply texture to walls and ceilings, and are available for rent. While they are relatively easy to use, get an operator's manual or lesson at the rental center, then practice on a scrap of cardboard before attempting your project.

## How to Clean Wallboard Finishing Tools

**1** Taping tools can be cleaned easily with water. Use a garden hose to spray off taping knives, mud pans, and mixing paddles immediately after use. Do not clean tools in a sink—compound can settle in pipes where it will harden and clog drains.

**2** Wipe down tools and allow to thoroughly dry to prevent rust. Hang taping knives to store, so the blades will not be bent or damaged by other tools.

# Installing Corner Bead

After the wallboard is hung, the next step is to install corner bead to protect outside corners, soffits, wallboard finished openings, and any other outside angles. Corner bead provides a clean, solid-edge wall corner that can withstand moderate abuse. It is available in a variety of styles for a variety of applications (see page 96). The three most common types are metal, vinyl and paper-faced beads.

Metal beads can be fastened with nails, screws, or a crimper tool. Vinyl beads are easily installed with spray adhesive and staples, or can be embedded in compound, similar to paper-faced beads. See pages 110 to 111 for installing paper-faced beads.

A number of specialty beads are also available, including flexible archway beads for curved corners and J-bead for covering panel ends that meet finished surfaces. Decorative bullnose beads and caps for 2- and 3-way corners are easy ways to add interesting detail to a room.

## Everything You Need

Tools: Aviation snips, screwgun or drill, tape measure, utility knife, stapler, screwdriver, hammer.

Materials: Corner bead, 1¼" wallboard screws, spray adhesive (for vinyl bead), ½" staples, archway bead, bullnose corner caps.

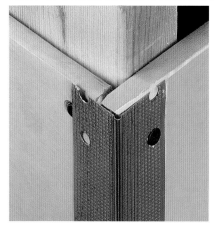

**Metal corner bead** installed over steel framing can be fastened using a crimper tool. Cut the bead to size and position in the corner (see Step 1 below), then crimp ever 4-in. to 6-in.

## How to Install Metal Corner Bead

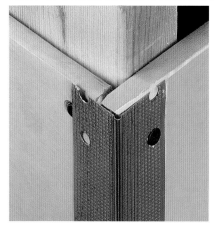

**1** Cut metal corner bead to length so there will be a ½" gap at the floor, using aviation snips. Position the bead so the raised spine is centered over the corner and the flanges are flat against both walls.

**2** Starting at the top, fasten the bead flanges with 1¼" drywall screws, driven every 9" and about ¼" from the edge. Alternate sides with each screw to keep the bead centered. The screws must not project beyond the raised spine.

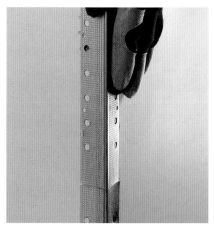

**3** Use full lengths of corner bead where possible. If you must join to lengths, cut the two pieces to size, though butt together the finished ends. Make sure the ends are perfectly aligned and the spine is straight along the length of the corner. File ends, if necessary.

## How to Install Vinyl Corner Bead

**1** Cut vinyl bead to length and test fit over corner. Spray vinyl adhesive evenly along the entire length of the corner, then along the bead.

**2** Quickly install the bead, pressing the flanges into the adhesive. Fasten the bead in place with 1/2-in. staples every 8-in.

## How to Install Corner Bead at Two- and Three-way Corners

**1** Where two or more outside corners meet, trim back the overlapping flanges of each bead to 45° mitered ends, using aviation snips. The ends don't have to match perfectly, but they should not overlap.

**2** Fasten the first bead in place, then test fit each subsequent piece, trimming any overlapping flanges. Align the tips of the two pieces and fasten in place. Install additional beads in the same way.

**Tip:** Blunt any sharp edges or points created by metal bead at three-way corners, using a metal file.

## How to Install Flexible Bead for an Archway

**1** Install standard corner bead on the straight lengths of the corners (see pages 100 to 101), so it is ½" from the floor and 2-in. from the start of the arch.

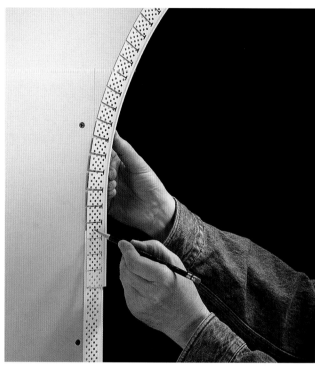

**2** Flatten flexible vinyl bead along the archway to determine the length needed, then add 3". Cut two pieces of bead to this length, one for each side of the archway.

**3** Spray one side of the archway with vinyl adhesive, then spray the bead. Immediately install the bead—work from one end, pushing the bead tight into the corner along the arch. Secure with ½-in. staples every 2-in. Trim the overlapping end so it meets the end of the straight length of corner bead.

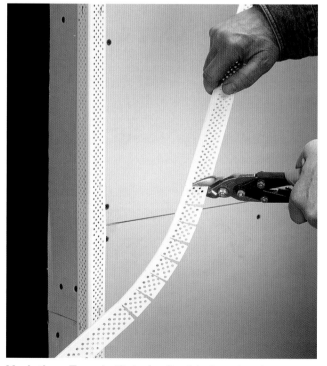

**Variation:** To substitute for flexible bead, snip one flange of standard vinyl bead at 1-in. intervals. Be careful not to cut into or through the spine.

## How to Install L-Bead

**1** L-bead caps the ends of wallboard panels that abut finished surfaces, such as paneling or wood trim, providing a finished edge. The wallboard is installed ⅛" from the finished surface, then the L-bead is positioned tight against the wallboard, so its finished edge covers the edge of the adjacent surface.

**2** Fasten L-bead to the wallboard with ½" staples or wallboard screws every 6-in., then finish with a minimum of three coats of compound (see pages 110 to 111). After final sanding, peel back the protective strip to expose the finished edge of the L-bead.

## Tips for Installing Vinyl Bullnose Corner Bead

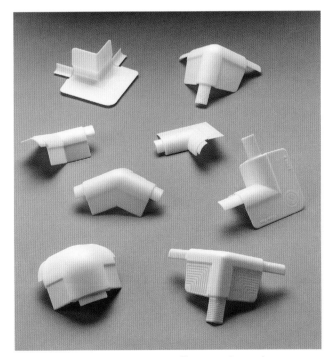

**Bullnose vinyl corner bead** is installed with vinyl adhesive and ½" staples, just like standard vinyl bead (see page 101). However, bullnose beads that have shallow curves may require that the ends of wallboard panels be cut back (inset).

**Wallboard manufacturers** offer a variety of corner caps to ease the finishing process of soffits and other openings trimmed out with wallboard.

# Recommended Levels of Wallboard Finish

The main purpose of finishing wallboard is to create an acceptable base surface for the desired decorative finish. For example, walls and ceiling that will be illuminated by bright light, or finished with gloss paint or thin wallcovering require a smooth, consistent surface to prevent taped seams, covered fasteners and minor imperfections from showing through, a condition termed as "photographing" (see page 122). On the other hand, surfaces that will be sprayed with a texture don't need as polished a wallboard finish, and areas that only need to meet fire codes may be acceptable with a single tape coat.

For years, there were no universal guidelines for what was considered an "acceptable" wallboard finish, which often left contractors and homeowners at odds over what "industry standard finish" actually meant. But recently four major trade associations devised a set of guidelines that have been accepted industry-wide. Below are their recommendations for finishing wallboard, as found in document GA-214-96, entitled "Recommended Levels of Gypsum Board Finish." Each entry describes the minimum level of finish recommended. The full document can be downloaded from the Gypsum Association's website (gypsum.org/downloads.html).

### Level 0

"No taping, finishing, or accessories required."

This level of finish may be useful in temporary construction or whenever the final decoration has not been determined.

### Level 1

"All joints and interior angles shall have tape set in joint compound. Surface shall be free of excess joint compound. Tool marks and ridges are acceptable."

Frequently specified in plenum areas above ceilings, in attics, in areas where the assembly would generally be concealed or in building service corridors, and other areas not normally open to public view. Accessories (beads, trims, or moldings) optional at specifier discretion in corridors and other areas with pedestrian traffic.

Some degree of sound and smoke control is provided; in some geographic areas this level is referred to as "firetaping." Where a fire-resistance rating is required for the gypsum board assembly, details of construction shall be in accordance with reports of fire tests of assemblies that have met the fire-rating requirement. Tape and fastener heads need not be covered with joint compound.

### Level 2

"All joints and interior angles shall have tape embedded in joint compound and wiped with a joint knife leaving a thin coating of joint compound over all joints and interior angles. Fastener heads and accessories shall be covered with a coat of joint compound. Surface shall be free of excess joint compound. Tool marks and ridges are acceptable. Joint compound applied over the body of the tape at the time of tape embedment shall be considered a separate coat of joint compound and shall satisfy the conditions of this level."

Specified where water-resistant gypsum backing board (ASTM C 630) is used as a substrate for tile; may be specified in garages, warehouse storage, or other similar areas where surface appearance is not of primary concern.

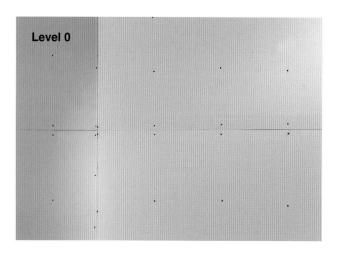

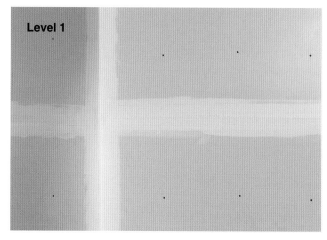

## Level 3

"All joints and interior angles shall have tape embedded in joint compound and one additional coat of joint compound applied over all joints and interior angles. Fastener heads and accessories shall be covered with two separate coats of joint compound. All joint compound shall be smooth and free of tool marks and ridges. Note: It is recommended that the prepared surface be coated with a wallboard primer prior to the application of final finishes. See painting/wallcovering specification in this regard."

Typically specified in appearance areas which are to receive heavy- or medium-texture (spray or hand applied) finishes before final painting, or where heavy-grade wallcoverings are to be applied as the final decoration. This level of finish is not recommended where smooth painted surfaces or light to medium wallcoverings are specified.

## Level 4

"All joints and interior angles shall have tape embedded in joint compound and two separate coats of joint compound applied over all flat joints and one separate coat of joint compound applied over interior angles. Fastener heads and accessories shall be covered with three separate coats of joint compound. All joint compound shall be smooth and free of tool marks and ridges. NOTE: It is recommended that the prepared surface be coated with a wallboard primer prior to the application of final finishes. See painting/wallcovering specification in this regard."

This level should be specified where flat paints, light textures, or wallcoverings are to be applied. In critical lighting areas, flat paints applied over light textures tend to reduce joint photographing. Gloss, semi-gloss, and enamel paints are not recommended over this level of finish.

The weight, texture, and sheen level of wallcoverings applied over this level of finish should be carefully evaluated. Joints and fasteners must be adequately concealed if the wallcovering material is lightweight, contains limited pattern, has a gloss finish, or any combination of these finishes is present. Unbacked vinyl wallcoverings are not recommended over this level of finish.

## Level 5

"All joints and interior angles shall have tape embedded in joint compound and two separate coats of joint compound applied over all flat joints and one separate coat of joint compound applied over interior angles. Fastener heads and accessories shall be covered with three separate coats of joint compound. A thin skim coat of joint compound or a material manufactured especially for this purpose, shall be applied to the entire surface. The surface shall be smooth and free of tool marks and ridges. NOTE: It is recommended that the prepared surface be coated with a wallboard primer prior to the application of finish paint. See painting specification in this regard."

This level of finish is highly recommended where gloss, semi-gloss, enamel, or non-textured flat paints are specified or where severe lighting conditions occur. This highest quality finish is the most effective method to provide a uniform surface and minimize the possibility of joint photographing and of fasteners showing through the final decoration.

Level 2

Levels 3, 4, 5

# Taping Wallboard Seams

Finishing newly installed drywall is satisfying work that requires patience and some basic skill, but it's easier than most people think. Beginners make their biggest, and most lasting, mistakes by rushing the job and applying too much compound in an attempt to eliminate coats. But even for professionals, drywall finishing involves three steps, and sometimes more, plus the final sanding.

The first step is the *taping* coat, when you tape the seams between the drywall panels. The taping is critical to the success of the entire job, so take your time here, and make sure the tape is smooth and fully adhered before it's allowed to dry. If you're using standard metal corner bead on the outside corners, install it before starting the taping coat; paper-faced beads go on after the tape. The screw heads get covered with compound at the beginning of each coat.

After the taping comes the second, or *filler*, coat. This is when you leave the most compound on the wall, filling in the majority of each depression. With the filler coat, the walls start to look pretty good, but they don't have to be perfect; the third coat will take care of minor imperfections. Lightly sand the second coat, then apply the *final* coat. If you're still left with imperfections, add more compound before sanding.

For best results, use a setting-type compound for the taping coat. It creates a strong bond and shrinks very little. Because setting-type compound hardens by chemical reaction, once it begins to set up the process cannot be slowed or stopped, rendering excess compound unusable. Make sure to prepare only as much setting-type compound as you can use in the amount of work time specified by the manufacturer. Choose lightweight setting-type compound because it is easier to sand.

For the other two coats, use an all-purpose compound. These drying-type compounds are available premixed and can be thinned with water if setup begins prematurely. Add small amounts of water to avoid over-thinning and mix using a hand masher. If compound is too thin, add thicker compound from another container. Remix periodically if the liquid begins to separate and rise to the top. If pre-mixed compound is moldy or foul-smelling, it is unusable and must be discarded.

Allow each coat of compound to set up and dry thoroughly before applying the next coat. Setting

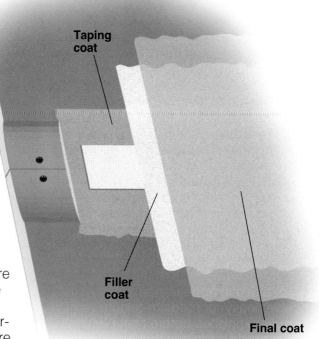

**Taping coat**

**Filler coat**

**Final coat**

time is dependent on a number of factors, such as size of project and type of compound used, but for most finishing projects, count on one day per coat—a total of three days. Refer to the manufacturer's instructions for product specifications. To speed up the process, compound accelerants are available.

Before you begin, make sure all wallboard panels are hung correctly, all corner beads are in place, and all damaged area are repaired. Use a screwdriver to drive any protruding screw heads. Finally, make sure the work area is free and clear of any unnecessary obstacles, tools, and materials.

As you work, keep your compound smooth and workable by mixing it in the mud pan frequently, folding it over with the drywall knife. Try to remove dried chunks, and throw away any mud that gets funky or has been added to and scraped off the wall too many times. Always let your compound dry completely between coats. If you have a large ceiling area to finish, it may be practical to rent a pair of drywall stilts.

## Everything You Need

Tools: Screwdriver; utility knife; 5-gallon bucket; ½" electric drill with mixing paddle; hand masher; 4", 6", 10", and 12" taping knives; inside corner taping knife; mud pan.

Materials: Setting-type joint compound (for tape coat), all-purpose compound (for filler and finish coat), cool potable water, paper joint tape, self-adhesive fiberglass mesh tape.

## How to Prepare Joint Compound

**1** Mix powdered setting-type compound with cool, potable water in a clean 5-gal. bucket, following the manufacturer's directions. All tools and materials must be clean—dirty water, old compound, and other contaminants will affect compound set time and quality.

**2** Use a heavy-duty drill with a mixing paddle to thoroughly mix compound to a stiff, yet workable consistency (see below). Use a low speed to avoid whipping air into the compound. Do not overwork setting-type compound, as it will begin setup. For powdered drying-type compound, remix after fifteen minutes. Clean tools thoroughly immediately after use.

**Use a hand masher** to loosen premixed compound. If the compound has been around a while and is stiff, add a little water and mix to an even consistency.

**Joint compound should appear smooth** in consistency and stiff enough so as not to slide off a trowel or taping knife.

## How to Apply the Taping Coat

**1** Inspect the entire drywall installation and fill any gaps wider than ¼" with compound. Smooth off excess compound so it's flush with the panel face. Also remove any loose paper from damaged areas and fill in with compound.

**2** Using a 4-in. or 6-in. taping knife, smear compound over each screw head, forcing it into the depression. Firmly drag the knife in the opposite direction, removing excess compound from the panel surface.

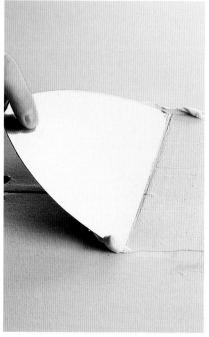

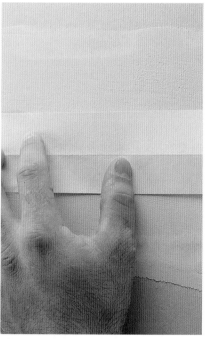

**Variation:** Cover an entire row of screw heads in the field of a panel with one steady, even pass of compound. Use a 6-in. taping knife and apply a thin coat.

**3** On tapered seams, apply an even bed layer of setting-type compound over the seam, about ⅛-in. thick and 6-in. wide, using a 6-in. taping knife. Note: With paper tape, you can also use premixed taping or all-purpose compound.

**4** Center the tape over the seam and lightly embed it in the compound, making sure the tape is smooth and straight. At the end of the seam, tear off the tape so it extends all the way into inside corners and up to the corner bead at outside corners.

**5** Smooth the tape with the taping knife, working out from the center. Apply enough pressure to force compound from underneath the tape, so the tape is flat and has a thin layer beneath it.

**6** At inside corners, smooth the final bit of tape by reversing the knife and carefully pushing it toward the corner. Carefully remove excess compound along the edges of the bed layer with the taping knife.

**7** On butt seams, apply an even $^{1}/_{8}$-in. thick, 4-in. wide bed layer of setting-type compound, using a 6-in. taping knife. Work in one direction and completely fill the V-notch.

**8** Center the tape over the butt seam, and lightly embed it in the compound. As you smooth the tape, apply only enough pressure to leave a $^{1}/_{16}$-in. layer of compound beneath the tape, then apply a thin layer of compound over the tape. Smooth the edges to remove excess compound.

(continued next page)

**9** Tape inside corners by folding precreased paper tape in half to create a 90° angle.

**10** Apply an even layer of setting-type compound, about ⅛-in. thick and 3-in. wide, to both sides of the corner, using a 4-in. taping knife. Embed the tape into the compound, using your fingers and a taping knife.

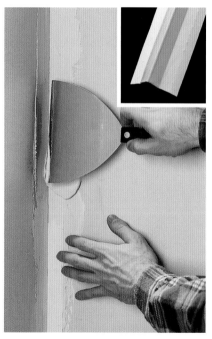

**11** Carefully smooth and flatten both sides of the tape, removing excess compound to leave only a thin layer beneath. Make sure the center of the tape is aligned straight with the corner.

**Tip:** An inside corner knife can embed both sides of the tape in one pass—draw the knife along the tape, applying enough pressure to leave a thin layer of compound beneath. Feather each side using a straight 6-in. taping knife, if necessary.

**Variation:** Paper-faced metal inside corner bead produces straight, durable corners with little fuss. To install the bead, embed it into a thin layer of compound, then smooth the paper, as with a paper-tape inside corner.

**12** Finish outside corner bead with a 6" knife. Apply the compound while dragging the knife along the raised spine of the bead. Make a second pass to feather the outside edge of the compound, then a third dragging along the bead again. Smooth any areas where the corner bead meets taped corners or seams.

**Variation:** To install paper-faced outside corner bead, spread an even layer of compound on each side of the corner, using a 6" taping knife. Press the bead into the compound and smooth the paper flanges with the knife.

## How to Apply Mesh Tape

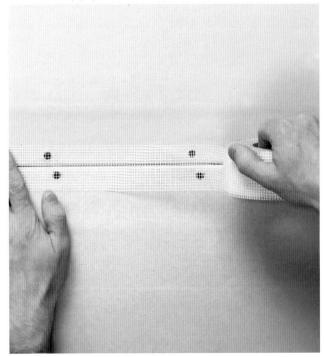

**1** To use self-adhesive mesh tape on seams, apply the tape over the seam center so it's straight and flat. Run mesh tape to corners, then cut using a sharp utility knife.

**2** Coat the mesh with an even layer of compound, about $\frac{1}{8}$-in. thick, using a 6-in. taping knife. Smooth the joint with a 10-in. or 12-in. knife, removing excess compound. NOTE: Use setting-type compound or drying-type taping compound.

## How to Apply the Filler Coat

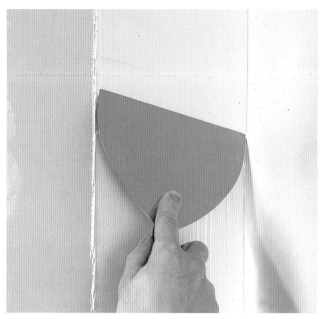

**1** After the taping coat has dried completely, scrape off any remaining ridges and chunks, then second-coat the screw heads, using a 6-in. taping knife and all-purpose compound (see page 108). Note: Setting-type compound and drying-type topping compound are also acceptable.

**2** Apply an even layer of compound to both sides of each inside corner, using a 6-in. taping knife. Smooth one side at a time, holding the blade about 15° from horizontal and lightly dragging the point along the corner. Make a second pass to remove excess compound along the outer edges. Repeat, if necessary.

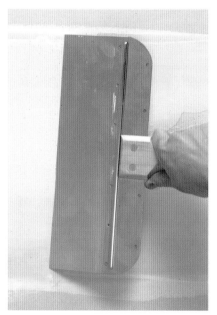

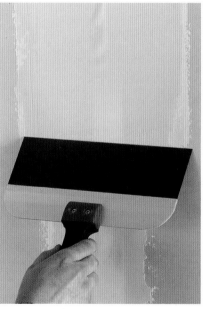

**3** Coat tapered seams with an even layer of all-purpose compound, using a 12-in. taping knife. Whenever possible, apply the coat in one direction and smooth it in the opposite. Feather the sides of the compound first, holding the blade almost flat and applying pressure to the outside of the blade, so the blade just skims over the center of the seam.

**4** After feathering both side edges of the compound, make a pass down the center of the seam, applying even pressure to the blade. This pass should leave the seam smooth and even, with the edges feathered out to nothing. The joint tape should be completely covered.

**5** For butt seams, use the same technique as for tapered seams, however, feather the edges out 8-in. to 10-in. on each side to help mask the seam. Apply compound in thin layers and smooth out as needed.

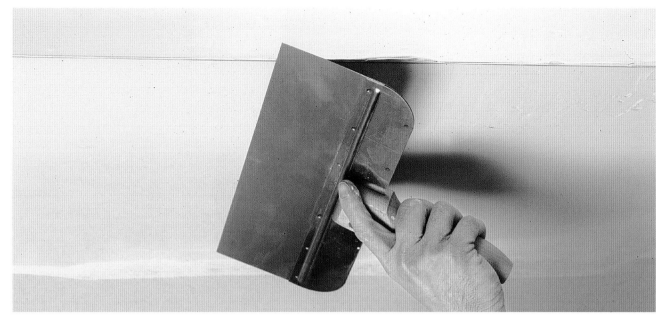

**6** Second-coat the outside corners, one side at a time, using a 12" knife. Apply an even layer of compound, then feather the outside edge by applying pressure to the outside of the knife—enough so that the blade flexes and removes most of the compound along the edge but leaves the corner intact. Make a second pass with the blade riding along the raised spine, applying even pressure.

## How to Apply the Final Coat

**1** After the filler coat has dried, lightly sand all of the joints (see pages 118 to 121), then third-coat the screws. Apply the final coat, following the same steps used for the filler coat but do the seams first, then the outside corners, followed by the inside corners. Use a 12" knife and spread the compound a few inches wider than the joints in the filler coat. Remove most of the compound, filling scratches and low spots but leaving only traces elsewhere. Make several passes, if necessary, until the surface is smooth and there are no knife tracks or other imperfections. Carefully blend intersecting joints so there's no visible transition.

## How to Flat Tape

**1** Trim any loose paper along the drywall edge with a utility knife. If the gap between the drywall and the object is wider than ¼", fill it with joint compound and let it dry. Cover the joint with self-adhesive mesh joint tape, butting the tape's edge against the object without overlapping the object.

**2** Cover the tape with a 4"-wide layer of setting-type or premixed taping compound. Smooth the joint, leaving just enough compound to conceal the tape. Let the first coat dry completely, then add two more thin coats, using a 6" taping knife. Feather the outside edge of the joint to nothing.

## How to Round Inside Corners

**1** To soften off-angle inside corners, round them off. Center self-adhesive fiberglass mesh tape over the seam, and smooth it flat. Apply a ⅛" thick layer of compound 4-in. wide along each side of the mesh, using a 6-in. taping knife. Note: Use setting-type compound to prevent significant shrinkage.

**2** Lightly drag the knife across the seam, perpendicular to the mesh tape, to sculpt a rounded base for the filler coat. Work in the same direction, along the entire length of the seam, then make a second pass, pulling the knife across in the opposite direction.

**3** Once the tape is completely covered, smooth out any ridges and feather the edges of the compound along the length of the seam.

**4** After the tape coat is dry, apply another ⅛" layer of setting-type compound along the seam, then use a 12" taping knife to create the rounded corner, following the same technique as in step 2.

**5** After the fill coat has dried, lightly sand ridges and high spots (see pages 118 to 121), then apply a thin layer of all-purpose or topping compound for the final coat, following the same technique as for the previous two coats.

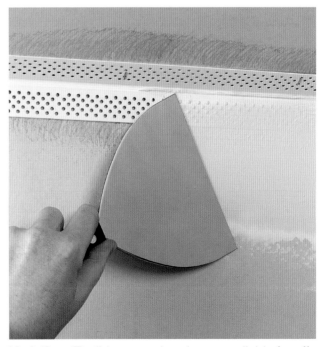

**Variation:** Flexible corner beads are available for off-angle joints that are prone to cracking, such as those between pitched ceilings and flat kneewalls. The vinyl center crease flexes along with normal structural shifts. Install flexible bead with adhesive or embed it in compound; keep the center crease free of compound.

# Final Inspection & Fixing Problems

After the final coat of joint compound has dried but before you begin sanding, inspect the entire finish job for flaws. If you discover scrapes, pitting, or other imperfections, add another coat of joint compound. Repair any damaged or overlooked areas such as cracked seams and overcut holes for electrical boxes prior to sanding.

During your inspection, make sure to check that all seams are acceptably feathered out. To check seams, hold a level or 12-in. taping knife perpendicularly across the seam; fill concave areas with extra layers of compound and correct any convex seams that crown more than 1/16".

### Everything You Need

Tools: 6-in. and 12-in. taping knives, sanding block or pole sander.

Materials: All-purpose joint compound, self-adhesive fiberglass mesh tape, 220-grit sanding screen or 150-grit sandpaper.

**Scratches, dents,** and other minor imperfections can be smoothed over with a thin coat of all-purpose compound.

## How to Fix Common Taping Problems

**Pitting occurs** when compound is overmixed or applied with too little pressure to force out trapped air bubbles. Pitting can be corrected easily with a thin coat of compound. If trapped air bubbles are present, sand lightly before covering with compound.

**Mis-cut holes** for electrical boxes can be flat taped. Cover the gap with self-adhesive mesh tape and cover with three coats of all-purpose compound. Precut repair patches are also available.

116

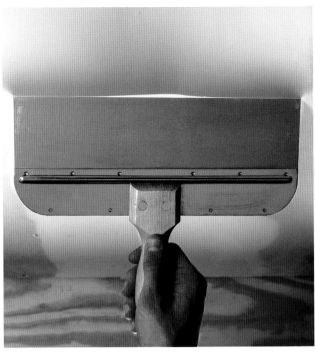

**Concave seams** can be filled with an extra layer or two of all-purpose compound, repeating the filler and final coats (see pages 112 to 113).

**For seams crowned** more than $1/16$", carefully sand along the center (see pages 118 to 121), but do not expose the tape. Check the seam with a level. If it's still crowned, add a layer of compound with a 12" knife, removing all of it along the seam's center and feathering it out toward the outside edges. After it dries, apply a final coat, if necessary.

**Bubbled or loose tape** occurs when the bed layer is too thin, which causes a faulty bond between the tape and compound. Cut out small, soft areas with a utility knife and retape. Large runs of loose tape will have to be fully removed before retaping.

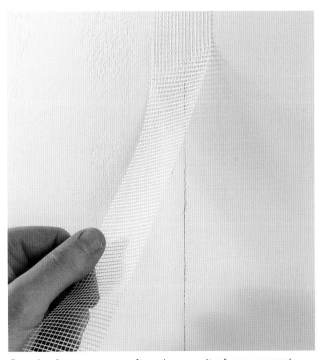

**Cracked seams** are often the result of compound that has dried too quickly or shrunk. Retape the seam if the existing tape and compound is intact; otherwise, cut out any loose material. In either case, make sure to fill the crack with compound.

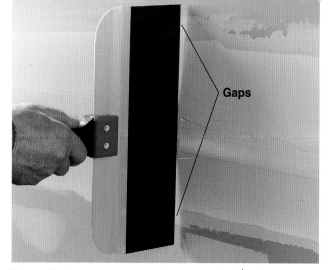

**Seam that crown or recess** more than 1/16" should be corrected with another coat of compound before sanding. To correct crowned and recessed seams, see page 117.

**Tip:** As you work, if you over-sand or discover low spots that require another coat of compound, mark the area with a piece of painter's tape for repair after you finish sanding. Make sure to wipe away dust so the tape sticks to the surface.

# Sanding Wallboard

Sanding is the final step in finishing wallboard. The goal is to remove excess joint compound and crowned seams, smooth out tool and lap marks, and feather the edges so they blend into the panel surface. Anywhere there is joint compound, you must sand. How much sanding is required depends on the quality of the taping job and the level of finish you need for the final decoration (see pages 104 to 105).

Sanding wallboard is a two-step process: Pole sanding to remove excess compound and feather edges, and hand sanding to take care of the final smoothing work.

Pole sanders have a flat head on a swivel that holds sandpaper or sanding screen. The length of the pole keeps you distanced from dust and brings ceiling seams within reach. You don't have to apply much pressure to get results, simply push the head along the seam and let the weight of the tool do the work. You can use 120-grit sanding screen or sandpaper for joints finished with all-purpose compound, though use 150-grit on lightweight or topping compounds, which are softer.

Hand sanding can be done with a block sander or dry sanding sponge. The object of this step is to smooth all the joints and create a uniform surface, so again you need not apply much pressure to get the job done. Use 150- to 220-grit sanding screen or sandpaper for final sanding.

As you work, make sure to sand only the compound rather than the panels. Face paper can scuff easily, necessitating a thin coat of com-

pound to repair. Do not use power sanders on wallboard; they are too difficult to control. A second's hesitation can remove too much compound or even mar panels.

Sanding wallboard is a messy job. The fine dust generated will easily find its way into all areas of the home if the work area is not contained. Sealing all doorways and cracks with sheet plastic and masking tape will help prevent dust from leaving the work zone, however wet sanding may be more practical in some instances. With wet sanding, or sponging, the abrasive papers and screens are replaced by a damp sponge that is used to smooth the water-soluble compound and blend it with the surface. Very little dust becomes airborne.

But if your goal is to eradicate dust, your best bet is to use a dust-free sanding system. Available at most rental centers, dust-free systems contain hoses with sanding attachments that connect to a wet/dry vacuum to cut dust by nearly ninety-five percent. A water filter can be added to the system to capture most of the dust and spare your vacuum's filter.

### Everything You Need

Tools: Swivel-joint pole sander, hand-sander block, work light, dry sanding sponge, wet sanding sponge, wet/dry shop vacuum, broom, dust mask, eye goggles.

Materials: Sheet plastic, 2-in. (blue) painter's tape, 120- and 150-grit sandpaper or 220-grit sanding screen.

## How to Minimize Dust

**Use sheet plastic** and 2-in. masking tape to help confine dust to the work area. Cover all doorways, cabinets, built-ins, and any gaps or other openings with plastic, sealing all four edges with tape—the fine dust produced by sanding can find its way through the smallest cracks.

**Prop a fan** in an open window so it blows outside to help pull dust out of the work area during sanding. Only open one window in the space to prevent a cross-breeze.

## How to Sand Wallboard

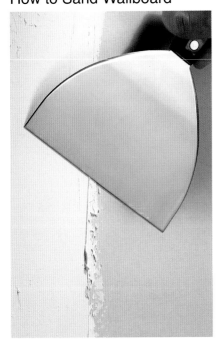

**1** Prior to sanding, knockdown any ridges, chunks or tool marks, using a 6-in. taping knife. Do not apply too much pressure—you don't want to dig into the compound, only remove the excess.

**2** Lightly sand all seams and outside corners, using a pole sander with 220-grit sanding screen or 150-grit sandpaper. Work in the direction of the joints, applying even pressure to smooth transitions and high areas. Don't sand out depressions; fill them with compound and resand. Be careful not to over-sand or expose joint tape.

119

**3** Inside corners often are finished with only one or two thin coats of compound over the tape. Sand the inside edge of joints only lightly and smooth the outside edge carefully; inside corners will be sanded by hand later.

**4** Fine-sand the seams, outside corners, and fastener heads using a sanding block with 150- to 220-grit sanding screen or sandpaper. As you work, use your hand to feel for defects along the compound. A bright work light angled to highlight seams can help reveal problem areas.

**5** To avoid damage from over-sanding, use a 150-grit dry sanding sponge to sand inside corners. The sides of sanding sponges also contain grit, allowing you to sand both sides of a corner at once to help prevent over-sanding.

**6** For tight or hard-to-reach corners, fold a piece of sanding screen or sandpaper in thirds and sand the area carefully. Rather than using just your fingertips, try to flatten your hand as much as possible to spread out the pressure to avoid sanding too deep.

**7** If necessary, repair depressions, scratches or exposed tape due to over-sanding after final sanding is complete. Wipe the area with a dry cloth to remove dust, then apply a thin coat of all-purpose compound. Allow to dry thoroughly, then resand.

**8** With sanding complete, remove dust from the panels with a dry towel or soft broom. Use a wet-dry vacuum to clean out all electrical boxes and around floors, windows, and doors, then carefully roll up sheet plastic and discard. Finally, damp mop the floor to remove any remaining dust.

## How to Wet Sand Wallboard

**Variation:** Wet sanding is a dust-free alternative to dry sanding. Use a high-density sponge made for wet sanding. Saturate it with cool, clean water, and wring it out just enough so it doesn't drip. Swipe joints and corners in the direction they run, and rinse the sponge frequently. Sponge sparingly, to avoid streaking.

**Variation:** Dust-free sanding systems come with both pole and hand sanding attachments that connect directly to your wet/dry vacuum or to a water filter that captures the bulk of the dust, keeping your vacuum's filter clean.

# Applying a Skim Coat

Joint compound and wallboard face paper have different porosities, which cause each to absorb paint and other decorative finishes differently. If taped walls and ceilings are not properly primed, seams and fastener heads can show through the finished paint job. This is called "photographing" and is readily apparent on surfaces that are under bright light or that are covered with high-gloss paint.

To combat photographing, apply a skim coat of thinned-down joint compound. A skim coat evens out surface textures to create a smooth, perfectly primed surface. Use all-purpose compound or drying-type topping compound for skim coating. Avoid setting-type compounds—if they dry too quickly they may not properly bond with the surface.

### Everything You Need

Tools: Heavy-duty drill with paddle mixer, 5-gal. bucket, paint screen or roller pan, paint roller, 12" to 14" taping knife.

Materials: Premixed all-purpose or drying-type topping compound, clean potable water.

**Photographing** is the term used to describe taped seams that show through painted walls and ceilings. It's caused by improperly primed taped surfaces.

## How to Apply a Skim Coat

**1** Thin compound with cool water to a paint-like consistency, using a drill and mixing paddle. Pour compound into a roller tray. NOTE: Use all-purpose compound or drying-type topping compound.

**2** Apply a thin coat of compound to the taped surface using a paint roller with a thin nap. Work in small sections so compound doesn't dry before you can smooth it.

**3** Once a section is covered with compound, smooth the surface using a 12-in. to 14-in. taping knife. Work from the top down, applying enough pressure to leave a thin film of compound over the surface and remove ridges.

# Texturing Walls & Ceilings

Wall and ceiling textures can take many forms, and today's texturing products make it easy to create a range of effects—from acoustical spray textures to custom hand-troweled designs.

Most textures are applied using hand tools, such as paint rollers and drywall knives, or pneumatic texturing guns, which you can find at rental centers. Spray equipment is not difficult to use, but make sure to get operating instructions or a lesson at the rental center. If you are hand-applying a texture on a ceiling, you may want to rent a pair of drywall stilts.

Home centers and paint stores carry a wide variety of do-it-yourself texturing products. One of the easiest to use is texture paint, because it combines a paint base (usually white) with texture additives and doesn't need to be painted after it's applied. You can also buy dry additives separately and mix them into the paint of your choice. For many texture treatments, you can also use all-purpose drywall compound, thinning it with water, if desired. Textures made with compound must be painted, however.

Texture products typically contain a lot of water and can be heavy if applied in thick coats. Drywalled ceilings that receive a popcorn texture or heavy coats of compound must be adequately supported to resist sagging. Standard $\frac{1}{2}$" drywall panels should be attached to joists that are 16" on-center. Where framing is 24" on-center, the drywall should be $\frac{5}{8}$" standard or $\frac{1}{2}$" ceiling panels. Texturing is not recommended on ceilings with $\frac{3}{8}$" drywall.

Before texturing, prepare new walls and ceilings with a coat of flat, white latex wall paint (or use a base-coat product made specifically for texturing). If you're texturing old surfaces, consult the manufacturer regarding prep work. To ensure consistent drying, texture when the air temperature, the wall or ceiling surface, and the texture material are at least 55°F. Ventilate the room only after application, and don't use heaters to speed the drying process.

## Tips for Protecting Surfaces from Overspray

**Before spraying ceilings,** cover walls with sheet plastic. Press the top half of 2-in. painter's tape along the joint between the ceiling and the wall, then hang plastic under the tape. After spraying, remove the loose edge as soon as the texture begins to setup.

**For wall applications,** cover windows, doors, and any other openings with sheet plastic and painter's tape to seal around the edges. Make sure to cover all jambs as oversprayed texture can make trim installation more difficult.

**Use drop cloths** to protect floors and for easy clean-up. Cover the entire floor area, overlapping drop cloths and sheet plastic protecting walls by 12-in.

**Stuff fiberglass insulation** into electrical boxes and HVAC ducts to protect wiring and ducting.

**Spraying texture** onto walls and ceilings is a messy job. Wear long sleeves and full-length pants, eye protection, and a dust mask.

# How to Apply a Popcorn Ceiling Texture

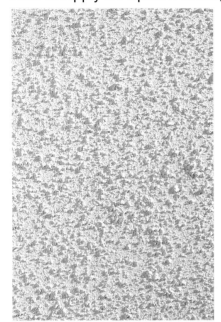

**Popcorn texture** is a popular treatment for ceilings. Its bumpy surface is created by tiny particles of vermiculite or polystyrene that give it sound-deadening properties. Mixtures are available in fine, medium, and coarse grades.

**Mix the dry texture** following the manufacturer's directions, and load the hopper of the texture gun. Apply the texture, holding the gun 2 ft. to 4 ft. below the ceiling. Spray in a side-to-side motion (not arching), leaving a thin, even layer over the entire ceiling. Immediately following the first layer, spray on a second thin layer, working in a direction perpendicular to the first. Allow the texture to dry. For a heavy texture, the manufacturer may recommend applying an additional coat.

# How to Apply an Orange Peel Texture

**Orange peel textures** are most commonly applied to walls. They have a distinctive, spattered look created by spraying a thin texturing product or water-thinned all-purpose drywall compound through a texturing gun. For a heavier spattered texture, repeat the step shown here, using less air pressure at the gun (atomizing air) and the compressor (feed pressure).

**Mix the texture product** or compound to the consistency of latex paint. Spray the surface with long, side-to-side strokes, keeping the gun perpendicular to the surface, and about 18" away from it. To apply a heavy spatter-coat, let the surface dry for 10 to 15 minutes, then spray with random motions, from about 6 ft. away.

## How to Create a Knock-down Texture

**A knock-down texture** is an orange peel texture that is partially smoothed with a drywall knife. Its relative flatness creates a subtle effect, and it's easier to paint and maintain than the heavier textures, making it a good choice for walls. Because of the light troweling required, this texture works best on smooth, flat surfaces.

**Mix the texture product** or all-purpose drywall compound to a heavy latex-paint consistency. Spray-texture the entire surface following the orange peel procedure on page 125. Let the texture dry for 10 to 15 minutes, then lightly trowel the surface with a 12" or larger drywall knife. Hold the knife almost flat, and work perpendicularly to the drywall seams.

## How to Apply a Stipple Texture

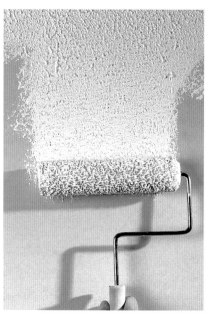

**Stipple textures** are made with a paint roller and texture paint or all-purpose drywall compound. Randomly shaped ridges have a noticeable grain orientation. The amount of texture is affected by the nap of the roller, which can vary from ¼" to 1". Stippling can be knocked down for a flatter finish.

**Mix paint or compound** to a heavy latex-paint consistency. Coat the roller and roll the surface, recoating the roller as needed to create an even layer over the entire work area. Let the texture dry to a dull-wet sheen, then roll the surface again—without loading the roller—to create the finished texture.

**Variation:** Knock down the stipple finish for a smoother texture. Apply the stipple texture with a roller, and let it dry for about 10 minutes. Smooth the surface with a 12" or larger drywall knife, holding the knife almost flat and applying very light pressure.

## How to Create a Swirl Texture

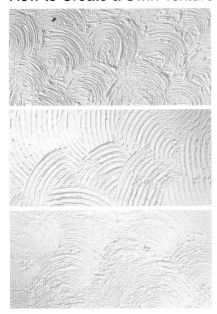

**Swirl textures** and other freehand designs can have the look of traditionally applied plaster. Swirls can be made with a wallpaper brush, whisk broom, or any type of raking or combing tool.

**Mix the texture product** or all-purpose drywall compound to a heavy latex-paint consistency. For a shallow texture, use a paint roller with a ½" nap to apply an even coat over the entire surface; for a deeper texture, apply an even, ⅛"-thick coat with a drywall knife. Let the surface dry to a dull-wet appearance. Brush the pattern into the material using arching or circular motions. Start at one end of the area and work backward, overlapping the starting and end points of previous swirls with each new row.

## How to Apply a Troweled Texture

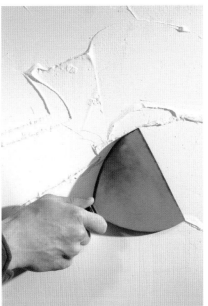

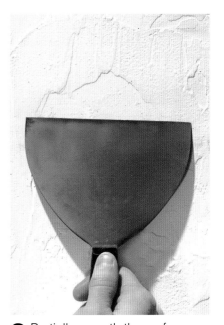

**A troweled texture** can have almost any design but should be applied with varied motions to create a random appearance. Premixed all-purpose drywall compound works well for most troweled textures, and it's usually best to work in small sections.

**1** Apply the compound to the surface using a 6" or 8" drywall knife. Vary the direction of the strokes and the thickness of compound. If desired, stipple the surface by stamping the knife into the compound and pulling it away sharply.

**2** Partially smooth the surface, using a 6", 8", or 12" knife. Flatten the tops of ridges and stipples without smoothing lower areas. When you're satisfied with the design, repeat step 1 in an adjacent section, overlapping the edges of the textured area by a few inches.

127

# Applying Veneer Plaster

While gypsum wallboard all but wiped out traditional plaster and lath in the 1940s, a new generation of plaster products now make plaster easier and cheaper to apply, leading to new popularity for this classic material.

Veneer plaster systems provide a solid, uniform wall surface that is highly resistant to nail pops, cracks and surface damage. A skim coat of plaster is troweled onto a gypsum wallboard base that has a distinctive blue color, commonly called blueboard. While blueboard is installed like standard wallboard, it has a highly absorptive face paper to which the wet-mix plaster bonds. Blueboard joints do not need to be taped as precisely as standard wallboard joints, and seams and fastener heads do not show through the finished plaster surface, a common problem with standard wallboard.

Veneer systems are available in one-coat and two-coat systems. One-coat systems have a single layer of finish plaster applied directly to the blueboard base; two-coat systems, a rough basecoat for the finish plaster

## Everything You Need

Tools: Stapler, hammer, heavy-duty ½" drill with mixing paddle, 16-gal. drum, mortar hawk, 12" trowel, fine-wire rake or broom (for basecoat), spray water bottle.

Materials: Metal corner bead with mesh flanges, 1¼" wallboard screws, non-adhesive fiberglass mesh tape, ¼" staples, clean potable water, dry-mix veneer basecoat plaster (for two-coat application), dry-mix veneer finish plaster.

**Tools and materials for installing veneer plaster** include: dry-mix veneer plaster basecoats (A); finish plaster (B), available for smooth or textured applications; spray bottle for moistening surfaces (C); non-adhesive fiberglass mesh tape for covering blueboard panel seams and inside corners (D); outside corner beads with metal beads and mesh flanges (E); mortar hawk (F); 12-in. trowel (G); thin-wire rake for roughening the base coat (H).

to mechanically "key" or bond to, providing a more rigid surface. Finish plaster can be troweled smooth or tooled for a texture. Sand and other additives can be used to create coarser textures.

Applying veneer plaster effectively does take some time to master, but no more so than that of any masonry technique that requires troweling. The key is to apply the plaster in quick, short strokes, called "scratching in," and then to immediately trowel it over with a steady, even stroke to smooth the plaster to a consistent thickness, typically $\frac{1}{16}$" to $\frac{1}{8}$.

Veneer plaster systems cost roughly 25 percent more to install than traditional wallboard, however, veneer plaster can be installed in a single day, rather than the minimum of three days required for a wallboard job. Additionally, veneer plaster does not need to be sanded, eliminating the additional setup and cleanup need for sanding wallboard.

For best results, maintain a consistent room temperature during all phases of the plaster application, until the material has dried completely. Plan your installation to allow for continuous application, from corner to corner, across a single surface. If you must stop partway through the application, use the trowel to cut a clean, sharp edge rather than feather out the coat. Do not overlap the applications, but rather use excess plaster to fill and bridge the joint during finish troweling.

NOTE: Each manufacturer has its own proprietary materials and methods for mixing, using, and applying its veneer plaster systems. Always follow the detailed instructions provided by the manufacturer for the products you use.

## One- and Two-coat Veneer Plaster Systems

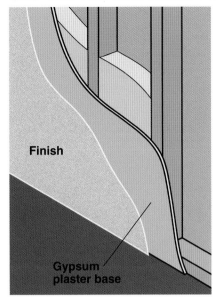

**One-coat veneer plaster systems** use a single, $\frac{1}{16}$" to $\frac{3}{32}$"-thick coat of finish plaster applied directly to a blueboard base. The coat can be troweled smooth or textured, resulting in a hard, monolithic surface.

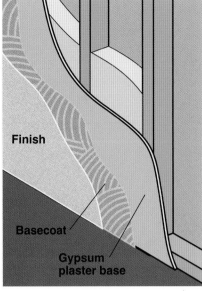

**Two-coat veneer plaster systems** are composed of a $\frac{1}{16}$" to $\frac{1}{8}$" basecoat plaster applied to blueboard, followed by a $\frac{1}{16}$" to $\frac{3}{32}$"-thick coat of finish plaster. The finish coat bonds with the scratched basecoat surface, forming a more uniform and monolithic surface than that of a one-coat system.

## Options of Veneer Plaster

**Veneer plaster** can be troweled smooth or textured using standard techniques (see pages 123 to 127). As an alternative to paint, many manufacturers also offer pigment additives in a variety of colors. Because the plaster itself is colored, scratches and other superficial flaws are less noticeable.

**Other materials** can be used as veneers to produce interesting walls and ceilings, such as concrete and clay. While most are applied using similar techniques to veneer plaster, always follow the manufacturer's instructions to achieve best results.

## How to Finish Blueboard Seams with Mesh Tape

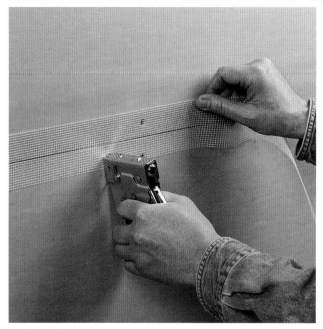

**1** Install metal outside corner bead with mesh flanges as you would standard metal corner bead (see page 100). To tape flat seams, center non-adhesive fiberglass mesh tape over the joint and fasten at one end with two ¼" staples. Pull the tape taut across the joint and fasten the opposite end with two staples, then secure the tape with staples on alternate sides of the joint, every 24-in.

**2** To tape inside corners, crease the tape in half lengthwise, and fasten to one surface only, with one staple at each end and then every 24-in. along the joint. At ceiling-to-wall joints, fasten tape to the ceiling-side; at wall-to-wall joints, fasten to either side. Avoid overlapping tape where possible.

## How to Mix Veneer Plaster

**1** Following the manufacturer's instructions, mix one bag of dry plaster with the specified amount of clear, potable water in a 16-gal. smooth-sided container. To prevent accelerated set times, make sure all tools and containers are clean, and never add anything to the mix that is not specified by the manufacturer.

**2** After all the plaster has been added, mix on high-speed for a couple minutes, stopping as soon as the plaster is smooth. Do not overmix plaster as it will decrease set time and reduce your trowel time. Clean mixing paddle and container immediately after use.

## How to Apply a One-Coat Veneer Plaster System

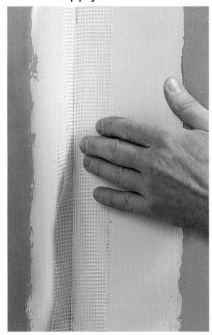

**1** Cover all seams first. Apply a thin layer of plaster along all flat seams and corner bead, feathering out the edges by 6-in. For inside corners, apply a thin bed of plaster and embed the loose tape, then cover with another thin layer. Allow all taped seams to set.

**Variation:** Blueboard joints can also be reinforced with paper tape. Embedded the tape in a thin plaster bed, then and cover with another thin layer to conceal the tape fully. NOTE: Some manufacturers recommend setting-type compound for embedding paper tape; always follow the manufacturer's directions for the products you use.

**2** After the seams have set, begin plastering the surface, beginning at one corner and moving to the opposite. Start with ceilings and then do the walls, completing one entire surface before moving on to the next. To apply the plaster, tightly scratch in the material up the wall (photo left), then immediately double-back over it, smoothing over the material to a thickness of $\frac{1}{16}$-in. to $\frac{3}{32}$-in., as specified by the manufacturer. Use tight, quick strokes to apply the plaster during the "scratch pass" and long, even strokes to achieve consistency during the "smooth pass."

**3** Continue to apply plaster by scratching in and smoothing over the surface. Don't worry about uniformity and trowel ridges at this point. Rather, make sure the entire surface is completely concealed with a relatively even plaster coat, 1/16-in. to 3/32-in.-thick.

**4** Once the plaster begins to firm (also called "taken up"), trowel the surface to fill any voids and remove tooling marks and imperfections, integrating the surface into a uniform smoothness.

**5** Prior to the plaster setting, make a final pass with the trowel to smooth the surface, using water sparingly. Do not over trowel; stop before the plaster begins to darken and sets.

**Variation:** For textured surfaces, skip the final troweling and work the surface with a texturing tool to achieve the desired results. See pages 123 to 127 for surface texturing techniques. NOTE: Sand or texture added to the plaster mixture does not require tooling.

# How to Apply Basecoat in a Two-Coat Veneer Plaster System

**1** Apply a thin layer of basecoat along all flat seams and corner bead, feathering out the edges by 6-in. For inside corners, apply a thin bed of basecoat and embed the loose tape, then cover with another thin layer. Allow all taped seams to set.

Scratch pass

Smooth pass

**2** After the seams have set, tightly scratch in basecoat, then immediately double-back over it, smoothing over the material to a thickness of 1/16-in. to 1/8-in., as specified by the manufacturer. Use tight, quick strokes to apply basecoat for the "scratch pass" and long, even strokes to achieve consistency for the "smooth pass."

**3** Once the plaster begins to firm or "take up," trowel the surface to fill any voids and remove tooling marks and imperfections, integrating the surface into a reasonably uniform surface—do not over-trowel to a smooth surface. Create keys for the final coat, using a thin-wire rake to roughen the basecoat.

**4** Approximately two hours after the basecoat has set, the finish coat can be applied using the same techniques as for a one-coat veneer plaster system (see pages 130 to 132).

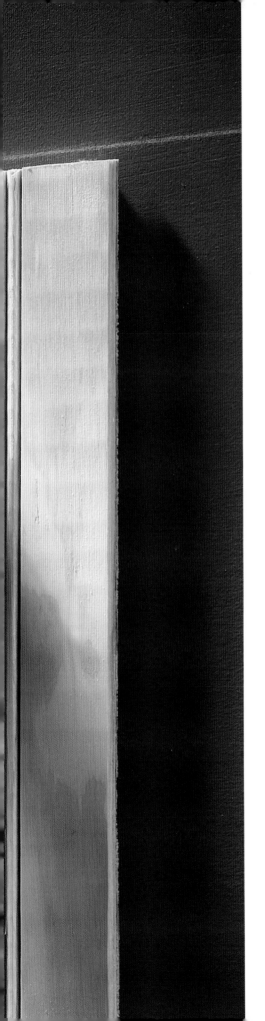

# Installing Paneling & Ceiling Systems

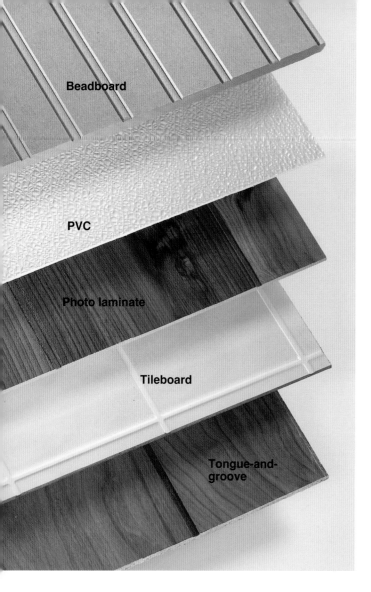

Beadboard

PVC

Photo laminate

Tileboard

Tongue-and-groove

# Installing Paneling

Paneling is a versatile wall-surfacing material that comes in a wide range of styles, colors, and prices. Paneling sheets are made from a variety of materials for numerous applications:

Solid and veneer wood paneling is durable and easy to clean. Available in finished and unfinished sheets, wood paneling brings a warm, rich tone to any room. It is often used as wainscoting (pages 140 to 143) and also can be used as an inexpensive cover-up for damaged plaster.

Laminate panels are sheets of MDF, particleboard, or plywood faced with paper, print or vinyl. Laminates are available in hundreds of colors, styles, and patterns, providing a durable alternative to paint or wallcoverings.

FRP (fiberglass reinforced plastic), extruded plastic, and vinyl panels contain solid material throughout the panel, creating a low-mainte-

nance, water-resistant wall surface for bathrooms, utility rooms, garages and workshops, as well as numerous commercial applications.

Tileboard is moisture-resistant hardboard coated with melamine, providing a durable, easy-to-clean plastic finish. It's designed to replicate the appearance of ceramic tile, for use in bathrooms, laundry rooms, and kitchens.

Bamboo paneling is gaining in popularity due to its unique look and green-friendly specs. Panels are constructed of strips of bamboo laminated to a fabric backing, which allows it to conform to any type of surface, flat or curved.

Most paneling is available in $4 \times 8$, $4 \times 9$, and $4 \times 10$ sheets. Some manufacturers also offer sheets in 60-in. widths. Paneling that is ¼-in. or less in thickness requires a solid backer of at least ½-in. wallboard; paneling ⅜-in. thick or more is rigid enough to be fastened directly to framing with 16-in. O.C. spacing. Installation typically involves a panel adhesive, either applied in beads along the wall or framing, or troweled onto the back surface of the panel. Make sure to check the manufacturer's instructions for the product you purchase.

Unlike wallboard, paneling is traditionally installed parallel to the framing. To estimate the number of sheets you'll need, measure the total width of the walls and divide by 48-in. For every door subtract half a sheet, for every window, a quarter sheet. For ceilings higher than 8-ft., purchase longer sheets or divide the extra height into 96-in. to determine how many additional panels you'll need.

Before installing paneling, condition it to the room it will be installed in for at least 24 hours. Stand sheets upright along their long edge, either separately or stacked together with wood spacers between each sheet to allow air to flow.

Exterior and basement walls must contain insulation and a vapor barrier behind the wallboard. For remodeling installations, remove all trimwork, fixtures and electrical coverplates, and shut off electricity to the work area.

## Everything You Need

Tools: Pry bar, stud finder, tape measure, plumb bob, circular saw, straightedge, hammer, carpenter's level, compass, jig saw, caulk gun.

Materials: Paneling sheets, 4d finish nails, wood stain, panel adhesive, powdered chalk.

## How to Install Wood Paneling

**1** Starting in the corner farthest from the entry, use a stud finder to locate the center of the stud closest to, but less than, 48-in. from the corner. Find and mark stud centers every 48-in. from this first stud. Snap a plumb chalk line down the wall at each location. Paneling seams will fall along these lines.

**2** Lay the first paneling sheet face-side down. Measure the distance from corner to the first plumb mark and add 1-in. to allow for scribing. Use a circular saw and clamped straightedge to cut paneling to this measurement.

**3** Position the first sheet of paneling against the wall so that the cut edge is 1-in. away from the corner, and the opposite, finished edge is plumb. Temporarily tack the top of the paneling to the wall.

**4** Spread the legs of a compass to 1¼", then run the compass down the full height of the wall to scribe the corner irregularities onto the face of the paneling. Remove paneling from wall.

(continued next page)

## How to Install Wood Paneling (continued)

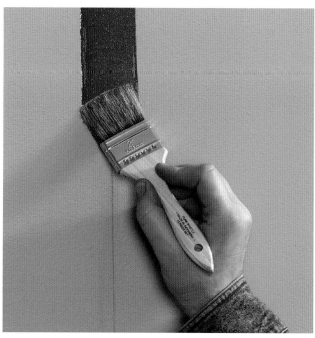

**5** Lay the paneling face-side up and cut along the scribe line with a jigsaw. To prevent splintering, use a fine-tooth woodcutting blade. The scribed edge will fit perfectly against the wall corner.

**6** Apply stain or paint to the wall at the plumb lines so the backer will not show through the slight gaps at joints. Select a stain that matches the color of the paneling edges, which may be darker than the paneling surface.

**7** Use a caulk gun to apply 2-in.-long beads of panel adhesive to the wall at 6-in. intervals and in a continuous, wavy bead about 1-in. back from plumb lines (to prevent adhesive from seeping out through the joints). For new construction, apply adhesive directly to the studs.

**8** Attach the paneling to the top of the wall, using 4d finishing nails driven every 16-in. Press the paneling against the adhesive, then pull it away from the wall. Press the paneling back against the wall when the adhesive is tacky, about 2 minutes.

**9** Hang the remaining paneling so that there is a slight space at the joints. This space allows paneling to expand in damp weather. Use a dime as a spacing gauge.

## How to Cut Openings in Paneling

**1** For window, door and other openings, measure the opening and mark the outline on the backside of the paneling. Cut to size using a circular saw and straightedge. Install as you would a full sheet of paneling (page 138).

**2** For receptacles, switches, fixtures, and heating vents, coat the edges of electrical boxes and ductwork with chalk.

**3** Press the paneling against the wall, so the back-side presses against the outlet or vent—the chalk outline will transfer to the paneling.

**4** Lay the paneling face-side down. Drill a hole at one corner of each outline, then use a jigsaw with a fine-tooth woodcutting blade to make the cutouts.

# Adding a Wainscot

A wainscot, by definition, is a wall treatment covering the lower portion of a wall. Virtually any material can be used as wainscoting, but the most common by far is wood. In most applications, the wainscot is covered along the bottom by a baseboard and along the top by a cap molding, rail, or shallow shelf.

Wainscots are useful not only for decoration but also as protective surfaces. Standard wainscot heights are between 32" and 36", a range at which the top cap can serve as a chair rail to protect the wall from furniture collisions. In hallways, mudrooms, and other functional areas, wainscots may run 48" and higher.

Wood wainscoting is available in a variety of species and styles. For price and ease of installation, the best types for do-it-yourselfers are 4 × 8-ft. sheets and tongue-&-groove boards, commonly called *beadboard*. Standard materials include: paint-grade pine (and other softwoods); hardwood veneers, such as oak and birch; molded polymers; and fiberboard.

There are two basic methods for installing wainscoting. Sheets and thinner boards (up to ⅜", in most cases) can be attached to drywall with construction adhesive and nails, or with nails alone. Thicker boards usually must be nailed, preferably blind-nailed—the technique of driving angled nails along the base of the tongue so the groove of the next board hides the nail heads. Thinner boards may have to be facenailed to avoid splitting the wood.

Wainscoting that is fastened only with nails must have blocking or backing to serve as a nailing surface. If the framing is exposed, you can install plywood backing over the wall studs in the area of the wainscot, then cover the rest of the wall with drywall of the same thickness (make sure the local building code permits installing wood directly over wall framing). You can also install 2 × 4 blocks between the studs, at 12" to 16" intervals, before hanging the drywall.

The project on pages 141 to 142 shows you how to install a tall wainscot of sheet paneling with a traditional molding treatment. A rail made from 1 × 6 clear pine runs along the top edge of paneling and is topped by a 1 × 3 pine cap with custom edges you mill with a router. Because of its height (60") and tall baseboard, this wainscot is especially suited to mudroom or hallway walls that receive some abuse, but it can work well in

bathrooms and other areas. You can install hooks for coats (or towels) along the rail or add a shelf for additional storage.

## Everything You Need

Tools: Chalk line, level, circular saw, caulk gun, drill, router with roundover bit, power miter saw, nail set.

Materials: Sheet paneling; construction adhesive; 10d, 6d, and 2d finish nails; 1 × 6 and 1 × 3 clear pine lumber; wood glue; cove molding; baseboard.

## How to Install a Wainscot with Sheet Paneling

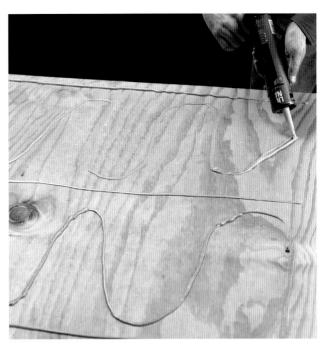

**1** Measure up from the floor and snap a chalk line to represent the top of the paneling. This line will be ¾" lower than the overall height of the wainscot. Use a pencil to mark the stud locations about 1" above the chalk line. Measure the length of the wall to plan the layout of the sheets. The last piece should be at least 3" wide, so you may have to trim the first sheet to make the last piece wider.

**2** Check the wall corner with a level to make sure it's plumb. If it's not plumb, scribe the first sheet to follow the angle or contours of the wall (see page 137). Cut the first sheet to length so its bottom edge will be ½" above the floor, using a circular saw. Unless you've scribed the sheet, cut from the back side to prevent splintering on the face. Using a caulk gun, apply construction adhesive to the back side.

**3** Apply the sheet to the wall so its top edge is flush with the chalk line and its side edge is set into the corner. Press the sheet firmly to bond it to the wall. Drive 6d finish nails at the stud locations, spacing them every 16", or so. Use only as many nails as needed to hold the sheet flat and to keep it in place.

**4** Install the remaining sheets in the wall section. If you are paneling an adjacent wall, check the paneled wall for plumb, and trim the first sheet, if necessary. Install the sheet butted against the end sheet on the paneled wall.

(continued next page)

# How to Install a Wainscot with Sheet Paneling (continued)

**5** Prepare the 1 × 6 rail material by sanding smooth the front face and bottom edge. If desired, round over the bottom, outside corner slightly with sand paper. Install the rail with its top edge flush with the chalk line, fastening it to each stud with two 10d finish nails driven through pilot holes. Butt together rail pieces at inside corners, and miter them at outside corners.

**6** Mill the 1 × 3 top cap material, using a router and roundover bit. Work on test pieces to find the desired amount of roundover, then rout your workpieces on both front corners. Sand the cap smooth. OPTION: Create a waterfall edge by rounding over only the top edge of the cap (top inset), or chamfer the front edges with a chamfer bit (bottom inset).

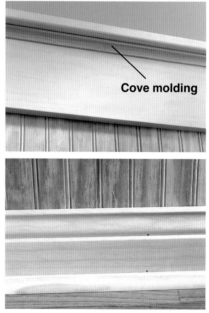

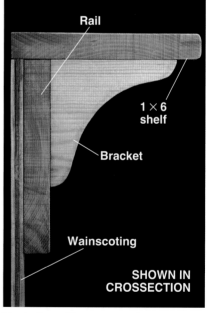

**7** Install the cap with wood glue and finish nails. Glue along the top edge of the rail and drive a 10d finish nail, angled at 45° through the cap and into each stud (drill pilot holes for the nails). Miter the rail at corners.

**8** Add cove molding to the joint between the cap and rail, fastening it to the rail with 2d finish nails. Install the baseboard along the bottom of the wainscot. Recess all nails with a nail set.

**Variation:** Top your wainscot with a shelf rather than a cap. Use 1 × 6 or wider boards, and mill them as shown in step 6. To support the shelf, add wooden brackets fastened to the wall studs.

# Tips for Installing Tongue-&-Groove Wainscoting

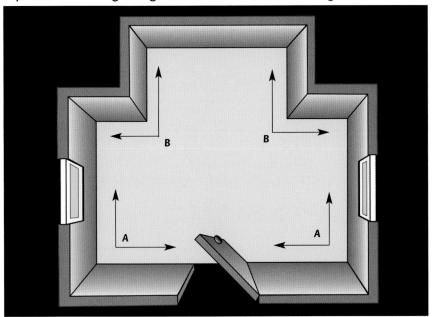

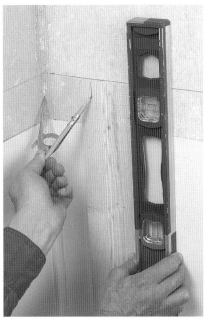

**Begin your installation at the corners**, either inside (A) or outside (B). Use the reveal dimension (see pages 150 to 151) to calculate the number of boards required for each wall: divide the length of the wall by the reveal, keeping in mind that a side edge may have to be trimmed from one or more of the corner boards. If the total number of boards includes a fraction of less than half a board, plan to trim the first board to avoid ending with a board cut to less than half its original width.

**Check corners for plumb**. If a corner isn't plumb, scribe and trim the first board to fit. At inside corners, use a level to hold the board plumb, then use a compass to transfer the contours of the wall to the board. At outside corners, overhang the wall edge and scribe along the board's back side.

Butted   Mitered

**Start inside corners** (left) by trimming off the tongue edge of the first board, or simply place the groove edge in the corner. Install the first board, leaving a ⅛" expansion gap in the corner. Butt the board on the adjacent wall against the face of the first board. At outside corners (right), join boards with butt joints or miter joints (insets). If necessary, drill pilot holes for the nails to prevent splitting. Drive the bottom and top nails where they'll be hidden by the molding. Set all nails with a nail set.

**Install subsequent boards** along the wall, following the panel manufacturer's directions regarding expansion gaps at the joints. Use a level to check every third board for plumb. If it's out of plumb, adjust the fourth board to compensate.

# Installing Wainscot Frames

Frame-and-panel wainscot adds depth, character, and a sense of Old-World charm to any room. Classic wainscot was built with grooved or rabbeted rails and stiles that captured a floating hardwood panel. In the project shown here, the classic appearance is mimicked, but the difficulties of machining precise parts and commanding craftsman-level joinery are eliminated. Paint-grade materials (mostly MDF) are used in the project shown; however, you can also build the project with solid hardwoods and finish-grade plywood if you prefer a clear-coat finish.

Installing wainscot frames that look like frame-and-panel wainscot can be done piece by piece, but it is often easier to assemble the main frame parts in your shop. Not only does working

in the shop allow you to join the frame parts together (we use pocket screws driven in the backs of the rails and stiles), it generally results in a more professional look.

Once the main frames are assembled, they can be attached to the wall at stud locations. If you prefer to site-build the wainscot piece by piece, you may need to replace the wallcovering material with plywood to create nailing surfaces for the individual pieces.

We primed all of the wainscot parts prior to installing them and then painted the wainscot (including the wall sections within the wainscot panel frames) a contrasting color from the wall above the wainscot cap.

## Everything You Need

Tools: Laser level, pencil, tape measure, circular saw or table saw, straightedge guide, power miter saw, drill with bits, carpenter's square, pocket hole jig with screws, pry bar, hammer, pneumatic finish nail gun with compressor, caulking gun.

Materials: $\frac{3}{4}$"-thick MDF sheet stock, $1\frac{1}{16}$" cove molding, $\frac{1}{2} \times \frac{3}{4}$" base shoe, $\frac{9}{16} \times 1\frac{1}{8}$" cap molding (10 ft. per panel), panel adhesive, paint and primer.

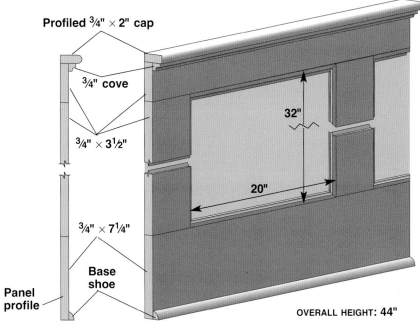

Profiled $\frac{3}{4}$" × 2" cap

$\frac{3}{4}$" cove

$\frac{3}{4}$" × $3\frac{1}{2}$"

$\frac{3}{4}$" × $7\frac{1}{4}$"

Base shoe

Panel profile

32"

20"

OVERALL HEIGHT: **44"**

# How to Install Wainscot Frames

**1** Use a laser level and a pencil to mark the height of the wainscot installation directly onto all walls in the project area. Also mark the height of the top rail (³⁄₄" below the overall height), since the cap rail will be installed after the rest of the wainscot is installed. Mark stud locations, using an electronic stud finder.

**2** Plot out the wainscot layout on paper and then test the layout by drawing lines on the wall to make sure you're happy with the design. Try to use a panel width that can be divided evenly into all project wall lengths. In some cases, you may need to make the panel widths slightly different from wall to wall, but make sure to maintain a consistent width within each wall's run.

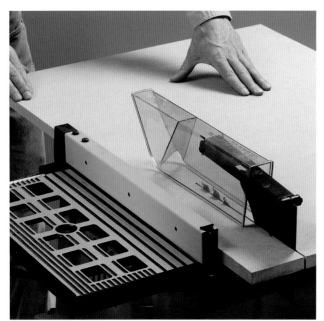

**3** Based on your plan, rip a sheet of MDF into strips to make all of the wainscot parts except the trim moldings. In our case, that included the cap rail (2" wide), the top rail and stiles (3½" wide), and the base rail (7¼" wide). Note: These are standard lumber dimensions. You can use 1 × 4 and 1 × 4 dimensional lumber for the rails and stiles (use 1 × 2 or rip stock for the cap rail).

**4** Cut top rails, base rails, and stiles (but not cap rails) to length and dry-assemble the parts into ladder frames based on your layout. Plan the layouts so wall sections longer than 8 ft. are cut with scarf joints in the rails meeting at a stud location. Dry-assemble the pieces on a flat work surface.

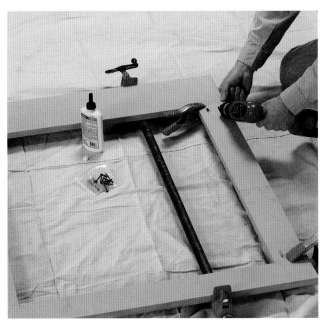

**5** Assemble the frames using glue and pocket screws or biscuits. Clamp the parts together first and check with a carpenter's square to make sure the stiles are perpendicular to both rails.

**6** Mount a ¾" roundover bit in your router or router table and shape a bullnose profile on the front edge of your cap rail stock.

**7** Prime all parts on both sides, including the milled moldings and uncut cap rail stock.

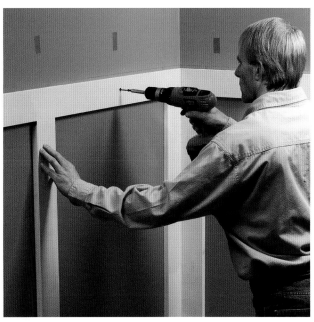

**8** Position the frames against the wall and shim underneath the bottom rails as necessary to bring them flush with the top rail marks on the wall (¾" below the overall height lines). Attach the wainscot sections by driving 3" drywall screws, countersunk, through the top rail and the bottom rail at each stud location. If you are using scarf joints, be sure to install the open half first.

(continued next page)

**9** Cut the cap rail to length and attach it to the top rail with panel adhesive and finish nails. Drive a 3" drywall screw through the cap rail and into the wall toenails style at each location. Be sure to carefully drill pilot holes and countersink holes for each screw. Miter-cut the cap rails at the corners.

**10** Install cove molding in the crotch where the cap rail and top rails meet, using glue and a brad nailer. Then, nail base shoe to conceal any gaps between the bottoms, rails and the floor. Miter all corners.

**11** Cut mitered frames to fit around the perimeter of each panel frame created by the rails and stiles. Use cap molding.

**12** Mask the wall above the cap rail and then prime and paint the wainscot frames. Generally, a lighter, contrasting color than the wall color above is most effective visually.

## Variation: Natural Wood Finish

**1** Snap a level line at the top rail height. Because the rails and stiles are the same thickness, the backer panel should run all the way from the floor to just shy of the top of the top rail. Cut the backers so the grain will run vertically when installed. Attach them to the walls with panel adhesive, notching to fit around obstructions, such as this window opening.

**2** Install the baseboard and top rail directly over the backer panels, using a finish nailer or by hand-nailing with 6d finish nails. The top edge of the top rail pieces should be slightly higher then the backer panels. Use your reference line as a guide for the top rail, but double-check with a level.

**3** Attach the cap rail pieces with a finish nailer. The caps should butt flush against the wall, concealing the top edges of the backer panels. Also butt the cap rails against the window and door casings.

**4** Cut the stile to fit between the top rail and the baseboard and install them. It's okay to vary the spacing slightly from wall to wall, but try to keep them evenly spaced on each wall. Where the wainscot meets door or window casing, butt the edges of the stiles against the casing. This can mean notching around window aprons or horns as well as door plinth blocks.

**5** Add decorative touches, such as the corbels we cut for this installation. The corbels provide some support for the cap rail but their function is primarily decorative. We glued and nailed one corbel at each end of each cap rail piece and above each stile, and then added an intermediate one between each pair of stiles.

# Paneling a Ceiling

Tongue-&-groove paneling offers a warm, attractive finish that's especially suited to vaulted ceilings. Pine is the most common material for tongue-&-groove paneling, but you can choose from many different wood species and panel styles. Panels typically are ⅜" to ¾" thick and are often attached directly to ceiling joists or rafters. Some building codes require the installation of drywall as a fire stop behind ceiling paneling that's thinner than ¼".

When purchasing your paneling, get enough material to cover about 15% more square footage than the actual ceiling size, to allow for waste. Since the tongue portions of the panels slip into the grooves of adjacent pieces, square footage for paneling is based on the *reveal*—the exposed face of the panel after it is installed.

Tongue-&-groove boards can be attached with flooring nails or finish nails. Flooring nails hold better because they have spiraled shanks, but they tend to have larger heads than finish nails. Whenever possible, drive the nails through the base of the tongue and into the framing. This is called *blind-nailing,* because the groove of the succeeding board covers the nail heads. Add facenails only at joints and in locations where more support is needed, such as along the first and last boards. To ensure clean cuts, use a compound miter saw. These saws are especially useful for ceilings with non-90° angles.

Layout is crucial to the success of a paneling project. Before you start, determine how many boards you'll need, using the reveal measurement. If the final board will be less than 2" wide, trim the first, or *starter*, board by cutting the long edge that abuts the wall. If the ceiling peak is not parallel to the side (starting) wall, rip the starter piece at an angle to match the wall. The leading edge of the starter piece, and every piece thereafter, must be parallel to the peak.

## Everything You Need

Tools: Chalk line, compound miter saw, circular saw, drill, nail set.

Materials: Tongue-&-groove paneling, 1¾" spiral flooring nails, trim molding.

# How to Panel a Ceiling

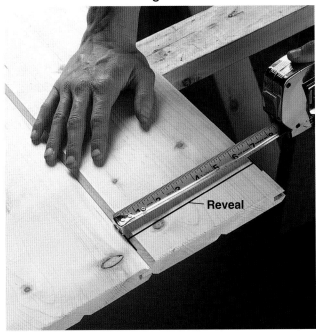

**1** To plan your layout, first measure the reveal of the boards. Fit two pieces together and measure from the bottom edge of the upper board to the bottom edge of the lower board. Calculate the number of boards needed to cover one side of the ceiling by dividing the reveal dimension into the overall distance between the top of the wall and the peak.

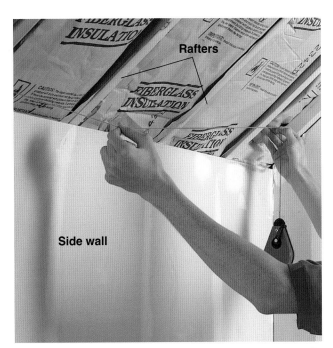

**2** Use the calculation from step 1 to make a control line for the first row of panels—the starter boards. At both ends of the ceiling, measure down from the peak an equal distance, and make a mark to represent the top (tongue) edges of the starter boards. Snap a chalk line through the marks.

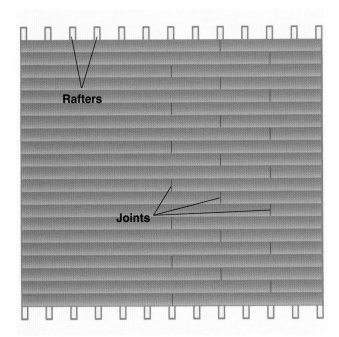

**3** If the boards aren't long enough to span the entire ceiling, plan the locations of the joints. Staggering the joints in a three-step pattern will make them less conspicuous. Note that each joint must fall over the middle of a rafter. For best appearance, select boards of similar coloring and grain for each row.

**4** Rip the first starter board to width by bevel-cutting the bottom (grooved) edge. If the starter row will have joints, cut the board to length using a 30° bevel cut on the joint end only. Two beveled ends joined together form a *scarf* joint (inset), which is less noticeable than a butt joint. If the board spans the ceiling, square-cut both ends.

(continued next page)

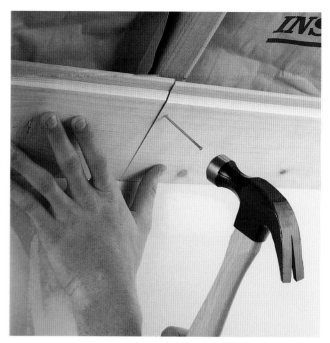

**5** Position the first starter board so the tongue is on the control line. Leave a ⅛" gap between the square board end and the end wall. Fasten the board by nailing through its face about 1" from the grooved edge and into the rafters. Then, blind-nail through the base of the tongue into each rafter, angling the nail backward at 45°. Drive the nail heads beneath the wood surface, using a nail set.

**6** Cut and install any remaining boards in the starter row one at a time, making sure the scarf joints fit together tightly. At each scarf joint, drive two nails through the face of the top board, angling the nail to capture the end of the board behind it. If necessary, predrill the nail holes to prevent splitting.

**7** Cut the first board for the next row, then fit its grooved edge over the tongue of the board in the starter row. Use a hammer and a scrap piece of paneling to drive downward on the tongue edge, seating the grooved edge over the tongue of the starter board. Fasten the second row with blind-nails only.

**8** As you install successive rows, measure down from the peak to make sure the rows remain parallel to the peak. Correct any misalignment by adjusting the tongue-&-groove joint slightly with each row. You can also snap additional control lines to help align the rows.

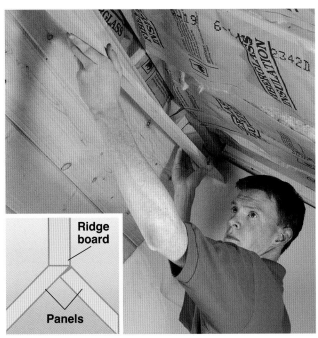

**9** Rip the boards for the last row to width, beveling the top edges so they fit flush against the ridge board. Facenail the boards in place. Install paneling on the other side of the ceiling, then cut and install the final row of panels to form a closed joint under the ridge board (inset).

**10** Install trim molding along walls, at joints around obstacles, and along inside and outside corners, if desired. (Select-grade 1 × 2 works well as trim along walls.) Where necessary, bevel the back edges of the trim or miter-cut the ends to accommodate the slope of the ceiling.

## Tips for Paneling an Attic Ceiling

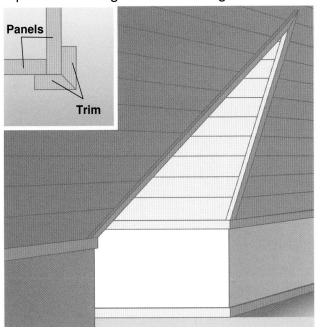

**Use mitered trim** to cover joints where panels meet at outside corners. Dormers and other roof elements create opposing ceiling angles that can be difficult to panel around. It may be easier to butt the panels together and hide the butt joints with custom-cut trim. The trim also makes a nice transition between angles.

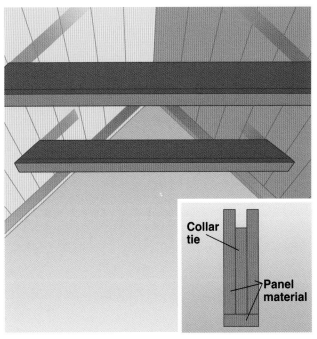

**Wrap collar ties or exposed beams** with custom-cut panels. Install the paneling on the ceiling first. Then, rip-cut panels to the desired width. You may want to include a tongue-&-groove joint as part of the trim detail. Angle-cut the ends of the trim so it fits tight to the ceiling panels.

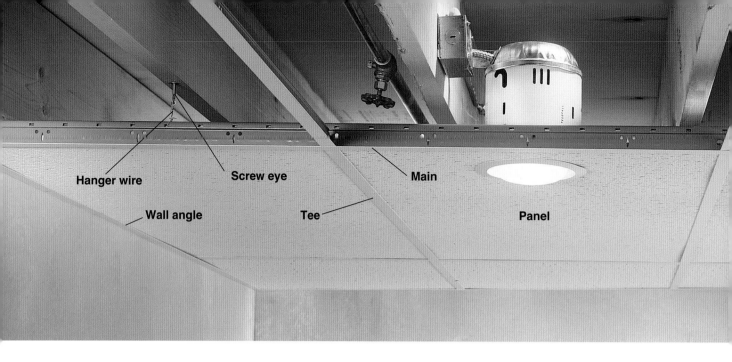

Hanger wire     Screw eye     Main

Wall angle     Tee     Panel

# Installing a Suspended Ceiling

Suspended ceilings are traditionally popular ceiling finishes for basements and utility areas, particularly because they hang below pipes and other mechanicals while providing easy access to them. However, the commercial appearance and grainy texture of basic ceiling tiles make them an unlikely choice for formal areas such as living rooms. Basic tiles are not your only option.

Suspended ceiling tile manufacturers have a wide array of ceiling tiles to choose from that go above and beyond traditional institutional tiles. Popular styles mimic historical tin tiles and add depth to the ceiling while minimizing sound and vibration noise.

A suspended ceiling is a grid framework made of lightweight metal brackets hung on wires attached to ceiling or floor joists. The frame consists of T-shaped main beams (mains), cross-tees (tees), and L-shaped wall angles. The grid supports ceiling panels, which rest on the flanges of the framing pieces. Panels are available in 2 × 2-ft. or 2 × 4-ft. sizes, in a variety of styles. Special options include insulated panels, acoustical panels that absorb sound, and light-diffuser screens for use with fluorescent lights. Generally, metal-frame ceiling systems are more durable than ones made of plastic.

To begin your ceiling project, devise the panel layout based on the size of the room, placing equally sized trimmed panels on opposite sides to create a balanced look. Your ceiling must also be level. For small rooms, a 4-ft. or 6-ft. level will work, but a water level is more effective for larger jobs. You can make a water level with two water-level ends (available at hardware stores and home centers) attached to flexible plastic tubing.

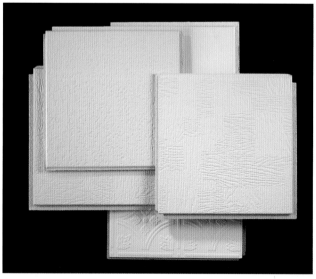

**Acoustical ceiling tiles** are available in a wide variety of styles. Some mimic the tin or plaster ceilings of the past.

### Everything You Need

Tools: Water level, chalk line, drill, aviation snips, string, lock-type clamps, screw-eye driver, pliers, straightedge, utility knife.

Materials: Suspended ceiling kit (frame), screw eyes, hanger wires, ceiling panels, 1½" drywall screws or masonry nails.

## Tips for Installing a Suspended Ceiling

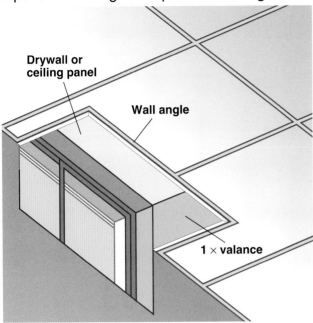

**Build a valance** around basement awning windows so they can be opened fully. Attach 1 × lumber of an appropriate width to joists or blocking. Install drywall (or a suspended-ceiling panel trimmed to fit) to the joists inside the valance.

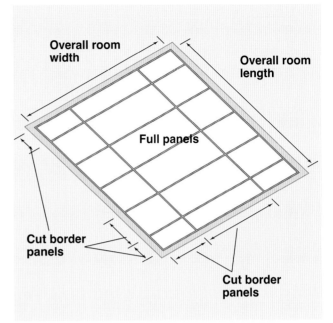

**Draw your ceiling layout** on paper, based on the exact dimensions of the room. Plan so that trimmed border panels on opposite sides of the room are of equal width and length (avoid panels smaller than ½-size). If you include lighting fixtures in your plan, make sure they follow the grid layout.

## How to Install a Suspended Ceiling

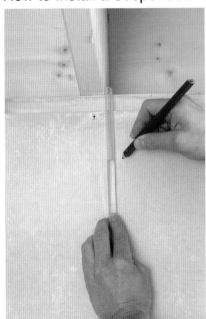

**1** Make a mark on one wall that represents the ceiling height plus the height of the wall angle. Use a water level to transfer that height to both ends of each wall. Snap a chalk line to connect the marks. This line represents the top of the ceiling's wall angle.

**2** Attach wall angle pieces to the studs on all walls, positioning the top of the wall angle flush with the chalk line. Use 1½" drywall screws (or short masonry nails driven into mortar joints on concrete block walls). Cut angle pieces using aviation snips.

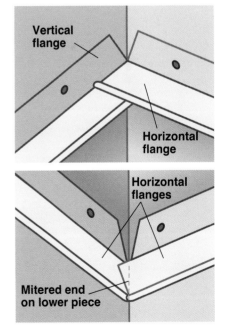

**Tip:** Trim wall angle pieces to fit around corners. At inside corners (top), back-cut the vertical flanges slightly, then overlap the horizontal flanges. At outside corners (bottom), miter-cut one horizontal flange, and overlap the flanges.

(continued next page)

**3** Mark the location of each main on the wall angles at the ends of the room. The mains must be parallel to each other and perpendicular to the ceiling joists. Set up a guide string for each main, using a thin string and lock-type clamps (inset). Clamp the strings to the opposing wall angles, stretching them very taut so there's no sagging.

**4** Install screw eyes for hanging the mains, using a drill and screw-eye driver. Drill pilot holes and drive the eyes into the joists every 4 ft., locating them directly above the guide strings. Attach hanger wire to the screw eyes by threading one end through the eye and twisting the wire on itself at least three times. Trim excess wire, leaving a few inches of wire hanging below the level of the guide string.

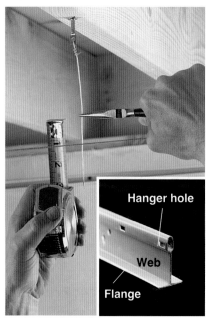

Hanger hole

Web

Flange

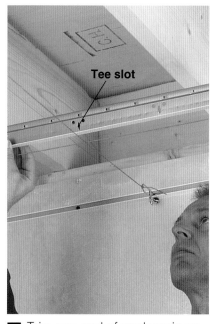

Tee slot

**5** Measure the distance from the bottom of a main's flange to the hanger hole in the web (inset). Use this measurement to prebend each hanger wire. Measure up from the guide string and make a 90° bend in the wire, using pliers.

**6** Following your ceiling plan, mark the placement of the first tee on opposite wall angles at one end of the room. Set up a guide string for the tee, using a string and clamps, as before. This string must be perpendicular to the guide strings for the mains.

**7** Trim one end of each main so that a tee slot in the main's web is aligned with the tee guide string, and the end of the main bears fully on a wall angle. Set the main in place to check the alignment of the tee slot with the string.

**8** Cut the other end of each main to fit, so that it rests on the opposing wall angle. If a single main cannot span the room, splice two mains together, end-to-end (the ends should be fashioned with male-female connectors). Make sure the tee slots remain aligned when splicing.

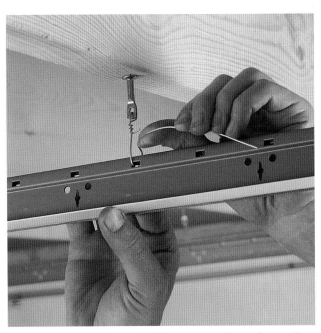

**9** Install the mains by setting the ends on the wall angle and threading the hanger wires through the hanger holes in the webs. The wires should be as close to vertical as possible. Wrap each wire around itself three times, making sure the main's flange is level with the main guide string. Also install a hanger near each main splice.

**10** Attach tees to the mains, slipping the tabbed ends into the tee slots on the mains. Align the first row of tees with the tee guide string; install the remaining rows at 4-ft. intervals. If you're using 2 × 2-ft. panels, install 2-ft. cross-tees between the midpoints of the 4-ft. tees. Cut and install the border tees, setting the tee ends on the wall angles. Remove all guide strings and clamps.

**11** Place full ceiling panels into the grid first, then install the border panels. Lift the panels in at an angle, and position them so they rest on the frame's flanges. Reach through adjacent openings to adjust the panels, if necessary. To trim the border panels to size, cut them face-up, using a straightedge and utility knife (inset).

# Installing Acoustical Ceiling Tile

Easy-to-install ceiling tile can lend character to a plain ceiling or help turn an unfinished basement or attic into beautiful living space. Made of pressed mineral and fiberboard, ceiling tiles are available in a variety of styles. They also provide moderate noise reduction.

Ceiling tiles typically can be attached directly to a drywall or plaster ceiling with adhesive. If your ceiling is damaged or uneven, or if you have an unfinished joist ceiling, install 1 × 2 furring strips as a base for the tiles, as shown in this project. Some systems include metal tracks for clip-on installation.

Unless your ceiling measures in even feet, you won't be able to install the 12" tiles without some cutting. To prevent an unattractive installation with small, irregular tiles along two sides, include a course of border tiles along the perimeter of the installation. Plan so that tiles at opposite ends of the room are cut to the same width and are at least ½ the width of a full tile.

Most ceiling tile comes prefinished, but it can be painted to match any decor. For best results, apply two coats of paint using a roller with a ¼" nap, and wait 24 hours between coats.

## Everything You Need

Tools: 4-ft. level, stepladder, chalk line, utility knife, straightedge, hammer or drill, handsaw, stapler.

Materials: 1 × 2 furring strips, 8d nails or 2" screws, string, ceiling tiles, staples, trim molding.

**Create an area rug effect** by covering only a portion of the ceiling with tiles. This technique helps to define living areas in open floor plans by breaking up bland expanses of white ceiling.

**Add a faux patina** by randomly dabbing the tiles with metallic green or blue paint, using a natural sea sponge.

# How to Install Ceiling Tile

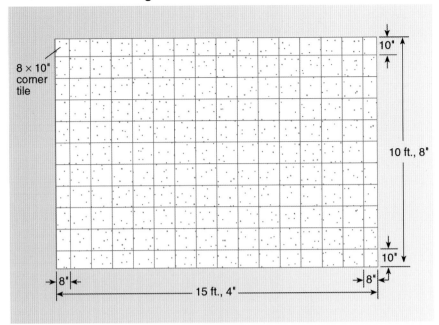

**1** Measure the ceiling and devise a layout. If the length (or width) doesn't measure in even feet, use this formula to determine the width of the border tiles: add 12 to the number of inches remaining and divide by 2. The result is the width of the border tile. (For example, if the room length is 15 ft., 4", add 12 to the 4, then divide 16 by 2, which results in an 8" border tile.)

**2** Install the first furring strip flush with the wall and perpendicular to the joists, fastening with two 8d nails or 2" screws at each joist. Measure out from the wall a distance equal to the border tile width minus ¾", and snap a chalk line. Install the second furring strip with its wall-side edge on the chalk line.

**3** Install the remaining strips 12" on-center from the second strip. Measure from the second strip and mark the joist nearest the wall every 12". Repeat along the joist on the opposite side of the room, then snap chalk lines between the marks. Install the furring strips along the lines. Install the last furring strip flush against the opposite side wall. Stagger the butted end joints of strips between rows so they aren't all on the same joist.

**4** Check the strips with a 4-ft. level. Insert wood shims between the strips and joists as necessary to bring the strips into a level plane.

(continued next page)

**5** Set up taut, perpendicular string lines along two adjacent walls to help guide the tile installation. Inset the strings from the wall by a distance that equals that wall's border tile width plus ½". Use a framing square to make sure the strings are square.

**6** Cut the corner border tile to size with a utility knife and straightedge. Cutting the border tiles ¼" short will ease fitting them. The resulting gap between the tile and wall will be covered by trim. Cut only on the edges without the stapling flange.

**7** Position the corner tile with the flange edges aligned with the two string lines and fasten it to the furring strips with four ½" staples. Cut and install two border tiles along each wall, making sure the tiles fit snugly together.

**8** Fill in between the border tiles with full-size tiles. Continue working diagonally in this manner, toward the opposite corner. For the border tiles along the far wall, trim off the flange edges and staple through the faces of the tiles, close to the wall.

**9** Install the final row of tiles, saving the far corner tile and its neighbor for last. Cut the last tile to size, then remove the tongue and nailing flange along the side edges. Finish the job by installing trim along the edges.

# Installing Tin Ceiling Tile

Today's metal ceilings offer the distinctive elegance of 19th-century tin tile in a durable, washable ceiling finish. Available at home centers and specialty distributors, metal ceiling systems include field panels (in 2 × 2-, 2 × 4-, and 2 × 8-ft. sizes), border panels that can be cut to fit your layout, and cornice molding for finishing the edges. The panels come in a variety of materials and finishes ready for installation, or they can be painted.

To simplify installation, the panels have round catches, called nailing buttons, that fit into one another to align the panels where they overlap. The buttons are also the nailing points for attaching the panels. Use 1" decorative conehead nails where nail heads will be exposed, and 1/2" wire nails where heads are hidden.

Install your metal ceiling over a smooth layer of 3/8" or 1/2" plywood, which can be fastened directly to the ceiling joists with drywall screws, or installed over an existing finish. The plywood

provides a flat nailing surface for the panels. As an alternative, some manufacturers offer a track system for clip-on installation.

Begin your installation by carefully measuring the ceiling and snapping chalk lines to establish the panel layout. For most tile patterns, it looks best to cover the center of the space with full tiles only, then fill in along the perimeter with border panels, which are not patterned. Make sure your layout is square.

### Everything You Need

Tools: Chalk line, level, tin snips, drill with 1/8" metal bit, compass, metal file.

Materials: 3/8" or 1/2" plywood, 2" drywall screws, field panels, border panels with molding edge, cornice molding, masking tape, 1/2" wire nails, 1" conehead nails, wood block.

# How to Install a Metal Tile Ceiling

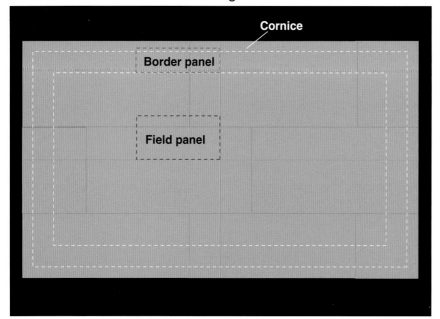

Cornice

Border panel

Field panel

**1** Measure to find the center of the ceiling, then snap perpendicular chalk lines intersecting the center. On the walls, mark a level reference line representing the bottom edges of the cornice molding. Where possible, plan to install the panels so they overlap toward the room's entrance, to help conceal the seams.

**2** Align the first field panel with the chalk lines at the ceiling's center, and attach it with ½" wire nails along the edges where another panel will overlap it. Drive the nails beside the nailing buttons—saving the buttons for nailing the overlapping panel.

**3** Continue to install field panels, working along the length of the area first, then overlapping the next row. Make sure the nailing buttons are aligned. Underlap panels by sliding the new panel into position beneath the installed panel, then fasten through both panels at the nailing buttons, using 1" conehead nails. Where field panels meet at corners, drill ⅛" pilot holes for the conehead nails.

**4** Cut the border panels to width so they will underlap the cornice by at least 1". Use sharp tin snips, and cut from the edge without edge molding. Install the panels so the nailing buttons on the molding align with those on the field panels. Fasten through the buttons with conehead nails, and along the cut edge with wire nails. At corners, miter-cut the panels, and drive conehead nails every 6" along the seam.

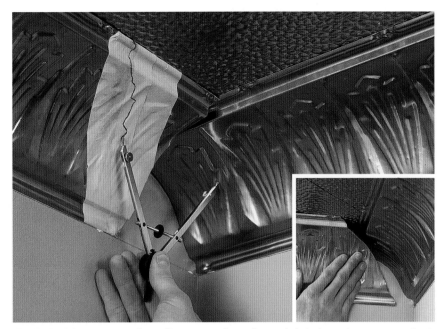

**5** Install each cornice piece with its bottom edge on the level line. Drive 1" conehead nails through the nailing buttons and into the wall studs. Don't nail the ends until the succeeding piece is in place. Fasten the top edges to the ceiling.

**6** At inside corners, install one cornice piece tightly into the corner, then scribe the mating piece to fit, using masking tape and a compass. Cut along the scribed line with tin snips, and make minor adjustments with a metal file. You may have to cut the mating piece several times, so start with plenty of length. If you have several corners, use this technique to cut templates for the corner pieces.

**7** At outside corners, cut the ends of two scrap pieces at a 33° angle. Fit the pieces together at the corner, then trim and mark each piece in turn, making minor adjustments until they fit well. Use the scrap pieces as templates for marking the work-pieces. Fasten near the corner only when both mating pieces are in place.

**8** Using a hammer and a piece of wood, carefully tap any loose joints to tighten them. If the cornice will be left unpainted, file the joints for a perfect fit. If you're painting the ceiling, seal the seams with paintable silicone caulk, then apply two coats of paint using a roller with a ¼" nap. Allow the first coat to dry for 24 hours before applying the second coat.

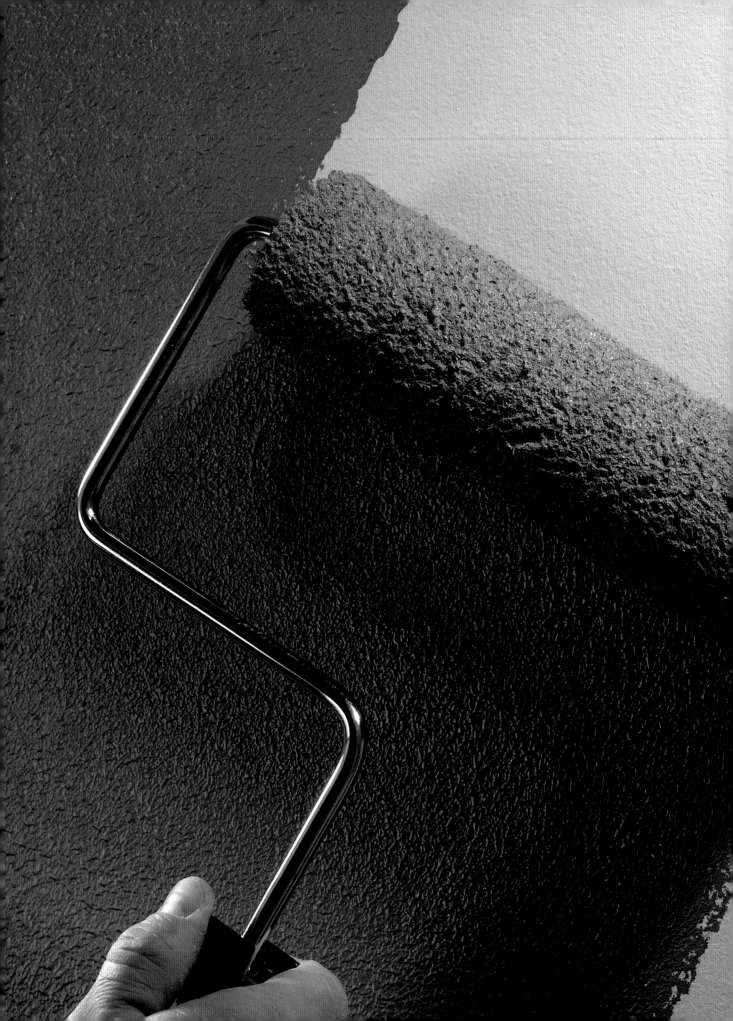

# Finishing Walls & Ceilings

**For large jobs,** mix paint together (called "boxing") in a large pail to eliminate slight color variations between cans. Stir the paint thoroughly with a wooden stick or power drill attachment.

# Basic Painting Techniques

Paints are either latex (water-based) or alkyd (oil-based). Latex paint is easy to apply and clean up, and the improved chemistry of today's latexes makes them suitable for nearly every application. Some painters feel that alkyd paint provides a smoother finish, but local regulations may restrict the use of alkyd products.

Paints come in various sheens. Paint finishes range from high-gloss to flat enamels. Gloss enamels dry to a shiny finish and are used for surfaces that need to be washed often, such as walls in bathrooms and kitchens, and woodwork. Flat paints are used for most wall and ceiling applications.

Paint prices typically are an accurate reflection of quality. As a general rule, buy the best paint your budget can afford. High-quality paints are easier to use, and they look better than cheaper paints. Quality paints last longer and cover better than budget paints, and because they often require fewer coats, they are usually less expensive in the long run.

Before applying the finish paint, prime all of the surfaces with a good-quality primer. Primer bonds well to all surfaces and provides a durable base that keeps the paint from cracking and peeling. Priming is particularly important when using a high-gloss paint on walls and ceilings, because the paint alone might not completely hide finished drywall joints and other variations in the surface. To avoid the need for additional coats of expensive finish paint, tint the primer to match the new color.

**Primers provide maximum adhesion** for paint on any surface. There are many specialty primers available, including: mold-resistant primers (A) that are especially useful in areas that tend to be damp, such as bathrooms; primers made for plaster and new drywall (B); stainblocking primers (C); and tinted primers (D) that reduce the need for multiple coats of paint (particularly for deep colors).

## How to Estimate Paint

| | |
|---|---|
| 1) Length of wall or ceiling (linear feet) | × |
| 2) Height of wall, or width of ceiling | = |
| 3) Surface area (square feet) | ÷ |
| 4) Coverage per gallon of chosen paint | = |
| 5) Gallons of paint needed | |

## How to Select a Quality Paint

**Paint coverage** (listed on can labels) of quality paint should be about 400 square feet per gallon. Bargain paints (left) may require two or even three coats to cover the same area as quality paints (right).

**High washability** is a feature of quality paint. The pigments in bargain paints (right) may "chalk" and wash away with mild scrubbing.

## Paint Sheens

**Paint comes in a variety of surface finishes**, or sheens, samples of which are shown here. Gloss enamel (A) provides a highly reflective finish for areas where high washability is important. All gloss paints tend to show surface flaws. Alkyd-base enamels have the highest gloss. Medium-gloss latex enamel creates a highly washable surface with a slightly less reflective finish. Like gloss enamels, medium-gloss paints (B) tend to show surface flaws. Eggshell enamel (C) combines the soft finish with the washability of enamel. Flat latex (D) is an all-purpose paint with a soft finish that hides surface irregularities.

# Painting Tools

Most painting jobs can be completed with a few quality tools. Purchase two or three premium brushes, a sturdy paint pan that can be attached to a stepladder, and one or two good rollers. With proper cleanup, these tools will last for years. See pages 170 to 175 for tips on how to use paintbrushes and rollers.

## Tips for Choosing a Paintbrush

**A quality brush** (left), has a shaped hardwood handle and a sturdy, reinforced ferrule made of noncorrosive metal. Multiple spacer plugs separate the bristles. A quality brush has flagged (split) bristles and a chiseled end for precise edging. A cheaper brush (right) will have a blunt end, unflagged bristles, and a cardboard spacer plug that may soften when wet.

**There's a proper brush for every job.** A 4" straight-edged brush (bottom) is good for cutting in along ceilings and corners. For woodwork, a 2" trim brush (middle) works well. A tapered sash brush (top) helps with corners on window sash. Use brushes made of hog or ox bristles only with alkyd (oil-based) paints. All-purpose brushes, suitable for all paints, are made with a blend of polyester, nylon, and sometimes animal bristles.

## Tips for Choosing Paint Rollers

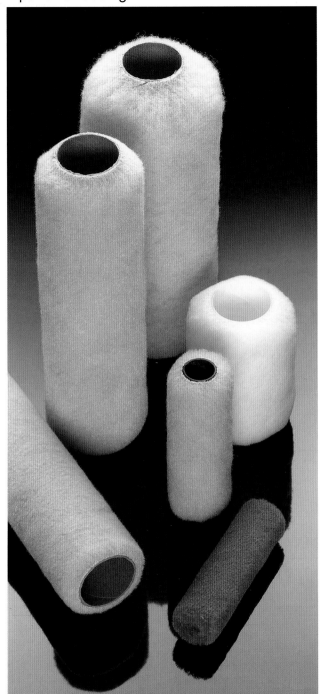

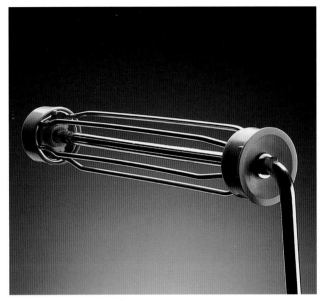

**Choose a sturdy roller** with a wire cage construction. Nylon bearings should roll smoothly and easily when you spin the cage. The handle end should be threaded for attaching an extension handle.

**Select the proper roller cover** for the surface you intend to paint. A ¼"-nap cover is used for very flat surfaces. A ⅜"-nap cover will cover the small flaws found in most flat walls and ceilings. A 1"-nap cover fills spaces in rough surfaces, such as concrete blocks or stucco walls. Foam rollers fit into small spaces and work well when painting furniture or doing touch-ups. Corner rollers have nap on the ends and make it easy to paint corners without cutting in the edges. Synthetic covers are good with most paints, especially latexes. Wool or mohair roller covers give an even finish with alkyd products. Always choose good-quality roller covers, which will be less likely to shed lint.

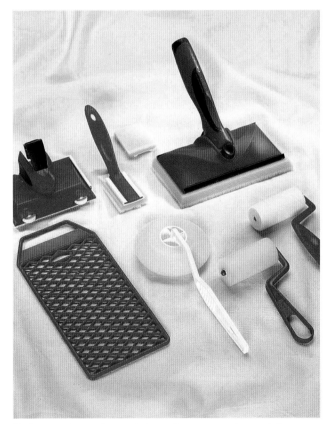

**Paint pads** and specialty rollers come in a wide range of sizes and shapes to fit different painting needs.

# How to Use a Paint Roller

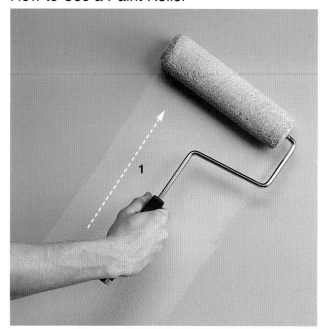

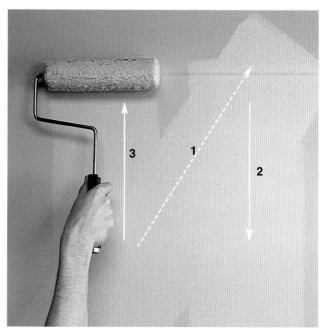

**1** Wet the roller cover with water (for latex paint) or mineral spirits (for alkyd enamel), to remove lint and prime the cover. Squeeze out excess liquid. Dip the roller fully into the paint pan reservoir and roll it over the textured ramp to distribute the paint evenly. The roller should be full, but not dripping. Make an upward diagonal sweep about 4 ft. long on the surface, using a slow stroke to avoid splattering.

**2** Draw the roller straight down (2) from the top of the diagonal sweep made in step 1. Lift and move the roller to the beginning of the diagonal sweep and roll up (3) to complete the unloading of the roller.

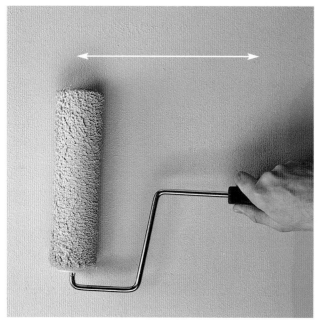

**3** Distribute the paint over the rest of the section with horizontal back-and-forth strokes.

**4** Smooth the area by lightly drawing the roller vertically from the top to the bottom of the painted area. Lift the roller and return it to the top of the area after each stroke.

## How to Use a Paintbrush

**1** Dip the brush into the paint, loading one-third of its bristle length. Tap the bristles against the side of the can to remove excess paint, but do not drag the bristles against the lip of the can.

**2** Paint along the edges (called "cutting in") using the narrow edge of the brush, pressing just enough to flex the bristles. Keep an eye on the paint edge, and paint with long, slow strokes. Always paint from a dry area back into wet paint to avoid lap marks.

**3** Brush wall corners using the wide edge of the brush. Paint open areas with a brush or roller before the brushed paint dries.

**4** To paint large areas with a brush, apply the paint with 2 or 3 diagonal strokes. Hold the brush at a 45° angle to the work surface, pressing just enough to flex the bristles. Distribute the paint evenly with horizontal strokes.

**5** Smooth the surface by drawing the brush vertically from the top to the bottom of the painted area. Use light strokes and lift the brush from the surface at the end of each stroke. This method is best for slow-drying alkyd enamels.

## Painting Walls & Ceilings

For a smooth finish on large wall and ceiling areas, paint in small sections. First use a paintbrush to cut in the edges, then immediately roll the section before moving on. If brushed edges are left to dry before the large surfaces are rolled, visible lap marks will be left on the finished wall. Working in natural light makes it easier to see missed areas.

Spread the paint evenly onto the work surface without letting it run, drip, or lap onto other areas. Excess paint will run on the surface and can drip onto woodwork and floors. Conversely, stretching paint too far leaves lap marks and results in patchy coverage.

For fast, mess-free painting, shield any surfaces that could get splattered. If you are painting only the ceiling, drape the walls and woodwork to prevent splatters. When painting walls, mask the baseboards and the window and door casings. (See top of opposite page.)

While the tried-and-true method of aligning painter's tape with the edge of moldings and casings is perfectly adequate, the job goes much faster and smoother with a tape applicator. Similarly, painter's tape can be used to cover door hinges and window glass, but hinge masks and corner masks simplify the job enormously. Evaluate the available choices and the project at hand: there are many new, easy-to-use options available.

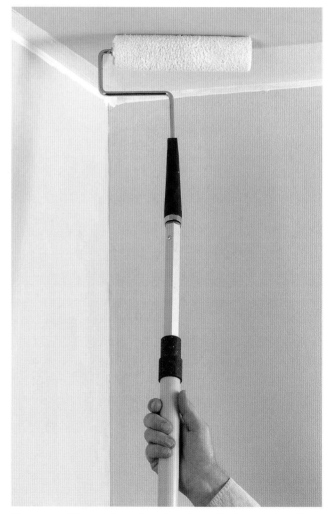

**Use an adjustable extension handle** to paint ceilings and tall walls easily without a ladder.

## How to Tape and Drape for Walls and Ceilings

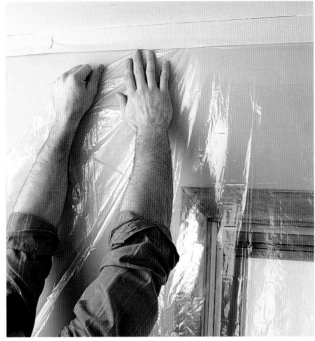

**1** Align wide masking tape with the inside edge of the molding; press in place. Run the tip of a putty knife along the inside edge of the tape to seal it against seeping paint. After painting, remove the tape as soon as the paint is too dry to run.

**2** Press the top half of 2" masking tape along the joint between the ceiling and the wall, leaving the bottom half of the tape loose. Hang sheet plastic under the tape, draping the walls and baseboards. After painting, remove the loose edge as soon as the paint is too dry to run.

## Tips for Painting Walls and Ceilings

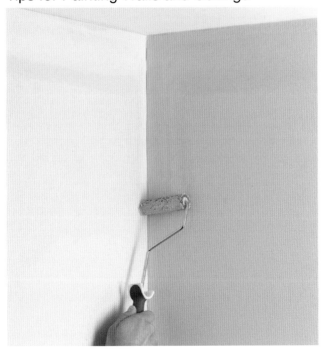

**Paint to a wet edge**. Cut in the edges on small sections with a paintbrush, then immediately roll the section. (Using a corner roller makes it unnecessary to cut in inside corners.) With two painters, have one cut in with a brush while the other rolls the large areas.

**Minimize brush marks**. Slide the roller cover slightly off of the roller cage when rolling near wall corners or a ceiling line. Brushed areas dry to a different finish than rolled paint.

## How to Paint Ceilings

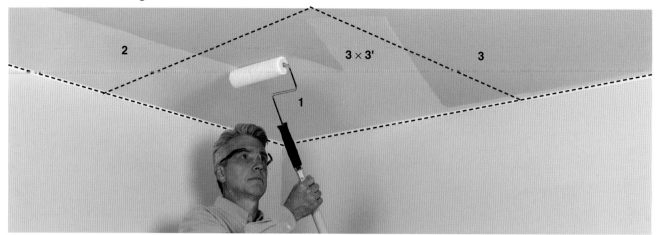

**Paint ceilings** with a roller handle extension. Use eye protection while painting overhead. Start at the corner farthest from the entry door. Paint the ceiling along the narrow end in 3 × 3' sections, cutting in the edges with a brush before rolling. Apply the paint with a diagonal stroke. Distribute the paint evenly with back-and-forth strokes. For the final smoothing strokes, roll each section toward the wall containing the entry door, lifting the roller at the end of each sweep.

## How to Paint Walls

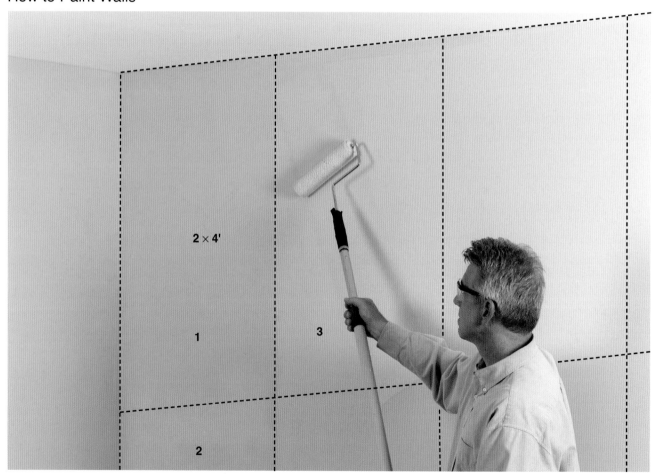

**Paint walls** in 2 × 4' sections. Start in an upper corner, cutting in the ceiling and wall corners with a brush, then rolling the section. Make the initial diagonal roller stroke from the bottom of the section upward, to avoid dripping paint. Distribute the paint evenly with horizontal strokes, then finish with downward sweeps of the roller. Next, cut in and roll the section directly underneath. Continue with adjacent areas, cutting in and rolling the top sections before the bottom sections. Roll all finish strokes toward the floor.

# Cleaning Up

At the end of a paint job you may choose to throw away the roller covers, but the paint pans, roller handles, and brushes can be cleaned and stored for future use. Always follow the paint manufacturer's guidelines for disposing of paint wastes.

The easiest way to clean brushes and roller covers you'd like to use again is to use a spinner tool to remove paint and solvent. Wash the roller cover or brush with solvent, then attach it to the spinner. Pumping the handle throws liquids out of the roller cover or brush. Hold the spinner inside a cardboard box or 5-gallon bucket to catch paint and avoid splatters. Once clean, store brushes in their original wrappers, or fold the bristles inside brown wrapping paper. Store washed roller covers on end to avoid flattening the nap.

Stray paint drips can be wiped away if they are still wet. A putty knife or razor will remove many dried paint spots on hardwood or glass. You can use a chemical cleaner to remove stubborn

paint from most surfaces, though make sure to test the product on an inconspicuous area to make sure the surface is colorfast.

**Cleaning products** include (from left): chemical cleaner, spinner tool, cleaner tool for brushes and roller covers.

## How to Use a Comb Brush

**Comb brush bristles** with the spiked side of a cleaner tool. This aligns the bristles so they dry properly.

**Scrape paint from a roller cover** with the curved side of cleaner tool. Remove as much paint as possible before washing the tools with solvent or water, depending on your paint.

# Hanging Wallcoverings

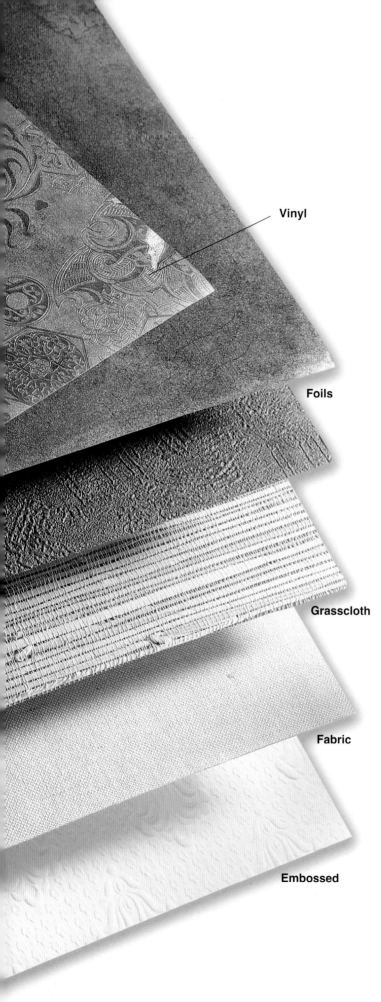

**Vinyl**

**Foils**

**Grasscloth**

**Fabric**

**Embossed**

Very few modern "wallpapers" are actually made of paper. Today's wallcoverings may be made of vinyl, vinyl-coated paper or cloth, textiles, natural grasses, foil, or Mylar. Vinyl or coated vinyl coverings are the easiest to hang, clean, and remove. Other types of wallcoverings offer specific decorative effects but may require special handling.

Tools for hanging wallcovering include ordinary items and a few specialty tools. Use a bubble-stick or 4-ft. level and a pencil to mark layout lines. Never mark with ink pens or chalk lines, which can bleed through the wet wallcovering or ooze from the seams. Cut wallcovering with a sharp utility knife and a straightedge. Use non-corrosive paint pails to hold wash water, and a natural or high-quality plastic sponge to wash wallcovering.

To smooth the wallcovering as you apply it, use a smoothing brush. Brushes come in various nap lengths. Use a short-nap brush for vinyl wallcoverings and a soft, long-nap brush for fragile materials, such as grasscloths. A seam roller makes it easy to smooth the joints between strips. Pages 178 to 179 show you the basic wallcovering tools and handling techniques.

If your wallcovering is not prepasted, you'll need one or more types of adhesive. For most vinyl or vinyl-backed wallcoverings, choose a heavy-duty premixed vinyl adhesive that contains a mildew inhibitor. Vinyl wallcoverings also require a special vinyl-on-vinyl adhesive for areas where the wallcovering strips overlap or for installing vinyl borders over wallcovering. Specialty wallcoverings may need special adhesives; check the label or ask a dealer about the correct adhesive for your application. You can apply adhesives with an ordinary paint roller.

Before hanging wallcovering, make sure the wall surfaces are both sealed and sized to prevent the adhesives from soaking into the surface. Today's premixed primer-sealers do both jobs with a single application.

# Tips for Choosing Wallcovering

**Removability:** Strippable wallcoverings (left) can be pulled away from the wall by hand, leaving little or no film or residue. Peelable wallcoverings (right) can be removed but may leave a thin paper layer on the wall, which can usually be removed with soap and water. Check the back of the sample or the wallcovering package for its strippability rating. Choose a strippable product to make future redecorating easier.

**Cleaning:** *Washable* wallcoverings can be cleaned with mild soap and water and a sponge. *Scrubbable* wallcoverings are durable enough to be scrubbed with a soft brush. Choose a scrubbable type for heavy-use areas.

**Application:** Prepasted wallcoverings (left) are factory-coated with water-based adhesive that is activated when the wallcovering is wetted in a water tray. Unpasted wallcoverings (right) must be coated with an adhesive for hanging. Prepasted products are easier to prepare and just as durable as those requiring an adhesive coat.

**Dye-lot:** To avoid slight color differences, make sure all of the wallcovering you use comes from the same dye lot. Also, record dye-lot numbers for future reference.

 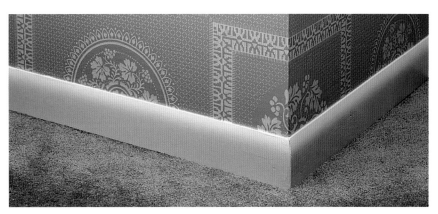

**Packaging:** Wallcoverings are sold in continuous triple-, double-, and single-roll bolts.

**Patterns:** There is always more waste with large patterns. A wallcovering with a large drop pattern can be more expensive to hang than one with a smaller repeat. With large designs, it may also be difficult to avoid pattern interruptions at baseboards or corners.

## How to Handle Prepasted Wallcovering

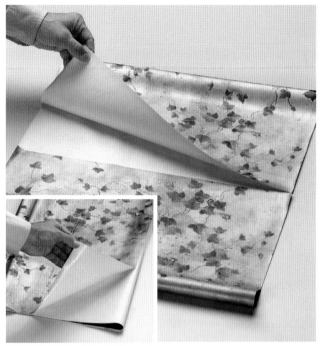

**1** Fill a water tray half-full of lukewarm water. Roll the cut strip loosely with the pattern side in. Soak the roll in the tray as directed by the manufacturer, usually about 1 minute. Pulling from one end, lift the strip from the water, making sure the back side is evenly wetted.

**2** "Book" the strip by folding both ends into the center, with the pasted side in. Do not crease the folds. Let the strip cure for about 10 minutes. Some wallcoverings should not be booked; follow the manufacturer's directions. For ceiling strips or wallcovering borders, use an "accordion" book (inset).

## How to Position & Smooth Wallcovering

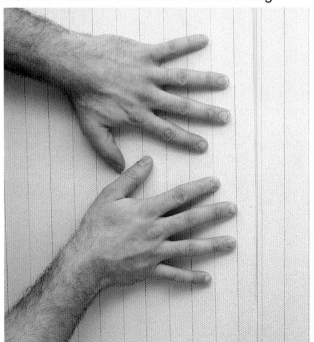

**1** Unfold the booked strip and position it lightly with its edge butted against a plumb line or previously hung strip. Use flat palms to slide the strip precisely into place. Flatten the top of the strip with a smoothing brush.

**2** Beginning at the top, smooth the wallcovering out from the center in both directions. Check for bubbles, and make sure the seams are properly butted. If necessary, pull the strip away and reposition it.

## How to Trim Wallcovering

**1** Position a 10" or 12" drywall knife along the intended cut, then cut along the edge with a sharp utility knife. Keep the utility knife blade in place while changing the position of the drywall knife.

**2** With wallcovered ceilings, crease the wall strips with the drywall knife, then cut along the crease with scissors. Cutting with a utility knife may puncture the ceiling strip.

## How to Roll Seams

**Let the strips stand** for about ½ hour. Then, roll the seam gently with a seam roller. Do not press out the adhesive by rolling too much or too forcefully. Do not roll seams on foils, fabrics, or embossed wallcoverings. Instead, tap the seams gently with a smoothing brush.

## How to Rinse Wallcovering

**Use clear water** and a sponge to rinse adhesive from the surface. Change the water after every 3 or 4 strips. Do not let water run along the seams. Do not use water on grasscloths, embossed wallcoverings, or fabrics.

# Measuring & Estimating for Wallcovering

Calculate the square footage of your walls and ceilings, then refer to the coverage information listed on the wallcovering package to estimate the correct amount of wallcovering to buy. Because of normal trimming waste, the actual per-roll coverage of wallcovering will be at least 15% less than the coverage listed on the package. The waste percentage can be higher depending on how much space it takes for the wallcovering pattern to repeat itself. This "pattern repeat" measurement is listed on the wallcovering package. When estimating, add the pattern repeat measurement to the wall height measurement of the room.

## Measure the room:

*Walls:* Measure the length and height of the walls to the nearest ½ ft. Include window and door openings but not baseboards or crown moldings.

*Ceilings:* Measure the length and the width of ceiling to the nearest ½ ft.

### How to Figure Actual Per-roll Coverage

| | |
|---|---|
| 1) Total per-roll coverage (square feet) | × .85 |
| 2) Adjust for waste factor | = |
| 3) Actual per-roll coverage (square feet) | |

### How to Calculate Rolls Needed for a Ceiling

| | |
|---|---|
| 1) Room length (feet) | + |
| 2) Wallcovering pattern repeat (feet) | = |
| 3) Adjusted length (feet) | × |
| 4) Room width (feet) | = |
| 5) Ceiling area (square feet) | ÷ |
| 6) Actual per-roll coverage (figured above; square feet) | = |
| 7) Number of rolls needed for ceiling | |

### How to Calculate Rolls Needed for Walls

| | |
|---|---|
| 1) Wall height (feet) | + |
| 2) Wallcovering pattern repeat (feet) | = |
| 3) Adjusted height (feet) | × |
| 4) Wall length; or room perimeter (feet) | = |
| 5) Wall area (square feet) | ÷ |
| 6) Actual per-roll coverage (figured above; square feet) | = |
| 7) Number of rolls | + |
| 8) Add 1 roll for each archway or recessed window | = |
| 9) Number of rolls needed for walls | |

## How to Measure Unusual Surfaces

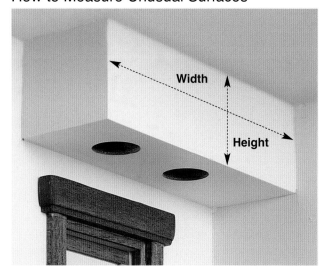

**Soffits:** If you're covering the sides of a soffit, add the width and height of each side to the wall measurement.

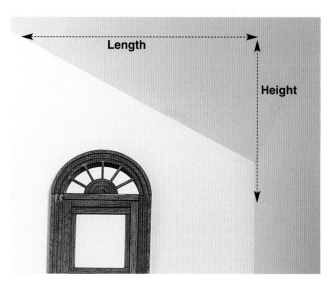

**Triangular walls:** Measure as though the surface is square: length × height.

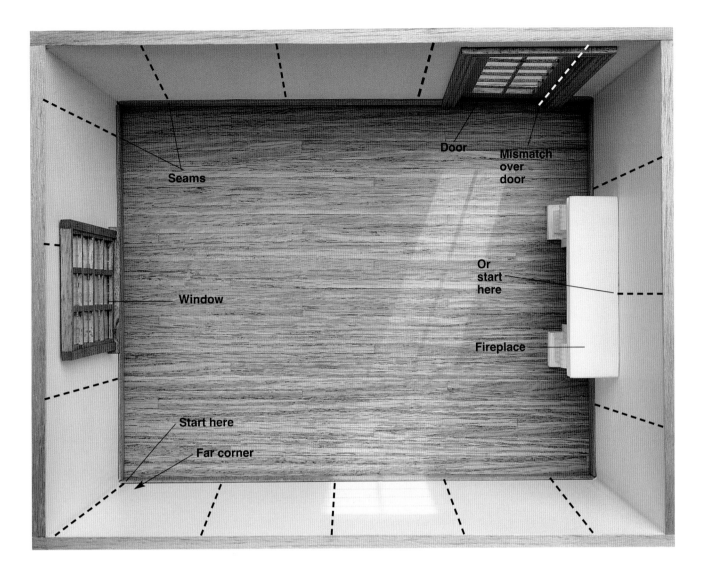

Seams

Door

Mismatch over door

Window

Or start here

Fireplace

Start here

Far corner

## The Hanging Plan

For best results, devise a hanging plan by sketching out the seam locations. When hanging any patterned wallcovering, there will be one seam where a full strip meets a partial strip, usually resulting in a mismatch of the pattern. Plan so that this seam falls in an inconspicuous spot, like behind a door or above an entrance. If one or more seams falls in a bad spot, adjust your plumb line a few inches to compensate. Follow these tips for a successful hanging plan:

• *Plan the mismatch.* If the room has no obvious focal point, start at the corner farthest from the entry. Measure out a distance equal to the wallcovering width and mark a point. Work in both directions, marking each seam location.

• *Start at a focal point,* like a fireplace or large window. Center a plumb line on the focal point,

then sketch a plan in both directions from the centerline.

• *Adjust for corners* that fall exactly on seam lines. Make sure you have at least ½" overlap on inside corners, and 1" on outside corners.

• *Adjust for seams* that fall in difficult locations, such as near the edges of windows or doors. Shift your starting point so that the seams leave you with workable widths of wallcovering around these obstacles.

• *Plan a ceiling layout* so that any pattern interruption will fall along the least conspicuous side of the room. Pattern interruptions occur on the last ceiling strip, so start the layout on the side opposite the entry.

## Installing Wallcovering

Working with wallcovering is easier with a helper, especially on ceilings. Shut off the electricity to the room at the main service panel, and remove the receptacle and switch coverplates. Cover the outlets with masking tape.

For ceilings, remember that the pattern on the last strip may be broken by the ceiling line. Since the least visible edge is usually on the entry wall, begin hanging strips at the far end of the room, and work toward the entryway. If you're covering the walls as well as the ceiling, remember that the ceiling pattern can blend perfectly into only one wall.

### Everything You Need

Tools: Bubblestick or level, pencil, smoothing brush, water tray (for prepasted wallcovering), paint roller and tray (for unpasted wallcovering), scissors, utility knife, drywall knives, sponge, bucket, seam roller.

Materials: Wallcovering, adhesive (for unpasted wallcovering), vinyl-on-vinyl adhesive (for vinyl wallcovering).

## How to Apply Wallcovering to Ceilings

**1** Measure the width of the wallcovering strip and subtract ½". Near a corner, measure this distance away from the wall at several points, and mark points on the ceiling with a pencil.

**2** Using the marks as guides, draw a guide line along the length of the ceiling with a pencil and straightedge. Cut and prepare the first wallcovering strip (see pages 178).

182

**3** Working in small sections, position the strip against the guide line. Overlap the side wall by ½", and the end wall by 2". Flatten the strip with a smoothing brush as you work. Trim each strip after it is smoothed.

**4** Cut out a small wedge of wallcovering in the corner so that the strip will lie flat. Press the wallcovering into the corner with a drywall knife.

**5** If the end walls will also be covered, trim the ceiling overlap to ½". Leave a ½" overlap on all walls that will be covered with matching wallcovering.

**Variation:** Trim the excess at the corner. Continue hanging strips, butting the edges so that the pattern matches.

# How to Apply Wallcovering to Walls

**1** Measure from your starting point a distance equal to the wallpaper width minus ½" and mark a point. At that point draw a vertical plumb line from the ceiling to the floor, using a bubblestick or level.

**2** Cut the first strip to length with about 2" of excess at each end. Prepare the strip according to the manufacturer's directions. Unfold the top portion of the booked strip and position it against the line so the strip overlaps onto the ceiling about 2".

**3** Snip the top corner of the strip so the wallcovering wraps around the corner without wrinkling. Slide the strip into position with open palms then smooth it with a smoothing brush.

**4** Unfold the bottom of the strip and use flat palms to position the strip against the plumb line. Smooth the strip flat with a smoothing brush, carefully pressing out any bubbles.

**5** Trim the excess wallcovering with a drywall knife and a sharp utility knife. Rinse any adhesive from the surface using clear water and a sponge.

**6** Hang additional strips, butting the edges so that the pattern matches. Let the strips stand for about ½ hour, then use a seam roller to roll the seams lightly. (On embossed wallcoverings or fabrics, tap the seams gently with a smoothing brush.)

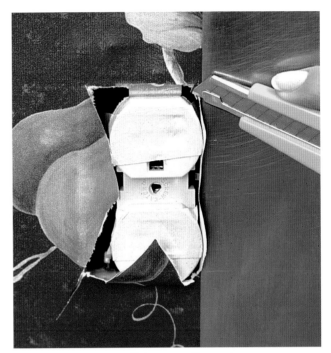

**7** With the power off, hang wallcovering over receptacle and switch boxes, then use a drywall knife and utility knife to trim back the paper to the edges of the box.

## How to Apply Wallcovering Around Corners

**1** Measure from the edge of the preceding strip to the corner at several points, then add ½" to the longest of these measurements. Align the edges of a booked strip, then measure from the edge and mark the above distance at two points. Cut the strip using a straightedge and utility knife.

**2** Position the strip on the wall, overlapping slightly onto the uncovered wall. Cut slits at the top and bottom so the strip wraps smoothly. Flatten the strip with a smoothing brush and trim the excess at the top and bottom.

(continued next page)

**3** On the uncovered wall, measure from the corner and mark at a distance equal to the width of the leftover strip plus ½". Draw a plumb line from the ceiling to the floor. Using the same measurement, cut a new strip to that width, starting from the leading edge of the new strip, so the pattern will match at the corner.

**4** Position the new cut strip on the wall with the cut edge in the corner and the leading (uncut) edge along the plumb line. Press the strip flat and smooth it with a smoothing brush, then trim the excess at the ceiling and baseboard.

**5** If you are using vinyl wallcovering, peel back the edge at the corner and apply vinyl-on-vinyl adhesive to the seam. Press the overlapping strip flat and let it stand for ½ hour, then roll the seam and rinse the area with a damp sponge.

**Variation:** Outside corners usually can be wrapped around without cutting the strip and drawing a new plumb line. If the corner is not plumb, follow the directions for inside corners, except add 1" to the measurement in step 1, rather than ½". If necessary, trim the top wallcovering strip to follow the corner.

# How to Apply Wallcovering Around a Window or Door

**1** Position the strip on the wall, running over the window or door casing. Butt the seam against the edge of the preceding strip. Smooth the flat areas with a smoothing brush and press the strip tightly against the casing.

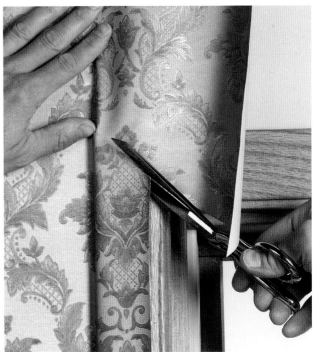

**2** Use scissors to cut diagonally from the edge of the strip to the corners of the casing. Then trim away the excess wallcovering using a drywall knife and a utility knife. Rinse the wallcovering and casing with a damp sponge.

**3** Cut a short strip for the section above the door, or for the sections above and below the window. Hang these strips exactly vertically to ensure a pattern match for the next full strip.

**4** Repeat steps 1 and 2 to install the strip along the other side of the casing, matching the edges.

# Installing Ceramic Wall Tile

Ceramic wall tile is one of the most durable surface materials for bathroom walls and ceilings because it's virtually impervious to water and easy to clean. However, a tiled surface surround for a bathtub or shower must be prepared using the proper materials to ensure that the wall system will be protected if water does get through the surface.

Install tile over cementboard (pages 190 to 191). Made from cement and fiberglass, cementboard cannot be damaged by water, though moisture can pass through it. To protect the framing, install a waterproof membrane, such as roofing felt or polyethylene sheeting, between the framing members and the cementboard. Be sure to tape and finish the seams between cementboard panels before laying the tile.

When shopping for tile, keep in mind that tiles that are at least 6" × 6" are easier to install than small tile, because they require less cutting and cover more surface area. Larger tiles also have fewer grout lines that must be cleaned and maintained. Check out the selection of trim and specialty tiles and ceramic accessories that are available to help you customize your project.

Most wall tile is designed to have narrow grout lines (less than ⅛" wide) filled with unsanded grout. Grout lines wider than ⅛" should be filled with sanded floor-tile grout. Either type will last longer if it contains, or is mixed with, a latex additive. To prevent staining, it's a good idea to seal your grout after it fully cures, then once a year thereafter.

If you are planning to tile all the walls in your bathroom, you can use standard drywall or water-resistant drywall (called "greenboard") as a backer for walls in dry areas. See page 195 for information on laying out full rooms.

## Everything You Need

Tools: Tile-cutting tools, marker, tape measure, 4-ft. level, notched trowel, mallet, grout float, sponge, small paintbrush, caulk gun.

Materials: Straight 1 × 2, dry-set tile mortar with latex additive, ceramic wall tile, ceramic trim tile (as needed), 2 × 4, carpet scrap, tile grout with latex additive, tub & tile caulk, alkaline grout sealer, cardboard.

## Materials for Wall Tiling Projects

**Use planning brochures** and design catalogs to help you create decorative patterns and borders for your ceramic tile projects. Brochures and catalogs are available free of charge from many tile manufacturers.

**Choose moisture-resistant backing materials.** Water-resistant drywall (A), or greenboard, is made from gypsum and has a water-resistant facing. Use it only in moderately damp or dry areas. Cementboard (B) is a rigid material with a fiberglass facing and a cement core. Because water does not damage cementboard, use it as a tile backer in bathtub and shower surrounds.

**Ceramic wall tile** is available in a wide range of shapes, styles, and colors. The most basic types of tile are: 4 × 4 glazed wall tiles (A); self-spacing mosaic sheet tiles (B); and trim tiles for borders (C) and accents (D).

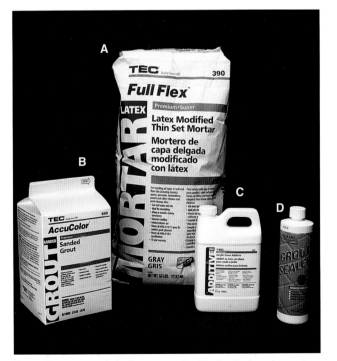

**Bonding materials** for ceramic tile include: dry-set mortar (A); grout mix (B); and latex grout additive (C). Latex additive makes grout lines stronger and more crack-resistant. Grout sealer (D) is used to protect grout lines from staining.

## How to Lay Out Tile Walls in a Bathtub Alcove

**1** Make a story pole to mark the tile layout on walls. For square tiles, set a row of tiles (and plastic spacers, if they will be used) in the selected pattern on a flat surface. Mark a straight 1 × 2 to match the tile spacing. Include any narrow trim tiles or accent tiles. For rectangular and odd-shaped tiles, make separate sticks for the horizontal and vertical layouts.

**2** Beginning with the back wall, measure up and mark a point at a distance equal to the height of one ceramic tile (if the tub edge is not level, measure up from the lowest spot). Draw a level line through this point, along the entire back wall. This line represents a tile grout line and will be used as a reference line for making the entire tile layout.

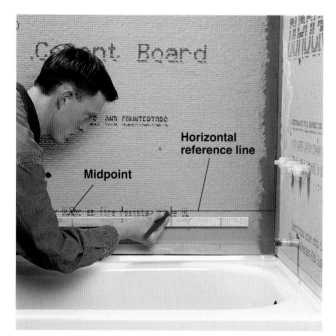

**3** Measure and mark the midpoint on the horizontal reference line. Using the story pole, mark along the reference line where the vertical grout joints will be located. If the story pole shows that the corner tiles will be less than half of a full tile width, move the midpoint half the width of a tile in either direction and mark (shown in next step).

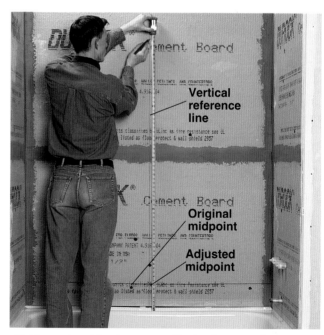

**4** Use a level to draw a vertical reference line through the adjusted midpoint from the tub edge to the ceiling. Measure up from the tub edge along the vertical reference line and mark the rough height of the top row of tiles.

**5** Use the story pole to mark the horizontal grout joints along the vertical reference line, beginning at the mark for the top row of tiles. If the cut tiles at the tub edge will be less than half the height of a full tile, move the top row up half the height of a tile. NOTE: If tiling to a ceiling, evenly divide the tiles to be cut at the ceiling and tub edge, as for the corner tiles in steps 3 and 4.

**6** Use a level to draw an adjusted horizontal reference line through the vertical reference line at a grout joint mark close to the center of the layout. This splits the tile area into four workable quadrants.

Adjusted horizontal reference line

Tile shown installed for clarity

**7** Use a level to transfer the adjusted horizontal reference line from the back wall to both side walls, then follow step 3 through step 6 to lay out both side walls. Adjust the layout as needed so the final column of tiles ends at the outside edge of the tub. Use only the adjusted horizontal and vertical reference lines for ceramic tile installation.

**Variation:** To wrap the final column of tile around the outside edge of the bathtub, begin your layout on a side wall. Make adjustments based on the tile to be notch-cut for the edge of the bathtub—the tile should be at least half a tile width and height. Transfer the adjusted horizontal reference line to the other walls and finish the layout.

## How to Install Ceramic Wall Tile in a Bathtub Alcove

**1** After marking the tile layout, fix a small batch of thin-set mortar containing a latex additive. (Some mortar has additive mixed in by the manufacturer and some must have additive mixed separately.) Spread adhesive on a small section of the wall, along both legs of one quadrant, using a ¼" notched trowel.

**2** Use the edge of the trowel to create furrows in the mortar. Set the first tile in the corner of the quadrant where the lines intersect, using a slight twisting motion. Align the tile exactly with both reference lines. When placing cut tiles, position the cut edges where they will be least visible.

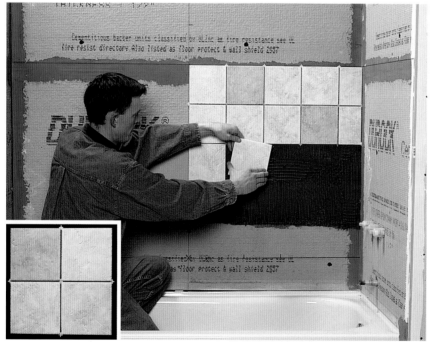

**3** Continue installing tiles, working from the center out into the field of the quadrant. Keep the tiles aligned with the reference lines and tile in one quadrant at a time. If the tiles are not self-spacing, use plastic spacers inserted in the corner joints to maintain even grout lines (inset). The base row against the tub edge should be the last row of tiles installed. To cut tiles at inside corners, see step 5 on the opposite page.

**Variation:** In some instances it is more practical to apply mortar to the tile rather than the wall. Cover the back of the tile with mortar, then press the tile in position with a slight twisting motion.

**4** As small sections are completed, set the tile by laying a scrap of 2 × 4 wrapped with carpet onto the tile and rapping it lightly with a mallet. This embeds the tile solidly in the adhesive and creates a flat, even surface.

**5** To mark tiles for straight cuts, begin by taping ⅛"-thick spacers against the surfaces below and to the side of the tile. Position a tile directly over the last full tile installed (A), then place a third tile so the edge butts against the spacers (B). Trace the edge of the top tile onto the middle tile to mark it for cutting.

**6** Install trim tiles, such as the bullnose tiles shown above, at border areas. Wipe away excess mortar along the top edges of the edge tiles.

**7** Mark and cut tiles to fit around all plumbing accessories or plumbing fixtures.

(continued next page)

**8** Install any ceramic accessories, such as soap dishes, by applying thin-set mortar to the back side, then pressing the accessory into place. Use masking tape to support the weight until the mortar dries (INSET).

**9** Let mortar dry completely (12 to 24 hours), then mix a batch of grout containing latex additive. Apply the grout with a rubber grout float, using a sweeping motion, and hold at a 30° angle to force it deep into the joints. Do not grout the joints adjoining the bathtub, floor, and corners. These will serve as expansion joints and will be caulked later.

**10** Wipe a damp grout sponge diagonally over the tiles, rinsing between wipes. Wipe only once; repeated wiping can pull grout from the joints. Let grout dry for about 4 hours, then buff the tile surface with a soft cloth to remove any remaining grout film.

**11** When the grout has cured completely, use a small foam brush to apply grout sealer to the joints, following the manufacturer's directions. Avoid brushing sealer on the tile surfaces, and wipe up excess sealer immediately.

**12** Fill the tub with water, then seal expansion joints around the bathtub, floor, and corners with silicone caulk. After the caulk dries, drain the tub and then buff the tile with a dry, soft cloth.

## Variation: How to Tile Bathroom Walls

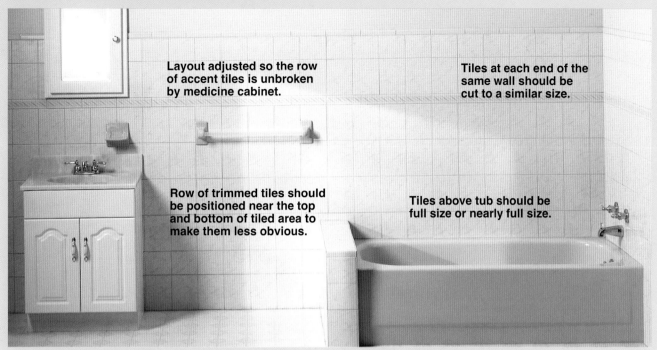

Layout adjusted so the row of accent tiles is unbroken by medicine cabinet.

Tiles at each end of the same wall should be cut to a similar size.

Row of trimmed tiles should be positioned near the top and bottom of tiled area to make them less obvious.

Tiles above tub should be full size or nearly full size.

**Tiling an entire bathroom** requires careful planning. The bathroom shown here was designed so that the tiles directly above the bathtub (the most visible surface) are nearly full height. To accomplish this, cut tiles were used in the second row up from the floor.

The short second row also allows the row of accent tiles to run uninterrupted below the medicine cabinet. Cut tiles in both corners should be of similar width to maintain a symmetrical look in the room.

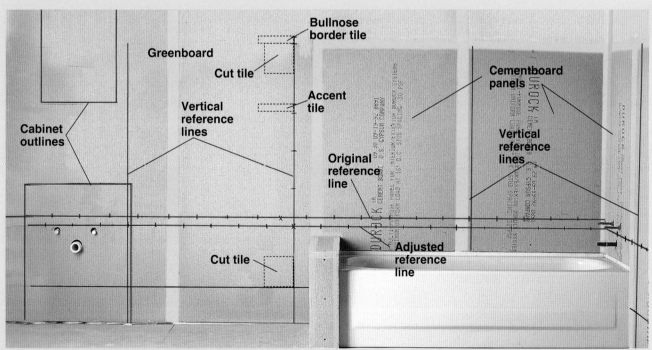

Bullnose border tile

Greenboard

Cut tile

Accent tile

Cementboard panels

Vertical reference lines

Cabinet outlines

Original reference line

Vertical reference lines

Cut tile

Adjusted reference line

**The key to a successful wall-tile project** is the layout. Mark the wall to show the planned location of all wall cabinets, fixtures, and wall accessories, then locate the most visible horizontal line in the bathroom, which is usually the top edge of the bathtub. Follow steps on pages 190 to 191 to establish the layout, using a story pole to see how the tile pattern will run in relation to the

other features in the room. After establishing the working reference lines, mark additional vertical reference lines on the walls every 5 to 6 tile spaces along the adjusted horizontal reference line to split large walls into smaller, workable sections, then install the tile. NOTE: Premixed, latex mastic adhesives generally are acceptable for wall tile in dry areas.

# Tiling a Kitchen Backsplash

There are few spaces in your home with as much potential for creativity and visual impact as the space between your kitchen countertop and cupboards. A well-designed backsplash can transform the ordinary into the extraordinary.

Tiles for the backsplash can be attached directly to wallboard or plaster and do not require backerboard. When purchasing the tile, order 10 percent extra to cover breakage and cutting. Remove switch and receptacle coverplates and install box extenders to make up for the extra thickness of the tile. Protect the countertop from scratches by covering it with a drop cloth. See page 223 for tile cutting tips.

**Tools and Materials**

Tools: Level, tape measure, pencil, tile cutter, rod saw, notched trowel, rubber grout float, beating block, rubber mallet, sponge, bucket.

Materials: Straight 1 × 2, wall tile, tile spacers (if needed), bullnose trim tile, mastic tile adhesive, masking tape, grout, caulk, drop cloth, grout sealer.

## Tips for Planning Tile Layouts

**Gather planning brochures** and design catalogs to help you create decorative patterns and borders for the backsplash.

**Break tiles into fragments** and make a mosaic backsplash. Always use a sanded grout for joints wider than ⅛".

**Add painted mural tiles** to create a focal point. Mixing various tile styles adds an appealing contrast.

## How to Tile a Kitchen Backsplash

**1** Make a story stick by marking a board at least half as long as the backsplash area to match the tile spacing.

**2** Starting at the midpoint of the installation area, use the story stick to make layout marks along the wall. If an end piece is too small (less than half a tile), adjust the midpoint to give you larger, more attractive end pieces. Use a level to mark this point with a vertical reference line.

**3** While it may appear straight, your countertop may not be level and therefore is not a reliable reference line. Run a level along the counter to find the lowest point on the countertop. Mark a point two tiles up from the low point and extend a level line across the entire work area.

(continued next page)

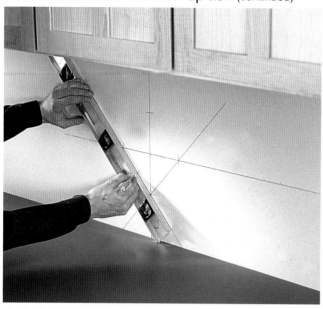

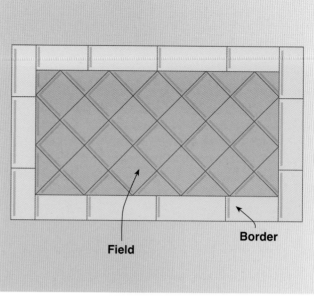

Field

Border

**Variation: Diagonal Layout.** Mark vertical and horizontal reference lines, making sure the angle is 90°. To establish diagonal layout lines, measure out equal distances from the crosspoint, then connect the points with a line. Additional layout lines can be extended from these as needed. To avoid the numerous, unattractive perimeter cuts common to diagonal layouts, try using a standard border pattern as shown. Diagonally set a field of full tiles only, then cut enough half tiles to fill out the perimeter. Finally, border the diagonal field with tiles set square to the field.

**4** Apply mastic adhesive evenly to the area beneath the horizontal reference line, using a notched trowel. Comb the adhesive horizontally with the notched edge.

**5** Starting at the vertical reference line, press tiles into the adhesive with a slight twisting motion. If the tiles are not self-spacing, use plastic spacers to maintain even grout lines. If the tiles do not hang in place, use masking tape to hold them in place until the adhesive sets.

**6** Install a whole row along the reference line, checking occasionally to make sure the tiles are level. Continue installing tiles below the first row, trimming tiles that butt against the countertop as needed.

**7** Apply adhesive to an area above the line and continue placing tiles, working from the center to the sides. Install trim tile, such as bullnose tile, to the edges of the rows.

**8** When the tiles are in place, make sure they are flat and firmly embedded by laying a beating block against the tile and rapping it lightly with a mallet. Remove the spacers. Allow the mastic to dry for at least 24 hours, or as directed by the manufacturer.

**9** Mix the grout and apply it with a rubber grout float. Spread it over the tiles, keeping the float at a low 30° angle, pressing the grout deep into the joints. Note: For grout joints ⅛" and smaller, be sure to use a non-sanded grout.

**10** Wipe off excess grout, holding the float at a right angle to the tile, working diagonally so as not to remove grout from the joints. Clean any remaining grout from the tiles with a damp sponge, working in a circular motion. Rinse the sponge thoroughly and often.

**11** Shape the grout joints by making slow, short passes with the sponge, shaving down any high spots; rinse the sponge frequently. Fill any voids with a fingerful of grout. When the grout has dried to a haze, buff the tile clean with a soft cloth. Apply a bead of caulk between the countertop and tiles. Reinstall any electrical fixtures you removed. After the grout has completely cured, apply a grout sealer.

# Installing Interior Trim

The term "trim" refers to all of the moldings that dress up walls and ceilings, hide gaps and joints between surfaces, and adorn window and door frames. As a decorating tool, trim lends a sculptural quality to otherwise flat surfaces and can have a dramatic effect on any room in the house. Working with trim involves a few specific cuts and techniques, but once you learn them, you can install almost any type.

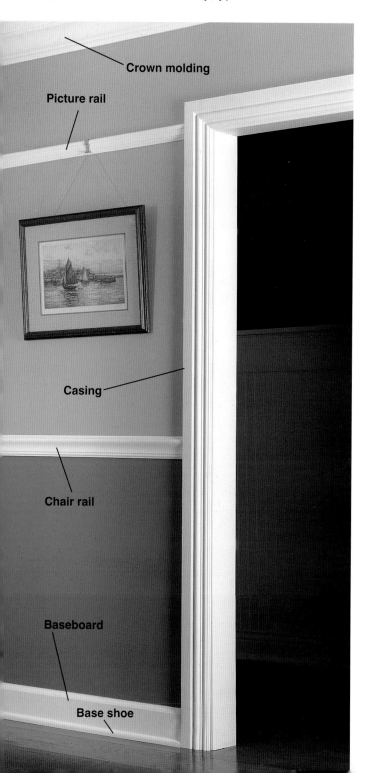

Crown molding

Picture rail

Casing

Chair rail

Baseboard

Base shoe

**Crown molding** decorates the intersection of walls and ceilings. Most crown molding is "sprung," meaning it is installed at an angle to its nailing surfaces, leaving a hollow space behind it. It can be built-up with several styles to create custom looks. In addition to wood, crown moldings can be made with plastic polymers, often in ornate, one-piece styles.

**Casing** is trim that covers the edges of door and window jambs.

**Picture rail** is a traditional molding that installs parallel to crown molding and has a protruding, rounded edge that holds hooks for hanging pictures. Similarly, chair rail runs horizontally along walls, though at a height of 30" to 36" to serve as a border for wallpaper or wainscot, or as a transition between different paint colors. Both chair and picture rail are installed like baseboard.

**Baseboard** covers the bottoms of walls along floor. Styles range from single-piece to built-up versions that include a base cap and a base shoe. Base shoe is a small, flexible molding that can follow contours in the floor to hide gaps left by baseboard.

Baseboard covers the bottoms of walls along the floor. Styles range from single-piece to built-up versions that include a base cap and a base shoe installed at the floor. Base shoe is small, typically rounded molding that is flexible and can follow contours in the floor to hide gaps left by the baseboard

To avoid problems due to shrinkage after installation, stack the trim in the room where it will be installed and allow it to acclimate for several days. Apply a coat of primer or sealer to all sides of each piece, and let it dry thoroughly before installing it. You may also choose to paint or stain the trim before installing it.

Attach wood trim with finish nails, which have small heads that you drive below the surface using a nail set. Nails for most trim are size 6d or smaller, depending on the thickness of the trim and the wall surface. At a minimum, nails should be long enough to penetrate the framing by at least 3/4"; heavier trim requires nails with more holding power. Use finish screws for securing trim to steel studs. After the trim is installed and all the nails are set, fill the nail holes with wood putty, and touch up the areas with paint or stain.

## How to Plan Your Trim Layout

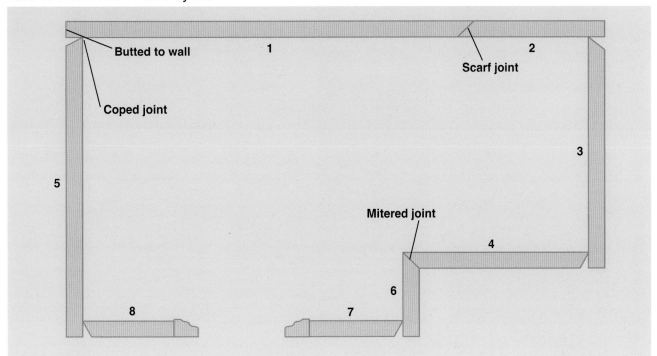

**Butted to wall**
**Coped joint**
1
2
**Scarf joint**
3
5
**Mitered joint**
4
6
7
8

**Plan the order** of your trim installation to minimize the number of difficult cuts on individual pieces. Use the longest pieces of molding for the most visible walls, saving the shorter ones for less conspicuous areas. When possible, place the joints so they point away from the direct line of sight from the room's entrance. At inside corners, butted and coped joints are preferable to mitered joints. If a piece will be coped on one end and mitered on the other, such as #4 above, cut and fit the coped end first. Also keep in mind the nailing points—mark all framing members you'll be nailing into before starting the installation (see below). At a minimum, all trim should be nailed at every wall stud, and every ceiling joist, if applicable. Install door and window casing before installing horizontal molding that will butt into it.

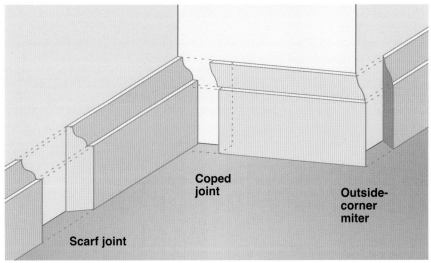

**Coped joint**
**Outside-corner miter**
**Scarf joint**

**The basic joints** for trim are shown here. A scarf joint (see page 203) joins two pieces along a length of wall. Coped joints join contoured molding at inside corners. The first piece is butted into the corner; the second piece is cut and fitted against the face of the first (see page 203). Miter joints are made with two 45°-angle cuts. To help with measuring and fitting miter joints, make a pattern by miter-cutting both ends of a scrap piece of trim. Hold the pattern against the wall at outside corners to test-fit and position cut pieces.

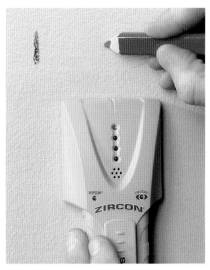

**Mark stud locations** throughout the project area, using a pencil or painter's tape placed 6-in. above the molding height. Use a stud finder—an electronic device that uses sonic waves to locate the edges of framing behind walls and ceiling surfaces—to determine the center of studs and joists.

# Tips for Cutting Trim

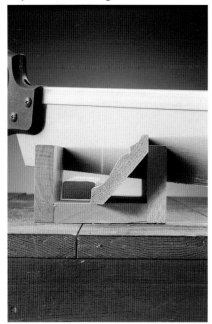  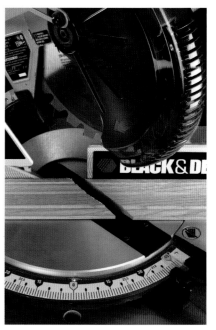

**A basic miter box**, made of wood or metal, and a backsaw are the simplest tools for making clean cuts in trim. These typically cut only 90° and 45° angles. A backsaw is a short handsaw with a stiff spine that keeps the blade straight while cutting. To cut crown molding, see below.

**Swivel-type miter boxes** rotate and lock the blade into position for cutting a wide range of angles. Some types have a special saw used only for the miter box; other types have clamps that accept standard backsaws.

**Power miter saws** make very accurate cuts. Their bases swivel and lock into position, and their large blades cut cleanly with minimal tearout. Standard miter saws are fixed vertically, while compound miter saws tilt to make bevel- and miter-cuts in one stroke.

 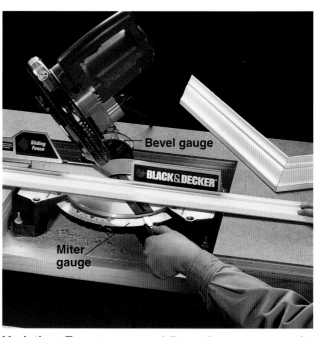

**To miter-cut crown molding** using a miter box or standard miter saw, flip the molding upside down, and place the flats on the back side of the molding against the table and fence of the saw (think of the table as the ceiling and the fence as the wall).

**Variation:** To cut crown molding using a compound miter saw, lay the molding flat on the saw table and set the miter and bevel angles. For outside-corner miters, the standard settings are 33° (miter) and 31.62° (bevel). These settings on the gauges often are highlighted for easy identification.

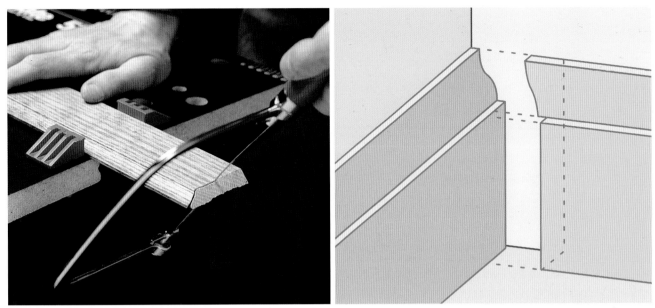

**Coped joints** form neat inside corners for contoured molding. To make a coped cut, cut the end of the molding at a 45° angle, so that the back side is longer than the front side. Using a coping saw, cut along the front edge of the molding, following the contour exactly. Angle the saw slightly toward the back side to create a sharp edge along the contour. Test-fit the cut using a scrap piece of molding. The coped piece should fit snugly against the profile of the scrap piece. If necessary, make small adjustments to the contoured edge, using sandpaper or a utility knife.

## Making Scarf Joints & Mitered Returns

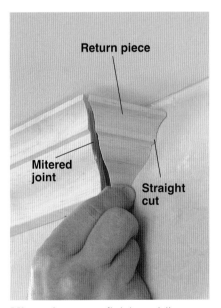

**Scarf joints** (or field joints) are used for joining molding on long runs. They help hide gaps if the wood shrinks. To make a scarf joint, cut the first piece at 45° so the end grain shows at the front. Install the piece, but don't nail it within 2 ft. of the joint. Cut the second piece at 45° in the opposite direction from the first. Fit the joint together, then fasten both pieces.

**For crown molding** and other sprung molding, cut the first piece at a 30° angle. Install the first piece, but nail only to within 2 ft. of the joint. Cut the second piece at 30° in the opposite direction—it's best to do this without adjusting the saw between cuts. Test-fit the joint, then apply wood glue to the mating surfaces and fasten both pieces completely.

**Mitered returns** finish molding ends that would otherwise be exposed. Miter the main piece as you would at an outside corner. Cut a miter on the return piece, then cut it to length with a straight cut so it butts to the wall. Attach the return piece with wood glue.

# Tips for Fastening Trim

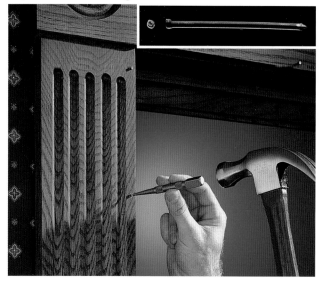

**Finish nails** are the best fasteners for most trim (inset). Drive the nails close to the surface with a hammer, then countersink, or set, them about 1⁄16" deep into the wood, using a nail set with a point slightly smaller than the nail head. Drill pilot holes for the nails in hardwood or small pieces of trim, to prevent splitting. At a minimum, nails should be long enough to penetrate the supporting material by 3⁄4"; heavier moldings require longer nails.

**Power nailers** automatically drive and set special finish nails. Traditional models use compressed air, but a variety of battery-powered consumer nailers are now available at home centers. Either style can also be rented. Power nailers simplify your work considerably by allowing you to hold the trim while nailing and eliminating the banging caused by hammering. They also eliminate the need for pilot holes, and they countersink the nails automatically.

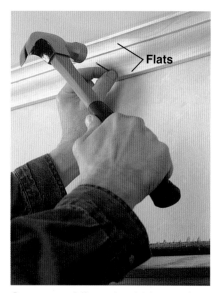

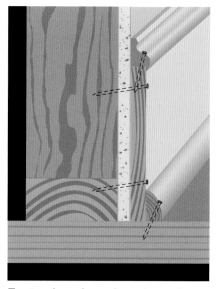

**Crown molding** should be positioned so the flats are flush against the wall and ceiling. Drill pilot holes, and drive finish nails through the flats of the molding at the stud and ceiling-joist locations. Note: To prevent splitting, slightly offset the nails so they are not in line vertically.

**Where there's no framing** to nail into, such as along walls parallel to joists, secure the top edge of molding with construction adhesive. Using power nailer, drive pairs of nails at opposing angles every 16" along the top flat. Nail the bottom edge at each stud location.

**Fasten baseboard** as shown here, nailing the main baseboard into the wall studs and the bottom plate at each stud location. If you're installing a built-up molding, run the main baseboard first, then add the cap and base shoe. Nail the cap into the baseboard or the wall studs, depending on the thickness of the baseboard. Nail the shoe to the floor only, to prevent gapping if the baseboard shrinks.

# How to Install Baseboard

**1** Locate and mark the wall studs. Following your trim layout plan (page 201) cut the ends of the first piece to fit from corner to corner. For butted and coped joint at the inside corners, cut the piece long by about $\frac{1}{16}$" then bend it out at the center and spring it into place against the wall. Nail the first piece as shown in the illustration opposite (page 204). Butt the second piece tightly against the face of the first piece and fasten it.

**Variation:** If you have contoured molding and you're coping the inside corners, cope the second piece to follow the profile of the first (see page 203). If the other end of the second piece is butted into a corner, cut the piece long by $\frac{1}{16}$", and spring it into place.

**2** Mark molding at outside corner by fitting the end of the piece into the corner (butting, mitering, or coping, according to your plan), then marking where the back side of the molding meets the outside corner of the wall.

**3** Cut the outside end of the base shoe piece at 45°, and test-fit it to ensure a tight fit. Use sandpaper or a file to shape the end. Fasten the piece, stopping about 2-ft. short of the outside corner. Complete the nailing when the mating piece is in place.

# Installing Polymer Crown Molding

Polymer moldings come in a variety of ornate, single-piece styles that offer easy installation and maintenance. The polystyrene or polyurethane material is as easy to cut as softwood, but unlike wood, the material won't shrink, and it can be repaired with vinyl spackling compound.

You can buy polymer moldings preprimed for painting, or you can stain it with a non-penetrating heavy-body stain or gel. Most polymers come in 12-ft. lengths, and some have corner blocks that eliminate corner cuts. There are even flexible moldings for curved walls.

## Everything You Need

Tools: Drill with countersink-piloting bit, power miter saw or hand miter box and fine-tooth saw, caulk gun, putty knife.

Materials: Crown molding, finish nails, 150-grit sandpaper, rag, mineral spirits, polymer adhesive, 2" drywall screws, vinyl spackling compound, paintable latex caulk.

## How to Install Polymer Crown Molding

**1** Plan the layout of the molding pieces by measuring the walls of the room and making light pencil marks at the joint locations. For each piece that starts or ends at a corner, add 12" to 24" to compensate for waste. If possible, avoid pieces shorter than 36", because short pieces are more difficult to fit.

**2** Hold a section of molding against the wall and ceiling in the finished position. Make light pencil marks on the wall every 12" along the bottom edge of the molding. Remove the molding, and tack a finish nail at each mark. The nails will hold the molding in place while the adhesive dries. If the wall surface is plaster, drill pilot holes for the nails.

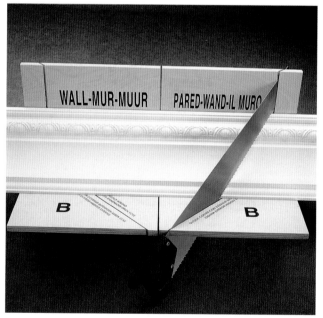

**3** To make the miter cuts for the first corner, position the molding faceup in a miter box. Set the ceiling side of the molding against the horizontal table of the miter box, and set the wall side against the vertical back fence (see page 202). Make the cut at 45°.

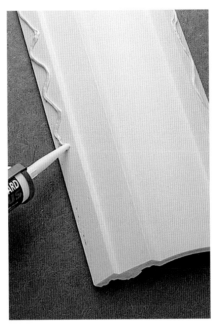

**4** Check the uncut ends of each molding piece before installing it. Make sure mating pieces will butt together squarely in a tight joint. Cut all square ends at 90°, using a miter saw or hand miter box.

**5** Lightly sand the backs of the molding that will contact the wall and ceiling, using 150-grit sandpaper. Slightly dampen a rag with mineral spirits, and wipe away the dust. Run a small bead of polymer adhesive (recommended or supplied by the manufacturer) along both sanded edges.

**6** Set the molding in place with the mitered end tight to the corner and the bottom edge resting on the nails. Press along the molding edges to create a good bond. At each end of the piece, drive 2" drywall screws through countersunk pilot holes through the flats and into the ceiling and wall.

**7** Cut, sand, and glue the next piece of molding. Apply a bead of adhesive to the end where the installed molding will meet the new piece. Install the new piece, and secure the ends with screws, making sure the ends are joined properly. Install the remaining molding pieces, and let the adhesive dry.

**8** Carefully remove the finish nails and fill the nail holes with vinyl spackling compound. Fill the screw holes in the molding and any gaps in the joints with paintable latex caulk or filler, and wipe away excess caulk with a damp cloth or a wet finger. Smooth the caulk over the holes so it's flush with the surface.

# Installing Door and Window Casing

Casings cover the gaps between window and door jambs and the surfaces of surrounding walls. In order for them to fit properly, the jambs and wall surfaces must lie in the same plane. If one of them protrudes, the casing will not lie flush. If the jambs protrude, shave them down with a block plane. If the jambs are shallow, which is often the case with 2 × 6 walls, build up the jamb with an extension of 1× finish-grade lumber.

Door and window casing should be installed before horizontal moldings that will butt into it. In most situations, it's easier to paint the walls before you install the casing. You can also save time by pre-painting or staining the casing before cutting and installing it. To help ensure tight joints, test fit all pieces prior to installation, and use a power nailer to fasten casing in place.

### Everything You Need

Tools: Tape measure, straightedge, pencil, miter saw, hammer and nail set or power nailer, plane or rasp.

Materials: Casing material, 4d and 6d finish nails, wood putty.

## How to Install Door or Window Casing

**On each jamb**, mark a reveal line ⅛" from the inside edge. The casing will be installed flush with these lines. NOTE: You can set the reveal at whatever dimension you choose, but make sure it's equal on all jambs.

**Place a length of casing** along one side jamb, flush with the reveal line. At the top and bottom of the molding, mark the points where horizontal and vertical reveal lines meet. (When working with doors, mark the molding at the top only.)

**Make 45° miter cuts** on the ends of the moldings. Measure and cut the other vertical molding pieces, using the same method.

**Drill pilot holes** spaced every 12" to prevent splitting, and attach the vertical casings with 4d finish nails driven through the casings and into the jambs. Drive 6d finish nails into the framing members near the outside edge of the casings.

**Measure the distance** between the side casings, and cut top and bottom casings to fit, with ends mitered at 45°. If window or door unit is not perfectly square, make test cuts on scrap pieces to find the correct angle of the joints. Drill pilot holes and attach with 4d and 6d finish nails.

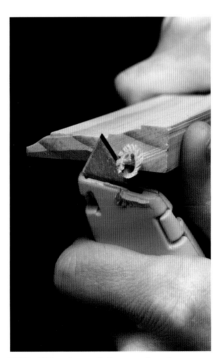

**TIP:** "Black-cut" the ends of casing pieces where needed to help create tight joints, using a sharp utility knife.

**Locknail the corner joints.** Drill pilot holes and drive 4d finish nails through each corner, or drive finishing nails through each corner with power nailer, as shown. If necessary, drive all nail heads below the wood surface, using a nail set, then fill the nail holes with wood putty.

# Repairing
# Walls & Ceilings

# Repairing Wallboard

**Most wallboard problems** can be remedied with basic wallboard materials and specialty materials: wallboard screws (A); paper joint tape (B); self-adhesive fiberglass mesh tape (C); corner bead (D); paintable latex or silicone caulk (E); all-purpose joint compound (F); lightweight spackling compound (G); wallboard repair patches (H); scraps of wallboard (I); and wallboard repair clips (J).

Patching holes and concealing popped nails are common wallboard repairs. Small holes can be filled directly, but larger patches must be supported with some kind of backing, such as plywood. To repair holes left by nails or screws, dimple the hole slightly with the handle of a utility knife or wallboard knife and fill it with spackle or joint compound.

Use joint tape anywhere the wallboard's face paper or joint tape has torn or peeled away. Always cut away any loose wallboard material, face paper, or joint tape from the damaged area, trimming back to solid wallboard material.

All wallboard repairs require three coats of joint compound, just like in new installations. Lightly sand your repairs before painting, or adding texture.

**To repair a popped nail**, drive a wallboard screw 2" above or below the nail, so it pulls the panel tight to the framing. Scrape away loose paint or compound, then drive the popped nail 1/16" below the surface. Apply three coats of joint compound to cover the holes.

**If wallboard is dented**, without cracks or tears in the face paper, just fill the hole with lightweight spackling or all-purpose joint compound, let it dry, and sand it smooth.

## Everything You Need

Tools: Drill or screwgun, hammer, utility knife, wallboard knives, framing square, wallboard saw, rasp, hacksaw, fine metal file.

Materials: 1¼" wallboard screws, all-purpose joint compound, lightweight spackle, 150-grit sandpaper, wood scraps, paper joint tape, self-adhesive fiberglass mesh joint tape, wallboard repair patch, wallboard repair clips.

# How to Repair Cracks & Gashes

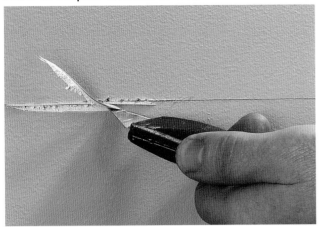

**1** Use a utility knife to cut away loose wallboard or face paper and widen the crack into a "V"; the notch will help hold the joint compound.

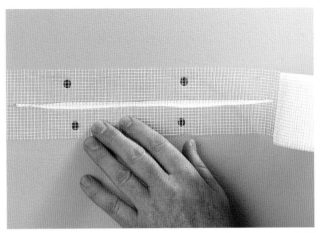

**2** Push along the sides of the crack with your hand. If the wallboard moves, secure the panel with 1¼" wallboard screws driven into the nearest framing members. Cover the crack and screws with self-adhesive mesh tape.

**3** Cover the tape with compound, lightly forcing it into the mesh, then smooth it off, leaving just enough to conceal the tape. Add two more coats, in successively broader and thinner coats to blend the patch into the surrounding area.

**4** For cracks at corners or ceilings, cut through the existing seam and cut away any loose wallboard material or tape, then apply a new length of tape or inside-corner bead and two coats of joint compound.

**Variation:** For small cracks at corners, apply a thin bead of paintable latex or silicone caulk over the crack, then use your finger to smooth the caulk into the corner.

## How to Patch Small Holes in Wallboard

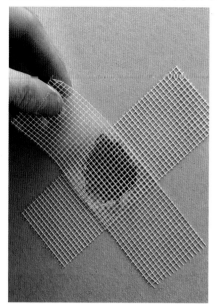

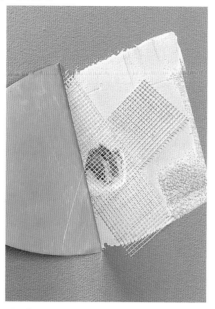

**1** Trim away any broken wall-board, face paper, or joint tape around the hole, using a utility knife. Cover the hole with crossed strips of self-adhesive mesh tape.

**2** Cover the tape with all-purpose joint compound, lightly forcing it into the mesh, then smooth it off, leaving just enough to conceal the tape.

**3** Add two more coats of compound in successively broader and thinner coats to blend the patch into the surrounding area. Use a wallboard wet sander to smooth the repair area.

## Other Options for Patching Small Holes in Wallboard

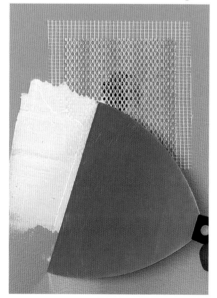

**Wallboard repair patches:** Cover the damaged area with the self-adhesive patch; the thin metal plate provides support and the fiberglass mesh helps hold the joint compound.

**Beveled wallboard patch:** Bevel the edges of the hole with a wall-board saw, then cut a wallboard patch to fit. Trim the beveled patch until it fits tight and flush with the panel surface. Apply plenty of compound to the beveled edges, then push the patch into the hole. Finish with paper tape and three coats of compound.

**Wallboard paper-flange patch:** Cut a wallboard patch a couple inches larger than the hole. Mark the hole on the backside of the patch, then score and snap along the lines. Remove the waste material, keeping the face paper "flange" intact. Apply compound around the hole, insert the patch, and embed the flange into the compound. Finish with two additional coats.

## How to Patch Large Holes in Wallboard

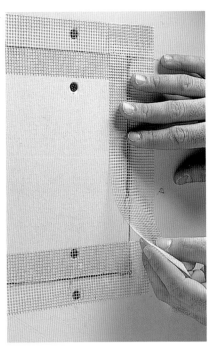

**1** Outline the damaged area, using a framing square. (Cutting four right angles makes it easier to measure and cut the patch.) Use a drywall saw to cut along the outline.

**2** Cut plywood or lumber backer strips a few inches longer than the height of the cutout. Fasten the strips to the back side of the drywall, using 1¼" drywall screws.

**3** Cut a drywall patch ⅛" smaller than the cutout dimensions, and fasten it to the backer strips with screws. Apply mesh joint tape over the seams. Finish the seams with three coats of compound.

## How to Patch Large Holes with Repair Clips

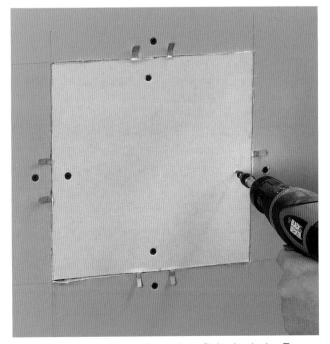

**1** Cut out the damaged area, using a wallboard saw. Center one repair clip on each edge of the hole. Using the provided wallboard screws, drive one screw through the wall and into the clips; position the screws ¾" from the edge and centered between the clip's tabs.

**2** Cut a new wallboard patch to fit in the hole. Fasten the patch to the clips, placing wallboard screws adjacent to the previous screw locations and ¾" from the edge. Remove the tabs from the clips, then finish the joints with tape and three coats of compound.

## How to Patch Over a Removed Door or Window

**1** Frame the opening with studs spaced 16" O.C. and partially beneath the existing wallboard—the new joints should break at the center of framing. Secure the existing wallboard to the framing with screws driven every 12" around the perimeter. If the wall is insulated, fill the stud cavity with insulation (See pages 42 to 43).

**2** Using wallboard the same thickness as the existing panel, cut the patch piece about ¼" shorter than the opening. Position the patch against the framing so there is a ⅛" joint around the perimeter, and fasten in place with wallboard screws every 12". Finish the butt joints with paper tape and three coats of compound (See pages 106 to 115).

## How to Repair Metal Corner Bead

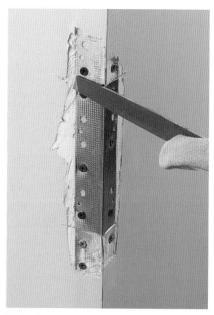

**Secure the bead** above and below the damaged area with 1¼" wallboard screws. To remove the damaged section, cut through the spine and then the flanges, using a hacksaw held parallel to the floor. Remove the damaged section, and scrape away any loose wallboard and compound.

**Cut a new corner bead** to fit the opening exactly, then align the spine perfectly with the existing piece and secure with wallboard screws driven ¼" from the flange edge; alternate sides with each screw to keep the piece straight.

**File the seams** with a fine metal file to ensure a smooth transition between pieces. If you can't easily smooth the seams, cut a new replacement piece and start over. Hide the repair with three coats of wallboard compound.

# Repairing Plaster

Plaster walls are created by building up layers of plaster to form a hard, durable wall surface. Behind the plaster itself is a gridlike layer of wood, metal, or rock lath that holds the plaster in place. Keys, formed when the base plaster is squeezed through the lath, hold the dried plaster to the ceiling or walls.

Before you begin any plaster repair, make sure the surrounding area is in good shape. If the lath is deteriorated or the plaster in the damaged area is soft, call a professional.

Use a latex bonding liquid to ensure a good bond and a tight, crack-free patch. Bonding liquid also eliminates the need to wet the plaster and lath to prevent premature drying and shrinkage, which could ruin the repair.

### Everything You Need

Tools: Wallboard knives, paintbrush, utility knife.

Materials: Lightweight spackle, all-purpose joint compound, patching plaster, fiberglass mesh tape, latex bonding liquid, 150-grit sandpaper, paint.

**Spackle is used to conceal cracks**, gashes, and small holes in plaster. Some new spackling compounds start out pink and dry white so you can see when they're ready to be sanded and painted. Use lightweight spackle for low-shrinkage and one-application fills.

## How to Fill Dents & Small Holes in Plaster

**1** Scrape or sand away any loose plaster or peeling paint to establish a solid base for the new plaster.

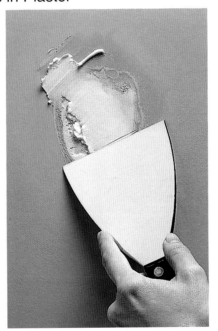

**2** Fill the hole with lightweight spackle. Apply the spackle with the smallest knife that will span the damaged area. Let the spackle dry, following the manufacturer's instructions.

**3** Sand the patch lightly with 150-grit production sandpaper. Wipe the dust away with a clean cloth, then prime and paint the area, feathering the paint to blend the edges.

## How to Patch Large Holes in Plaster

**1** Sand or scrape any texture or loose paint from the area around the hole to create a smooth, firm edge. Use a wallboard knife to test the plaster around the edges of the damaged area. Scrape away all loose or soft plaster.

**2** Apply latex bonding liquid liberally around the edges of the hole and over the base lath to ensure a crack-free bond between the old and new plaster.

**3** Mix patching plaster as directed by the manufacturer, and use a wallboard knife or trowel to apply it to the hole. Fill shallow holes with a single coat of plaster.

**4** For deeper holes, apply a shallow first coat, then scratch a crosshatch pattern in the wet plaster. Let it dry, then apply second coat of plaster. Let the plaster dry, and sand it lightly.

**5** Use texture paint or wallboard compound to recreate any surface texture. Practice on heavy cardboard until you can duplicate the wall's surface. Prime and paint the area to finish the repair.

**Variation:** Holes in plaster can also be patched with wallboard. Score the damaged surface with a utility knife and chisel out the plaster back to the center of the closest framing members. Cut a wallboard patch to size, then secure in place with wallboard screws driven every 4" into the framing. Finish joints as you would standard wallboard joints.

## How to Patch Holes Cut in Plaster

**Cut a piece of wire mesh** larger than the hole, using aviation snips. Tie a length of twine at the center of the mesh and insert the mesh into the wall cavity. Twist the wire around a dowel that is longer than the width of the hole, until the mesh pulls tight against the opening. Apply latex bonding liquid to the mesh and the edges of the hole.

**Apply a coat of patching plaster**, forcing it into the mesh and covering the edges of the hole. Scratch a cross-hatch pattern in the wet plaster, then allow it to dry. Remove the dowel and trim the wire holding the mesh. Apply a second coat, filling the hole completely. Add texture. Let dry, then scrape away any excess plaster. Sand, prime, and paint the area.

## How to Repair Cracks in Plaster

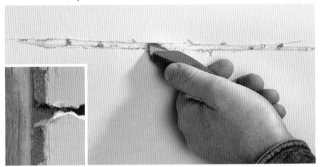

**1** Scrape away any texture or loose plaster around the crack. Using a utility knife, cut back the edges of the crack to create a keyway (inset). The keyway will help lock the patch in place and prevent recracking.

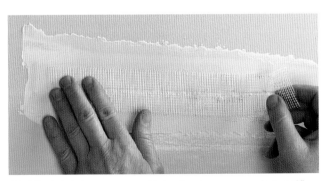

**2** Work joint compound into the keyway using a 6" knife, then embed mesh tape into the compound, lightly forcing the compound through the mesh. Smooth the compound, leaving just enough to conceal the tape.

**3** Add two more coat of compound, in successively broader and thinner coats, to blend the patch into the surrounding area. Lightly sand, then retexture the repair area to match the wall. Prime and paint it to finish the repair.

# Replacing Sheet Paneling

Despite its durability, prefinished sheet paneling occasionally requires repairs. Many scuff marks can be removed with a light coat of paste wax, and most small scratches can be disguised with a touchup stick.

Paneling manufacturers do not recommend trying to spot-sand or refinish prefinished paneling.

The most common forms of significant damage to paneling are water damage and punctures. If paneling has suffered major damage, the only way to repair it is to replace the affected sheets.

If the paneling is more than a few years old, it may be difficult to locate matching pieces. If you can't find any at lumber yards or building centers, try salvage yards. Buy the panels in advance so that you can condition them to the room before installing them. To condition the paneling, place it in the room, standing on its long edge. Place spacers between the sheets so air can circulate around each one. Let the paneling stand for 24 hours if it will be installed above grade, and 48 hours if it will be installed below grade.

**Most scuffs** in paneling can be polished out using paste wax. To use, make sure the panel surface is clean and dust free, then apply a thin even coat of paste wax using a clean soft cloth. Work in small areas using a circular motion. Allow to dry until a paste becomes hazy (5 to 10 minutes), then buff with a new cloth. Apply a second coat if necessary.

Before you go any further, find out what's behind the paneling. Building Codes often require that paneling be backed with wallboard. This is a good idea, even if Code doesn't require it. The support provided by the wallboard keeps the paneling from warping and provides an extra layer of sound protection. However, if there is wallboard behind the paneling, it may need repairs as well, particularly if you're dealing with water damage. And removing damaged paneling may be more difficult if it's glued to wallboard or a masonry wall. In any case, it's best to have a clear picture of the situation before you start cutting into a wall.

Finally, turn off the electricity to the area and remove all receptacle covers and switch plates on the sheets of paneling that need to be replaced.

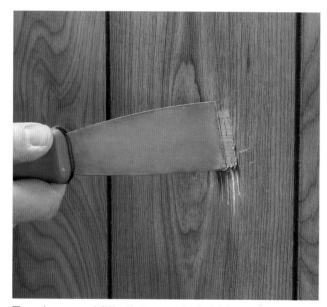

**Touch-up and fill sticks** can help hide most scratches in prefinished paneling. Wax touch-up sticks are like crayons—simply trace over the scratch with the stick. To use a fill stick, apply a small amount of the material into the surface and smooth it over the scratch using a flexible putty knife. Wipe away excess fill with a clean, soft cloth.

## Everything You Need

Tools: Wallboard knife, putty knife, flat pry bar, framing square, linoleum knife, hammer, chisel, caulk gun, rubber mallet, nail set.

Materials: Replacement panels, spray paint, panel adhesive, color-matched paneling nails, shims, finish nails, putty sticks, and wood filler.

# How to Replace a Strip of Paneling

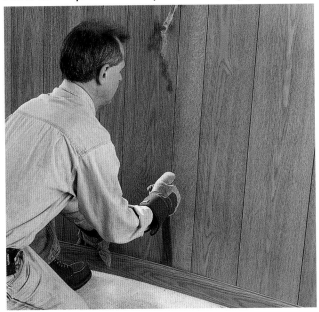

**1** Carefully remove the baseboard and top moldings. Use a wallboard or putty knife to create a gap, then insert a pry bar and pull the trim away from the wall. Remove all the nails.

**2** Draw a line on the panel from top to bottom, 3-in. to 4-in. from each edge of the panel. Hold a framing square along the line and cut with a linoleum knife. Using a fair amount of pressure, you should cut through the panel within two passes. If you have trouble, use a hammer and chisel to break the panel along the scored lines.

**3** Insert a pry bar under the panel at the bottom, and pull up and away from the wall, removing nails as you go. Once the center portion of the panel is removed, scrape away any old adhesive, using a putty knife. Repair the vapor barrier if damaged; below-grade applications may require a layer of 4mil polyethylene between outside walls and paneling. Measure and cut the new panel, including any necessary cutouts, and test-fit the panel.

**4** On the back of the panel, apply zigzag beads of panel adhesive from top to bottom every 16", about 2" in from each edge, and around cutouts. Tack the panel into position at the top, using color-matched paneling nails. When the adhesive has set up, press the panel to the wall and tap along stud lines with a rubber mallet, creating a tight bond between the adhesive and wall. Drive finish nails at the base of the panel to hold it while the adhesive dries. Replace all trim pieces and fill nail holes with wood filler.

# Repairing Ceramic Tile

Ceramic tile is durable and nearly maintenance free, but it can fail or develop problems. The most common problem involves damaged grout. Failed grout is unattractive, but the real danger is that it offers a point of entry for water. Given a chance to work its way beneath grout, water can destroy a tile base and eventually wreck an entire installation. It's important to regrout ceramic tile and replace any broken tiles as soon as you see signs of damage.

NOTE: Before the 1960s, ceramic tile was set in a masonry base. If your tile is of this vintage, contact a professional for repairs.

**Most tile repairs** involve removing grout. And although it's not difficult, doing it well takes more time than you might think. There are tools available that make the job relatively easy. A rotary tool with a straight carbide bit and joint guide makes short work of removing grout on big jobs, while a grout cutter is perfect for smaller projects. You can also use an awl or utility knife (see below).

### Everything You Need

Tools: Rotary tool, grout cutter, awl, or utility knife; grout float, hammer, chisel, small pry bar, sponge, eye protection.

Materials: Replacement tile, tile adhesive, masking tape, grout, cloth or rag, rubbing alcohol, mildew remover, silicone or latex caulk, sealer.

## How to Regrout Ceramic Tile

**1** Scrape out the old grout completely, leaving a clean bed for the new grout. Use a rotary tool or grout cutter (above), or an awl or utility knife.

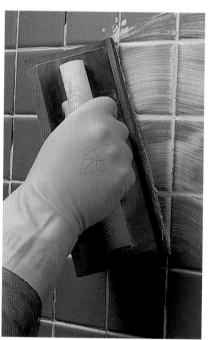

**2** Clean and rinse the grout joints, then spread grout over the entire project area, using a rubber grout float or sponge. Work the grout well into the joints and let it set slightly.

**3** Wipe away excess grout with a damp sponge. When the grout is dry, wipe away the residue and polish the tiles with a dry cloth.

## How to Replace a Broken Ceramic Tile

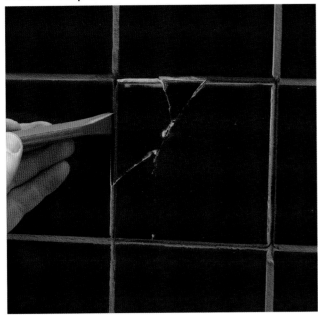

**1** Remove grout from the surrounding joints. Break the damaged tile into small pieces using a hammer and chisel. Remove the broken pieces, then use a utility knife to scrape any debris or old adhesive from the open area.

**2** Test fit the new tile and make sure it fits and sits flush with the old tile. (If the tile needs to be cut, see below.) Spread adhesive on the back of the replacement tile, then place it in the hole, twisting slightly to make sure the tile makes good contact with the wall. Use masking tape to hold the tile in place for 24 hours before grouting (see opposite page).

## Tips for Cutting Ceramic Tile

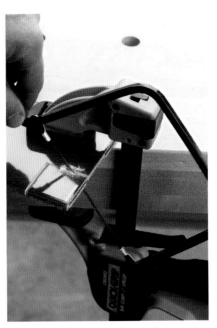

**For straight cuts**, use a tile cutter. Align the cutting wheel with the reference mark, press down the handle firmly to score a cutting line, then snap the handle to quickly break the tile cleanly.

**You can also cut tile with a rod saw:** Fit a tungsten carbide rod saw blade into a coping saw body. Firmly support the tile and use a sawing motion to cut the tile.

**For curved cuts**, mark the curve on the tile, then use the scoring wheel of a handheld tile cutter to score a cut line. Make several parallel scores, no more than 1/4" apart, in the waste portion of the tile. Use tile nippers to nibble away the scored portion of the tile.

# Repairing Wallcovering

Loosened seams and bubbles are common wall-covering problems, but both are easy to remedy using a little adhesive and a sponge. For papers that are compatible with water, use a clean, damp sponge. For other types of papers (grass-cloth or flocked wallcoverings, for example), clean fingers are probably the best choice.

Scratches, tears or obvious stains can be patched so successfully that the patch is difficult to spot. Whenever you hang wallcoverings, save remnants for future repairs. It's also a good idea to record the name of the manufacturer as well as the style and run numbers of the wallcoverings. Write this information on a piece of masking tape and put it on the back of a switchplate in the room.

If you need to patch an area of wallcovering but don't have remnants available, you can remove a section of wallcovering from an inconspicuous spot, such as inside a closet or behind a door. You can camouflage the spot by painting the hole with a color that blends into the background of the wallcovering.

## Everything You Need

Tools: Edge roller, syringe-type adhesive applicator, sponge, utility knife.

Materials: Adhesive, removable tape, wallcovering remnants.

## How to Fix a Bubble

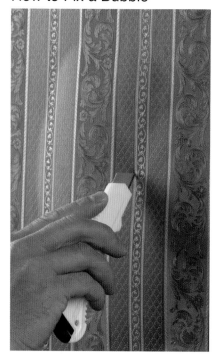

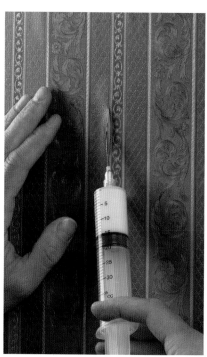

**1** Cut a slit through the bubble, using a sharp razor knife. If there is a pattern in the wallcovering, cut along a line in the pattern to hide the slit.

**2** Insert the tip of a glue applicator through the slit and apply adhesive sparingly to the wall under the wallcovering.

**3** Press the wallcovering gently to rebond it. Use a clean, damp sponge to press the flap down and wipe away excess glue.

# How to Patch Wallcovering

**1** Fasten a scrap of matching wallcovering over the damaged portion with drafting tape, so that the patterns match.

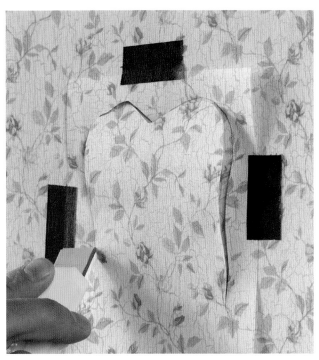

**2** Holding a razor knife blade at a 90° angle to the wall, cut through both layers of wallcovering. If the wallcovering has strong pattern lines, cut along the lines to hide the seams. With less definite patterns, cut irregular lines.

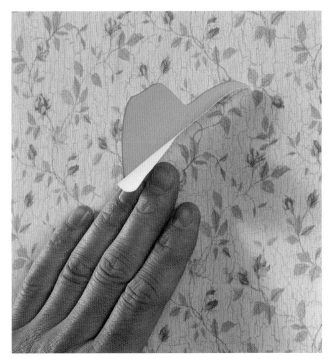

**3** Remove the scrap and patch, then peel away the damaged wallcovering. Apply adhesive to the back of the patch and position it in the hole so that the pattern matches. Rinse the patch area with a damp sponge.

# How to Fix a Seam

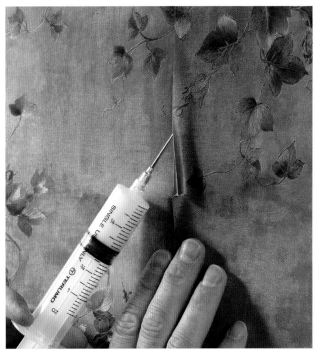

**Lift the edge** of the wallcovering and insert the tip of a glue applicator under it. Squirt adhesive onto the wall and gently press the seam flat. Let the repair stand for ½ hour, then smooth the seam lightly with a seam roller. Wipe the seam lightly with a damp sponge.

# Repairing Ceilings

**Aerosol touch-up products** are available for small repairs to ceilings with popcorn and orange peel textures. Use a wallboard knife to scrap away the existing texture at the damaged area and slightly around it. Make any necessary repairs, then spray on the aerosol texture carefully to blend the new texture with the existing ceiling.

Most ceiling repairs are relatively simple: the techniques used to repair wallboard walls apply to ceilings as well (pages 212 to 216), while sagging panels can be refastened or replaced easily; the tongue-and-groove edges of acoustical tiles make it easy to remove and replace a single tile; and textures such as acoustical "popcorn" can be matched with a little practice on a scrap of cardboard or simply removed altogether.

However, plaster, by contrast, is difficult to work with, and replastering is not an option for most homeowners. While minor repairs are manageable, widespread failure of the bond between the plaster coating and the lath foundation can be dangerous. If you find large spongy areas or extensive sags in your plaster ceiling, consult a professional.

## How to Remove Popcorn Ceiling Texture

**1** To protect floors and ease cleanup later, line floors with 6-mil plastic, then cover with corrugated cardboard to provide a non-slip surface. Caution: Popcorn ceilings in houses built prior to 1980 may contain asbestos. Contact your local building department for regulations governing asbestos removal.

**2** Using a pressure sprayer, dampen the ceiling with a mixture of a teaspoon of liquid detergent per gallon of water. Allow 20 minutes for the mixture to soak in, rewetting as necessary.

**3** Scrape texture from the ceiling using a 6-in. wallboard knife. Be careful not to cut into the wallboard surface. After all texture is removed, sand rough spots, then carefully roll up and dispose of the plastic and debris. Patch any damaged areas with joint compound, then prime and paint.

## How to Replace Acoustical Ceiling Tile

**1** Cut out the center section of the damaged tile with a utility knife. Slide the edges away from the surrounding tiles.

**2** Trim the upper lip of the grooved edges of the new tile, using a straightedge. If necessary, also remove one of the tongues.

**3** At the ceiling, apply construction adhesive to the furring strips. Install the new tile, tongue first, and press it into the adhesive. Tip: To hold large tiles in place while the glue dries, lay a flat board across the tile, then prop a 2 × 4 post between the board and the floor.

## How to Raise a Sagging Wallboard Ceiling

**1** Position a T-brace under the lowest point of the sagging area with the bottom end on a piece of plywood or hardboard on the floor. Nudge it forward until the sagging panels are tight to the joists. If fasteners pop through the surface, drive them back in.

**2** Remove loose tape and compound at joints between loose panels. Starting at one end, drive wallboard screws with broad, thin washers every 4" through the center of the joint and into the joists. In the field of panel, drive screws 2" from existing fasteners.

**3** When the area is securely fastened, remove the T-brace. Scrape off any loose chips of paint or wallboard around joints and screws, then fill with compound. Cover large cracks or gaps with fiberglass tape before applying the compound.

# Repairing Water Damaged Walls & Ceilings

A sure sign of a water problem is discoloration and bubbling on the ceiling surface. Water from a leaky roof or pipe above will quickly find a low spot or a joint between wallboard panels, soaking through to a visible surface in a matter of minutes. Water in joints is especially damaging because it ruins the edges of two panels at once. If you have a water problem, be sure to fix the leak and allow the damaged wallboard to dry thoroughly before making any repairs.

Whenever water or moisture infiltrates a house, there is always a concern regarding mold. Mold grows where water and nutrients are present—damp wallboard paper can provide such an environment. You can use a damp rag and baking soda or a small amount of detergent to clean up small areas of mold (less than one square yard), though you should wear goggles, rubber gloves, and a dust mask to prevent contact with mold spores. If mold occupies more area than this, you may have a more serious problem. Contact a mold abatement specialist for assessment and remediation. To help prevent mold growth, use exhaust fans and dehumidifiers to rid your home

of excess moisture and repair plumbing leaks as soon as they are found.

If damaged wallboard requires extensive repair, resurfacing walls and ceiling with a layer of new wallboard may be the best option. Resurfacing is essentially the same installation as hanging multiple layers of wallboard, and results in a smooth, flat surface. However, the added wall thickness can affect the appearance of window and door trim, which may need to be extended. Use ⅜" wallboard for resurfacing—while ¼" wallboard is thinner, it's fragile and can be difficult to work with.

## Everything You Need

Tools: Utility saw, utility knife, drill or screwgun, wallboard knives, 150-grit sandpaper, paint roller and tray.

Materials: Wallboard screws, wallboard (for patching or resurfacing), construction adhesive, stain-blocking primer/sealer, paper tape, joint compound.

## How to Repair Water Damaged Wallboard

**1** After the source for the water leak has been fixed, cut 4-in. holes at each end of joist and stud bays to help ventilation. Where possible, remove wet or damp insulation to dry out. Use fans and dehumidifiers to help speed up the drying process.

**2** Remove loose tape and compound using a utility knife. Cut back areas of soft wallboard to solid material. To prevent sagging, prop waterlogged ceiling panels against joists with T-braces (see page 227).

**3** Once wallboard is dry, refasten ceiling panels to framing (see page 227) or remove panels that are excessively bowed. Reinforce damaged wall panels with wallboard screws driven 2-in. from the existing fasteners.

**Tip:** If wallboard contains small areas (less than one square yard) of mold on the panel surface, clean with a damp rag and baking soda or detergent. Allow to dry, then continue the repair. Wear protective eyewear, rubber gloves, and a disposable dust mask when cleaning mold. Caution: Larger areas containing mold must be evaluated and treated by a mold abatement specialist.

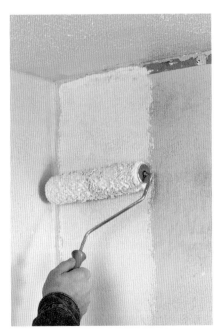

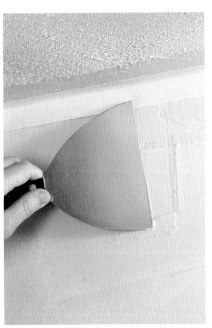

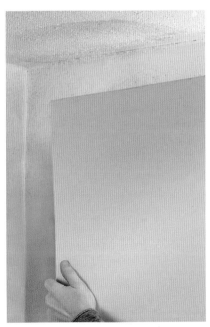

**4** Patch all vent holes and damaged areas with wallboard (see pages 212 to 216) and replace insulation. Apply a quality stain-blocking primer/sealer to the affected area. Use an oil-based sealer; latex-based sealers may allow water stains to bleed through.

**5** After the primer/sealer has dried, finish all joints and repairs with paper tape and three coats of compound. If water stains bleed through, reseal prior to final priming and painting.

**Variation:** Where damage is severe, resurface with a new layer of 1/4" or 3/8" wallboard. Hang new panels perpendicular to existing wallboard, and use panel adhesive to strengthen the bond. See pages 84 to 85 for more information on hanging multiple layers of wallboard.

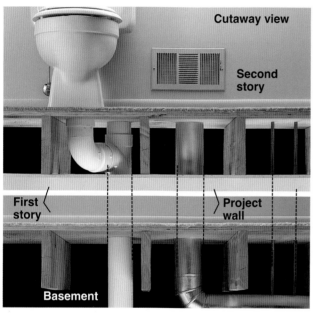

**Locate framing members** using a stud finder or by knocking on the wall and feeling for solid points. Verify the findings by driving finish nails through the wall surface. After finding the center of one stud, measure over 16" to locate neighboring studs.

**Cutaway view**

**Second story**

**First story**

**Project wall**

**Basement**

**Check for hidden plumbing lines**, ductwork, wiring, and gas pipes before cutting into a wall. To locate the lines, examine the areas directly below and above the project wall. In most cases, pipes, utility lines, and ductwork run through the wall vertically between floors. Original blueprints for your house should show the location of many of the utility lines.

## Lead Paint

Before removing any surface in a home built before 1980, test for lead, a hazardous substance. (Lead paint additives were banned in 1978, but supplies on hand were sold and used beyond that time.) You can find inexpensive test kits at hardware stores and home centers. If tests indicate lead, get expert advice. Most paint stores and the paint department in larger home centers carry free brochures on what's known as "lead abatement procedures." You can also find information at www.epa.gov.

# Removing Wall & Ceiling Surfaces

If a wall or ceiling surface is damaged or deteriorated beyond repair or if your remodeling project requires framing alterations or additional utility lines, you may need to remove the wall and ceiling surfaces.

Removing any wall surface is a messy job, but it's not a difficult one. But before you tear into a wall with a hammer or power saw, you need to know what lies inside. Start by checking for hidden mechanicals in the project area. Wiring that's in the way can be moved fairly easily, as can water supply pipes and drain vents. If it's gas piping, drain pipe, or ducting, however, you'll probably have to call a professional before you can move to the next step.

It's also a good idea to locate all of the framing members in the project area. Marking all of the studs, plates, and blocking will help guide your cuts and prevent unpleasant surprises.

When you're ready to begin demolition, prepare the work area to help contain dust and minimize damage to flooring and other surfaces—tearing out wallboard and plaster creates a very fine dust that easily finds its way into neighboring rooms. Cover doorways (even closed ones) and openings with plastic sheeting. Tape plastic over HVAC registers to prevent dust from circulating through the system. Protect floors with cardboard or hardboard and plastic or drop cloths. Also, carefully remove any trim from the project area, cutting painted joints with a utility knife to reduce the damage to the finish.

As an added precaution, turn off the power to all circuits in the work area, and shut off the main water supply if you'll be making cuts near water pipes.

### Everything You Need

Tools: Utility knife, pry bar, circular saw with demolition blade, straightedge, maul, masonry chisel, reciprocating saw with bimetal blade, heavy tarp, hammer, protective eyewear, dust mask.

## How to Remove Wallcovering

**Find a loose edge** and try to strip off the wallcovering. Vinyls often peel away easily. If the wallcovering does not strip by hand, cover the floor with layers of newspaper. Add wallcovering remover fluid to a bucket of water, as directed by the manufacturer.

**Pierce the wallcovering surface** with a wallpaper scorer (inset) to allow remover solution to enter and soften the adhesive. Use a pressure sprayer, paint roller, or sponge to apply the remover solution. Let it soak into the covering, according to the manufacturer's directions.

**Peel away loosened wallcovering** with a 6-in. wallboard knife. Be careful not to damage the plaster or wallboard. Remove all backing paper. Rinse adhesive residue from the wall with remover solution. Rinse with clear water and let the walls dry completely.

## How to Remove Ceramic Wall Tile

**1** Be sure the floor is covered with a heavy tarp, and the electricity and water are shut off. Knock a small starter hole into the bottom of the wall, using a maul and masonry chisel.

**2** Begin cutting out small sections of the wall by inserting a reciprocating saw with a bimetal blade into the hole, and cutting along grout lines. Be careful when sawing near pipes and wiring.

**3** Cut the entire wall surface into small sections, removing each section as it is cut. Be careful not to cut through studs.

## How to Remove Wallboard

**Remove baseboard** and other trim, and prepare the work area. Set a circular saw to the thickness of the wallboard, then cut from floor to ceiling. Use a utility knife to finish the cuts at the top and bottom and to cut through the taped horizontal seam where the wall meets the ceiling surface.

**Insert the end of a pry bar into the cut,** near a corner of the opening. Pull the pry bar until the wallboard breaks, then tear away the broken pieces. Take care to avoid damaging the wallboard outside the planned rough opening.

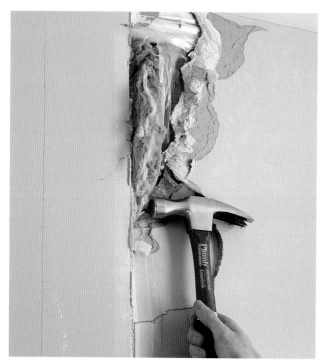

**Strike the wallboard** with the side of a hammer, then pull it away from the wall with the pry bar or your hands.

**Remove nails, screws,** and any remaining wallboard from the framing members, using a pry bar or drill (or screwgun). Check the vapor barrier and insulation for damage and replace if necessary.

# How to Remove Plaster

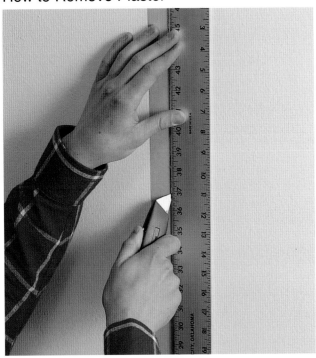

**Remove baseboards** and other trim and prepare the work area (page 230). Score the cutting line several times with a utility knife, using a straightedge as a guide. The line should be at least 1/8" deep.

**Break the plaster along the edges** by holding a scrap piece of 2 × 4 on edge just inside the scored lines, and rapping it with a hammer. Use a pry bar to remove the remaining plaster.

**Cut through the lath** along the edges of the plaster, using a reciprocating saw or jig saw. Remove the lath from the studs using a pry bar. Pry away any remaining nails. Check the vapor barrier and insulation for damage and replace if necessary.

**Variation:** If the wall has metal lath laid over the wood lath, use aviation snips to clip the edges of the metal lath. Press the jagged edges of the lath flat against the stud. The cut edges of metal lath are very sharp; be sure to wear heavy work gloves.

# Additional Resources

**Archcraft Products, Inc.**
Creative Corners
www.creativecorners.net
510 617 0400

**Flex - C Trac**
(flexible track for curved walls)
405-715-1799
www.flexc.com

**Georgia-Pacific**
(Dens-Shield® Tile Backer,
sound-deadening gypsum board)
800-225-6119
www.gp.com

**James Hardie Building Products**
(Hardibacker® Fiber-cement Board)
888-JHARDIE
www.jameshardie.com

**National Gypsum**
800-NATIONAL
www.nationalgypsum.com

**Outwater Plastics Industries Inc.**
(flexible polymer molding, specialty
architectural products)
888-OUTWATER
www.outwater.com

**Owens Corning**
(insulation, soundproofing products)
800-GET-PINK
www.owenscorning.com

**USG Corporation**
(cementboard and drywall products,
soundproofing insulation)
800-USG-4YOU
www.usg.com

# Photo Credits

**Armstrong Ceilings** Page 158
717-397-0611
www.armstrong.com

**Brian Greer's Tin-Ceilings** Page 161
519-570-1447
www.tinceilings.com

**Dal-Tile Corporation** Page 196 (top)
214-398-1411
www.daltile.com

**Fireclay Tile, Inc.** Page 196 (bottom right)
408-275-1182
www.fireclaytile.com

**Fypon, LTD** page 196 (bottom middle)
800-446-9373
www.fypon.com
Photo courtesy of Hi-Ho Industries, Inc./
Julie Caruso-photographer.

**USG Corporation** pp. 6 (top), 8 (bottom), 11 (bottom), 24
(top), 88, 128, 129 (bottom).
800-USG-4YOU
www.usg.com

## Photographers:

**Karen Melvin**
Minneapolis, MN
www.karenmelvin.com
© Karen Melvin: pp. 4-5, 6 (bottom), 7 (top, bottom left and
bottom right), 8 (top), 9 (top and bottom right), 10 (top and bottom), 11 (top left and top right), p. 90 (top), p. 150.

# Conversion Charts

## Metric Conversions

| To Convert: | To: | Multiply by: |
|---|---|---|
| Inches | Millimeters | 25.4 |
| Inches | Centimeters | 2.54 |
| Feet | Meters | 0.305 |
| Yards | Meters | 0.914 |
| Square inches | Square centimeters | 6.45 |
| Square feet | Square meters | 0.093 |
| Square yards | Square meters | 0.836 |
| Ounces | Milliliters | 30.0 |
| Pints (U.S.) | Liters | 0.473 (Imp. 0.568) |
| Quarts (U.S.) | Liters | 0.946 (Imp. 1.136) |
| Gallons (U.S.) | Liters | 3.785 (Imp. 4.546) |
| Ounces | Grams | 28.4 |
| Pounds | Kilograms | 0.454 |

| To Convert: | To: | Multiply by: |
|---|---|---|
| Millimeters | Inches | 0.039 |
| Centimeters | Inches | 0.394 |
| Meters | Feet | 3.28 |
| Meters | Yards | 1.09 |
| Square centimeters | Square inches | 0.155 |
| Square meters | Square feet | 10.8 |
| Square meters | Square yards | 1.2 |
| Milliliters | Ounces | .033 |
| Liters | Pints (U.S.) | 2.114 (Imp. 1.76) |
| Liters | Quarts (U.S.) | 1.057 (Imp. 0.88) |
| Liters | Gallons (U.S.) | 0.264 (Imp. 0.22) |
| Grams | Ounces | 0.035 |
| Kilograms | Pounds | 2.2 |

## Lumber Dimensions

| Nominal - U.S. | Actual - U.S. | Metric |
|---|---|---|
| 1 × 2 | ¾" × 1½" | 19 × 38 mm |
| 1 × 3 | ¾" × 2½" | 19 × 64 mm |
| 1 × 4 | ¾" × 3½" | 19 × 89 mm |
| 1 × 5 | ¾" × 4½" | 19 × 114 mm |
| 1 × 6 | ¾" × 5½" | 19 × 140 mm |
| 1 × 7 | ¾" × 6¼" | 19 × 159 mm |
| 1 × 8 | ¾" × 7¼" | 19 × 184 mm |
| 1 × 10 | ¾" × 9¼" | 19 × 235 mm |
| 1 × 12 | ¾" × 11¼" | 19 × 286 mm |
| 1¼ × 4 | 1" × 3½" | 25 × 89 mm |
| 1¼ × 6 | 1" × 5½" | 25 × 140 mm |
| 1¼ × 8 | 1" × 7¼" | 25 × 184 mm |
| 1¼ × 10 | 1" × 9¼" | 25 × 235 mm |
| 1¼ × 12 | 1" × 11¼" | 25 × 286 mm |

| Nominal - U.S. | Actual - U.S. | Metric |
|---|---|---|
| 1½ × 4 | 1¼" × 3½" | 32 × 89 mm |
| 1½ × 6 | 1¼" × 5½" | 32 × 140 mm |
| 1½ × 8 | 1¼" × 7¼" | 32 × 184 mm |
| 1½ × 10 | 1¼" × 9¼" | 32 × 235 mm |
| 1½ × 12 | 1¼" × 11¼" | 32 × 286 mm |
| 2 × 4 | 1½" × 3½" | 38 × 89 mm |
| 2 × 6 | 1½" × 5½" | 38 × 140 mm |
| 2 × 8 | 1½" × 7¼" | 38 × 184 mm |
| 2 × 10 | 1½" × 9¼" | 38 × 235 mm |
| 2 × 12 | 1½" × 11¼" | 38 × 286 mm |
| 3 × 6 | 2½" × 5½" | 64 × 140 mm |
| 4 × 4 | 3½" × 3½" | 89 × 89 mm |
| 4 × 6 | 3½" × 5½" | 89 × 140 mm |

## Counterbore, Shank & Pilot Hole Diameters

| Screw Size | Counterbore Diameter for Screw Head | Clearance Hole for Screw Shank | Pilot Hole Diameter Hard Wood | Pilot Hole Diameter Soft Wood |
|---|---|---|---|---|
| #1 | .146 (9/64) | 5/64 | 3/64 | 1/32 |
| #2 | 1/4 | 3/32 | 3/64 | 1/32 |
| #3 | 1/4 | 7/64 | 1/16 | 3/64 |
| #4 | 1/4 | 1/8 | 1/16 | 3/64 |
| #5 | 1/4 | 1/8 | 5/64 | 1/16 |
| #6 | 5/16 | 9/64 | 3/32 | 5/64 |
| #7 | 5/16 | 5/32 | 3/32 | 5/64 |
| #8 | 3/8 | 11/64 | 1/8 | 3/32 |
| #9 | 3/8 | 11/64 | 1/8 | 3/32 |
| #10 | 3/8 | 3/16 | 1/8 | 7/64 |
| #11 | 1/2 | 3/16 | 5/32 | 9/64 |
| #12 | 1/2 | 7/32 | 9/64 | 1/8 |

# Index

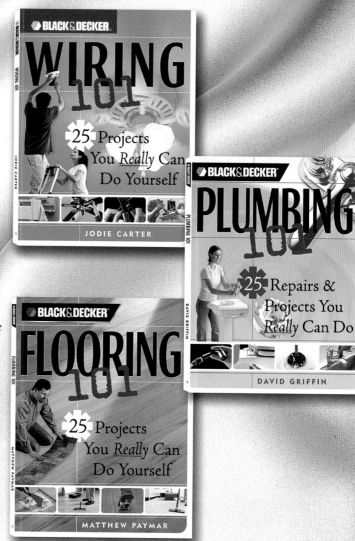
 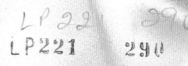